Osher Günsberg is one of Australia's most recognisable media personalities. His radio and television career spans over two decades, including Channel [v] in the early 2000s, seven seasons co-hosting *Australian Idol*, and host of *The Bachelor Australia*, *The Bachelorette Australia* and *Bachelor in Paradise*.

The Osher Günsberg Podcast began in 2013, features over 240 episodes and has thousands of daily listeners all over the world.

Osher lives with his wife, Audrey, and stepdaughter, Georgia, in Sydney's eastern suburbs. He is a cycling enthusiast, a coffee connoisseur and only eats plants.

Back,

After the Break

Osher Günsberg

■ HarperCollins*Publishers*

HarperCollins*Publishers*

First published in Australia in 2018
by HarperCollins*Publishers* Australia Pty Limited
ABN 36 009 913 517
harpercollins.com.au

HarperCollins*Publishers*
Level 13, 201 Elizabeth Street, Sydney NSW 2000, Australia
Unit D1, 63 Apollo Drive, Rosedale, Auckland 0632, New Zealand
A 53, Sector 57, Noida, UP, India
1 London Bridge Street, London SE1 9GF, United Kingdom
Bay Adelaide Centre, East Tower, 22 Adelaide Street West, 41st floor, Toronto,
  Ontario M5H 4E3, Canada
195 Broadway, New York NY 10007, USA

A catalogue record for this book is available from the National Library of Australia

ISBN: 978 1 4607 5624 9 (paperback)
ISBN: 978 1 4607 1024 1 (ebook)

Cover design by Mark Campbell, HarperCollins Design Studio
Cover photography by Steve Baccon
Styling by Melissa Byrne
Hair and make-up by Carla Mico
Typeset in Baskerville BE by Kirby Jones
Author photograph by Steve Baccon
Printed and bound in Australia by McPherson's Printing Group
The papers used by HarperCollins in the manufacture of this book are a natural,
recyclable product made from wood grown in sustainable plantation forests. The fibre
source and manufacturing processes meet recognised international environmental
standards, and carry certification.

For Audrey, who helped me believe that it was going to be OK.

*For Georgia, who showed me how to experience
another's joy as my own.*

*For my brothers, the three smartest, wisest, most incredible people
I know; for always being there when I needed them the most.*

* * *

This book deals with mental illness, suicidal ideation and drug use. If you, or a person you know, is in need of crisis or suicide prevention support, call Lifeline on 13 11 14, Kids Helpline on 1800 55 1800, or call 000 in an emergency.

If this book raises any issues for you, you can contact the SANE helpline on 1800 187 263 (weekdays 10am–10pm AEST) to talk to a mental health professional, or visit eheadspace.org.au or www.lifeline.org.au/gethelp

contents

preface

Hi. Thanks for being here. I used to be known as Andrew, but we'll get to that. Thanks for deciding that my story was good enough for you to want to part with your hard-earned cash.

In the radio and TV business, we talk about 'hooking'; finding ways of making you watch or listen longer. I suppose I had better 'hook' you by telling you what's in the pages ahead.

Better start with the big stuff then.

In sobriety, I've learned what rock bottom is. It's where your life has become so unmanageable that you lie there, often in a pile of your own filth, and realise that the only reason you're down there is because of decisions you have made. In the past you may have found yourself in the same place, but you had blamed your partner, your job, your parents, your country – anyone but yourself. You reach rock bottom when you have run out of people to blame for your own choices. It's only then that you're able to take responsibility for the decisions that have put you there, and start the long and painful climb out of the muck in a direction you've never gone before – a direction that involves healing the hurt you've caused and trying not to repeat the mistakes of the past.

For some people, rock bottom is a crystal clear and defined moment, after which their lives are irrevocably different. I got the bonus plan.

Sure I had a rock bottom with my drinking and using, but that was really just the first bounce along the asphalt as if my life was a ute that was hurtling down the road at 120 kilometres an hour in a school zone, and I'd just drunkenly fallen out the back of it. I'd spin in the air and bounce painfully again as my first marriage ended, once more as my career wound up in the toilet, and then just when I thought I'd come to a skidding halt I flipped and smashed face first into the ground once again as my own mental health became the most dangerous thing in my life, something that threatened to stop my journey permanently.

Because of the job I do, you probably heard or saw me a few times along the way as I was bouncing down to rock bottom. I probably had a big smile, one of three separate names, and I most definitely had a questionable haircut. But I can tell you that while you might have been familiar with the face that you saw, what was really going on behind those excited eyes and that TV smile was something far darker than would have ever been allowed on prime time.

But here it is. The whole story.

one
beginnings

Some time around 1970, Michael Günsberg walked alone through the residents' hall at Stoke-on-Trent hospital during a regular Friday night party. It was the end of a long week and like most other doctors he was enjoying a few English-temperature beers to take the edge off the stresses of being a junior doctor at a busy hospital.

He joined a few other resident doctors in animated discussion, and that's when he first laid eyes on a petite woman curled up on an armchair, her teeny miniskirt doing a terrible job of hiding her slender legs. A resident doctor herself, she looked up at him and saw a tall, dark and handsome stranger. That's how my parents met.

My mother was born Birute Magdalena Mikuzis in Kaunas, Lithuania. World War II saw her and her family flee their native land when the Russians took the country back from the occupying German army in 1944. I don't know what you were doing at four years old, but my mum and her family were fleeing with the retreating Germans; whatever the enemy were doing was less horrible than whatever the Soviets were promising.

Mum had lived for three years under German occupation – a dark time in Lithuania's history indeed. It took her years to tell us about it. Largely untouched because of their Catholic faith,

Mum's family had a front-row seat to the horrors inflicted on the Jews of their community, largely by members of the non-Jewish community. It's estimated that some 190,000 Jews were murdered during the German occupation of Lithuania. While many Lithuanians collaborated with the Nazis in destroying the Lithuanian Jewish population, I'm proud to say that my mother's family resisted the injustices wherever they could.

Both my Lithuanian grandparents were doctors, and the main hospital in Kaunas where they worked was right on the town square. One day, some local Nazi thugs were sadistically whipping a man in that very square. They had tied him to a pole and were flaying him for all the town to see. Infuriated by his wails of agony, my grandmother Aldona Mikuzis walked out the front door of the hospital and marched across the square, shouting the whole way at the Nazis. Not used to being challenged, let alone by a woman, they stopped in their tracks while she chastised them. She told them that she was sick of patching up their victims every day once they had had their fun, and told them to find something better to do. Amazingly, they let her go.

My grandfather Jonas Mikuzis was a prominent figure in town. A former lieutenant in the cavalry, he headed up the obstetrics and gynaecology department at the hospital. He and my grandmother owned a farm a little way out of town; it backed onto a train line between two stations. My grandmother had arranged with the train conductor to stop the train at the back fence, allowing her to get off and save travelling all the way back from the next station.

Under the guise of hiring young Jewish girls to help around the farm, my grandmother would arrange for them to come with her on the train. Perhaps the fact that she was putting

Jews to work allowed her to get the kids past the guards. When the train stopped at the farm's back fence there were no such police or guards, as there would have been at the station. My *babytė* was able to smuggle the girls off the train and very quickly hand them over to an underground organisation that helped them escape the country altogether.[1]

My *babytė* did all of this without my grandfather knowing. Once he found out he was terrified of retribution; the Nazis had executed many Lithuanians who had tried to help the Jews. By the time he had convinced my grandmother to stop, she had helped at least six young women escape certain death. Not every person could be Oscar Schindler, but it's important to know that all across Europe families did what they could to help their friends and neighbours.

When it was clear that the Russians were preparing to take back the country from the Germans, my grandparents buried their family treasures in the backyard, hitched Grandad's cavalry horse to the farm cart and headed for safety. They expected to be gone only for a few weeks, but they would never see their home again. Mum's family spent months wandering south from Lithuania, along with hundreds of thousands of others trying to find somewhere safe. Eventually they ended up in a refugee camp in Barenburg, Germany. Mum would sometimes talk about the horrible things that happened there, and it's fair to say that not much has changed in refugee camps since then. When you pack thousands of desperate people from many cultural backgrounds into a small space with little news or hope as to what happens next, bad things happen. However, Mum's family made a home there, spending the

---

1   One of the girls got to America and wrote a book about her experience and her flight from Lithuania: *I Jew*. If you ever see it in a bookstore, let me know, will you?

next few years living as normal a life as their conditions would allow.

By 1949, just before my mother's ninth birthday, things in Europe had started to calm down, and it was time for all 'displaced persons' to find a place they could call home.[2] Among them of course were my mother, her parents, her older sister and her younger brother. A large group of Lithuanians managed to get on the boat heading to the USA, but my aunt had a cough that the examining doctor thought was tuberculosis.[3] The boat heading to Australia had a Lithuanian examining doctor, and after a compassionate word between him and my grandfather where they both concluded it probably wasn't tuberculosis, they managed to get on board. As the weeks-long journey headed south through the tropics, instead of dying from disease my aunt recovered and was perfectly fine by the time they arrived in Adelaide. The front page of the paper was thrilled that two doctors were part of the boatload of new arrivals.

As the only languages that my mum, aunt and uncle knew were Lithuanian and German, they were bullied pretty intensely when they first arrived. However, soon enough Mum learned English and her natural intelligence shone through. While she wanted to study physics at university my grandfather, who was a very strict man, insisted that she study medicine instead, which she did at the University of Adelaide.

Soon Mum met a young British army officer named James Kelly, who was in South Australia working on the British nuclear tests. They were married, and when his tour of duty

_____

2   They weren't refugees then, they were 'displaced'. They couldn't go home but they couldn't stay where they were.

3   A disease which used to kill millions, but has now been largely controlled by the use of vaccines and antibiotics. Yay science!

was over he headed back to the UK, with Mum following soon after. It turned out that he wasn't the best human being after a few drinks, so Mum promptly left him and set about enjoying herself in the heady environment of England at the end of the swinging 1960s. She eventually took a job at a hospital in Stoke-on-Trent, and that was where she met Dad.

My father was born in London on D-Day, 6 June 1944, as the Allies stormed the beaches of Normandy to roll the Nazis back. His mother greatly admired the American general Dwight D. Eisenhower and named my father Dwight Michael Jan Antonin Günsberg. Dad hated the name and always went by Miša, the Czech variant of Michael.[4] Following the Nazi invasion of Prague, his father who was a Jewish political journalist managed to get smuggled out to London by the Associated Press. My grandmother soon escaped too and they were reunited. I guess even in war, bombings, fear and displacement there was time for intimacy, which was how Dad ended up being born in London. After the war the family went back to Prague in Czechoslovakia, where eventually Dad trained as a doctor.

Twenty-four years later, in August 1968, the Russians Mum had fled in the 1940s decided to crack down on the burgeoning pro-democracy movement that would come to be known as 'The Prague Spring'. With the walls of his house shaking as Soviet tanks rolled down the street, my father fled in the middle of the night, leaving his family, friends and all that he knew behind him as the communists clamped down. He told

---

4   The little birdy on the s makes it a 'sh' sound like if you were trying to get a person
    to be quiet, and the umlaut on the Günsberg makes it sound like 'ginzberg'. I could
    always tell when Mum was really mad at Dad because she would say, 'You can't
    get it through your thick skull that you're wrong, can you, Dwight?' spitting out the
    name in scorn.

the authorities he was going on holiday and because he also had a British passport, he was luckily allowed to leave. Dad's 'holiday' lasted for thirty years. His sister left too and found a home with her husband and daughter in Switzerland.

Once he had crossed the border into Austria, Dad hitchhiked his way across Europe with barely any English and ended up back in London, sleeping in the hallway of a friend's apartment. Imagine being twenty-four and knowing that you could never go back home to live. Those first few days and weeks must have been incredibly traumatic. Adding to the trauma was that Dad's father had suffered a massive stress-related heart attack soon after the Russians came. Defying the risk of not being able to leave again, Dad managed to find his way back into Czechoslovakia to say goodbye not only to his father but to his country. All his life my father had not a good word to say for the Russians – understandably, as they took his dad and his country from him. By the time he got back to London I can understand why he wanted to numb that pain. Dad used to tell us that while he was in London he would smoke huge joints with his friends and go to see psychedelic bands at a nearby nightclub called the Electric Circus where they projected strange lights on the walls and everyone would be dancing around in a trance. I asked him if one of the bands was Pink Floyd and he excitedly responded, 'Yes! That was them!' Fortunately one of Dad's Czech professors was able to smuggle Dad's paperwork out of Prague to prove that he was a doctor, and my father was able to find work in this new country he now had to call home.

And so it was a few years later that Mum and Dad ended up at that party, and ended up together. They were young doctors in a free and exciting new world just emerging into the light from under the dark rubble of war. Dad's mother – my grandmother – came from Prague and joined Dad and Mum when they went to live in Essex right after my big brother was born. Twenty-three months later I came into this world.

It was a Friday afternoon, 29 March 1974, around 3:30pm. Heavily pregnant and just back from doing the grocery shopping with Dad's mum, my mother decided to get the car washed. She found one of those mechanised car washes with the rails that you drive on to, and somewhere between the big automated rolling brushes and the spraying water she looked down and noticed that it was also wet inside the car. Realising her roof wasn't leaking, she knew that the only other explanation was that her water had just broken. With nowhere to go until the car wash cycle was complete, she calmly sat and waited for her Ford Anglia to be scrubbed clean. My grandmother in the passenger seat was far from calm, however, and by all reports flew into conniptions, which made the next few minutes in their above-water, sub-aquatic vehicle somewhat unpleasant. Now with a car that was spick and span and with a fresh coat of wax, Mum decided she didn't have time to get home to put the groceries in the fridge, and had better make her way to the hospital. Always with a keen sense of direction, she navigated through the rabbit warren of north London and drove to University College Hospital, found a parking place and made her way up the front steps.

I was apparently in quite a hurry to get going with life, a fact that was not lost on Mum. In her own very direct way, she promptly informed the triage staff that she was about to give birth, and told them to call the midwife while they found the nearest bed. I wasn't interested in waiting for the midwife, and so a trembling and wide-eyed student doctor got a crash course

9

in delivering babies as Mum calmly talked him through every step of my birth. By the time the midwife breathlessly burst into the room, there I was, little Andrew Günsberg,[5] resting peacefully on my mum's chest.

---

5   I'm unsure why the child of a Czech and a Litho would get a Scottish name, but it might have something to do with how much my mum was teased about her strange Euro name when she was a kid. While she was named 'Birute' she lived her whole life as 'Ruth'. 1974 was a big year for Andrews. Twenty years later, I'd play in a five-piece band which featured no less than three Andrews. We were differentiated by nicknames, but more about names later.

two
adelaide

Now with two small boys, Mum and Dad decided to leave the UK and join Mum's parents in Adelaide,[1] arriving in August 1974. Mum's father was dying of cancer, and the plan was to be with him for his last year. Though I was just an infant, the reason we had travelled to the other side of the world somehow got through to me. When I was about fifteen I asked Mum about my recurring vision of a blue wall to the left, a lot of light and strange shadows to my right, a large black crack in front of me and a grey-haired man with huge hands below me. She turned white and told me, 'You have just described meeting your grandfather when you were six months old.'

Turns out I was talking about my grandparents' house in Carrington Street, Adelaide. My grandfather Dr Jonas Mikuzis would see his patients in the front room of the house and the family lived in the back. The room where I met him was the kitchen, where they had put a single bed so that he

---

1 Adelaide is hot. Hot like your breath when you breathe on your hands in the cold to warm them. Except the air is your breath and your breath is cooler than the air around you. I was only a baby and had yet to grasp any concept of hot or cold or thermodynamics, and yet here we were – in a small city on the edge of a desert. Nothing but barren and unforgiving outback to the north, shark-infested waters to the south, and surrounded on all sides by the strange feeling of a town still haunted by the disappearance of the Beaumont children. These were three kids who went missing on 26 January 1966 on a packed beach. This was also the part of Australia where Snowtown happened. Let's just say that Adelaide is a strange place.

could see outside. The walls were indeed blue, the crack in front of me was actually a crack in the ceiling, the strange shadows on the right were the chickens pecking around in the backyard seen through the flyscreen doorway, he was below me because I was lying on my mum's lap as she sat next to the bed, and his hands were huge because when you're a baby I guess everything is huge.

I can't imagine what Adelaide was like for my parents, but it was probably hardest for Dad. The place was full of family for Mum, since many of the Lithuanians who came to Australia got off the boat there. While she may have had more family support than Dad, like him she was not untouched by trauma and displacement. Nowadays, we know about PTSD and intergenerational trauma, and since I have spent time in Israel, a country made up almost entirely of survivors of unspeakable trauma, I've come to learn how the pathology and behaviour of war survivors can be passed from one generation to the next. However, back then, if you were upwardly mobile, mostly functional, and got away with a socially accepted amount of self-medication,[2] people didn't think too much of it.

Later Dad told me his had been a particularly difficult transition. He had fled Prague less than six years before, he had come from the swinging sixties and seventies in London, he was a cultured, educated man, who thrived on great conversation, great wine and great art. He had got on a plane in London and left the doorstep of Europe to land in … Adelaide.

Not a single tree, plant, bird or meal looked anything like my parents knew. They also had to cope with the heat – and in

---

2   I often wondered if the RSL system and the cheap beers for veterans were the best ideas anyone had at the time for dealing with soldiers who came back from the war unable to speak about it or deal with their pain which we now know as PTSD.

Adelaide during summer the hot air can sit without a breath of wind for days, and it's no cooler after dark. Dad told me later that he felt very alone. A year in Adelaide turned into two, which turned into about five. We found a house in the suburb of Hyde Park, a nice middle-class part of town.

Dad did what he could to make himself feel at home in this strange new country. Thrilled to discover that South Australia has some of the best wine growers in the world, he set about filling the cellar in our home with bottles of 1970s vintage Penfolds that would probably buy a yacht now, had they not been enjoyed over meals with the family. Our cellar fascinated me; I was excited at being in a normal room that was underground. To get down there, you needed to lift a heavy trapdoor in the floor of our kitchen and go down a set of steep concrete stairs. I was too little to lift the cellar door by myself, so whenever the cellar was open I loved descending into this strangely cool, quiet room.

I was down there with Dad one day and I guess we were having some people over because he'd run out of hands to carry the bottles he wanted up the stairs. He loaded his arms with a few bottles and headed up the stairs to make his first delivery to the kitchen table. It was my first time alone down there. The sticky-sweet smell of bottles purchased straight from the vineyards mixed with the aroma of dusty concrete. I was still only two or three, so from my perspective rows of bottles stretched up into the sky and I was completely surrounded by them on all sides. I was becoming overwhelmed by this feeling when all of the bottles started tinkling, like the sound of glasses chinking together.

Dad called from above for me to come up to the kitchen. The urgency in his voice snapped me out of my trance and

I dashed up the steep stairs. In the kitchen the sound was there too, but here it was different. The air was thick with the cacophony of glasses on the shelves rattling, pots and pans lightly clanging together, and my father giggling. I don't know if his laugh was nervous or gleeful, but it made me feel much less frightened.

Dad said we were having an earthquake. Of course I had no idea what an earthquake was, so he explained it to me. Never one to give a simple explanation when a far more scientific and complex one was possible, he talked enthusiastically about changes in the earth's molten core causing tectonic plates to smash together, mountains being gouged out of the sea floor to form massive islands, houses being toppled and giant chasms in the earth that could swallow you whole opening up all over the place.

I could barely contain my excitement as I raced outside to witness the aftermath of this cataclysmic event. When I got to the front yard I was disappointed to find that our peaceful Adelaide suburb was still there, with all the houses still standing. But I froze with fear when I saw a crack in our driveway at least three centimetres across and as wide as the driveway itself. I gingerly got down on my hands and knees and peered into the crack to see if a chasm to the centre of the earth had indeed opened up, right in my own driveway. The cool air from below smelled of freshly turned dirt, but I could not see the bottom even though it was the middle of the day.

I've always been a curious person and I wanted to test out whether this fissure through the earth's crust opened up all the way to the molten core that until five minutes before I had known nothing about. I grabbed a couple of Lego men out of the toy box – Mum had always been keen on early childhood development – and dropped them down the crack, hoping for a report back from below, I suppose.[3] Yet there was nothing but silence. My research complete, I'd verified that we now had a hole that reached all the way to the centre of the earth right in our own driveway. From then on, I was convinced that every crack I saw in concrete must open to the same dark and frightening place. It took years for me to walk down the street normally instead of leaping from one side of the crack to the other like Indiana Jones leaping over a pit of spikes. This faded as I grew older, as most irrational childish fears do. However, a much darker part of my brain was just starting to fire up.

One day in particular sticks out to me as the start of my experience with anxiety. I was at kindergarten so I must have been at least three,[4] and I'd been playing on the tyre swing. It was one of those old-school playground toys before the days of excessive litigation changed everything to spongy surfaces and soft landings. This swing was suspended underneath an archway by four ropes attached at equal points on the wall of the tyre. I had figured out that if you spun the thing one way, it would unwind the other way and whizz around. I wanted to be on that swing as it spun, because that looked like fun. Exhibiting an early example of the proverb that too much is never enough, I wound the tyre up as far as it would go while still allowing space for me to squeeze in between the ropes as I lay across it.

---

3 Mum's keenness on early educational development included talking to us as adults from the first day, encouraging critical thinking and only having educational toys around that would challenge us. Lego was an important part of that, but I don't know if she'd intended the then-expensive Lego men and women in our collection to become expert spelunkers. I'm sure Lego was hard to get in Adelaide back in the mid-1970s. Regardless, down the crack they went, to see what they could see.

4 My brother and I both started school a year early, so I guess Mum's insistence on early childhood education paid off.

The moment my final foot left the ground the tyre began to spin. Much faster, I might add, than it had done during my pilotless test flight. My added weight had me spinning so fast I could no longer focus on even the ground below me. The trick with these things, as figure skaters and ballet dancers know, is to keep your head at the centre of the rotation. I was three so I'd never figure skated or even known what ballet was at this point, and with my head hanging out over one side I was not only rapidly becoming very dizzy but the centrifugal force was pushing blood up into my head, making my vision go very strange.

Like many things I would do for a thrill later in life, once fully committed I quickly realised that it was a terrible idea, but there was no way to stop the effects of it now and my only option was to hold on and try to ride it out until it was over. This was the first time I had felt utterly powerless in the face of something very frightening. The pack of kids going about their gleeful playtime business fell silent as they all focused on me, spinning in fear, wailing like a strange doppler siren.

Eventually the spinning of the tyre stopped but my brain most definitely did not. Completely confused and scared I did what most three-year-olds do in that situation – I screamed for help. A kind kindergarten teacher came to my aid and did her best to soothe me. She held me until my whimpering subsided and made me lie down on one of the trundle beds.

Long after the dizziness had abated, the shock of experiencing that fear was still with me. What if I felt so afraid again? I started to be terrified of feeling that fear again. This made me afraid. So now I was afraid of feeling *afraid* of *feeling afraid*. This was my first real experience with the downward spiral, except this time it wasn't a spinning tyre that I knew would eventually stop. The tears started again quickly, and not long after that the wailing followed. The older kindy teacher came to try and calm me down; I remember her telling me everything was going to be all right, and trying to talk me down from the terrified state that I was clearly in.

But the crying just intensified. Why didn't that teacher understand that I was falling into a dark hole of terror and I had no concept that anything would ever feel good again? As far as I was concerned, this was my new permanent state. How could she feel so calm when this darkness was coming to swallow all of us?

The teacher tried for a long time to make me feel better, but eventually became exasperated and called Mum. Knowing she was coming made a bit of a difference, but all I wanted to do was hide until she arrived. I didn't dare blink in case I missed her coming to rescue me from this horrible feeling. When she did arrive about an hour later, I could tell by the way she walked through the gate that she was upset. Being a busy anaesthetist – she had done her specialist training in the UK – she would probably have had to have someone cover for her so she could come and get me. She was probably also pissed off that these people she paid to look after me hadn't been able to calm me down. When she finally clapped eyes on me, though, her demeanour changed; her expression went from, 'What the hell is so bad that you had to pull me away from work?' to, 'Oh, shit.'

As we walked out through the front gate with me holding her hand, I immediately began to feel better. On the ride home in her Renault 16 I remember her trying to talk to me about what happened, but I just stared at my feet – I didn't know how to talk about what had gone on; I was three after all. Since she was off from work I guess she thought a quick trip to the shops was convenient.

I was still whimpering with the aftershocks of the wailing when we walked into our local butcher's shop. Knowing what I know now about moving through an anxiety attack, the change of scene did a lot to make me feel better. The cool air helped bring me back into my body, the vibrant colours of the eye-level display case helped me get present in the room. I put my hands on the glass, and it was very cold, misting up under my nostril's breath. I stared at all of those cuts of meat, the bones, the muscle, the blood, so red and so glistening. Way above me Mum asked for her order and as our butcher started to wrap the meat up in clean white paper he called out my name.[5] I looked up, and he was holding a thin slice of round pink meat he called 'fritz'.[6] He reached out and down over the display case and I stood on my tippytoes to grasp it. It was easy to chew, had a salty and spicy flavour, and both he and Mum seemed very happy that I was eating it, so I smiled too. Only ten minutes before I had been convinced that the world was going to end, and here I was grinning with a mouth full of lunch meat in a suburban butcher's shop. I'm not saying that this is where my association with eating and changing an emotional state came from, but it's the first time I can remember it happening.

5   Remember that super-boring company conference day you had where you were asked to brainstorm ideas, write all those ideas out on big sheets of paper mounted on an A-frame easel, and then the company took one of those ideas and made heaps of money from it? But all you got in return was your regular pay cheque, some bad conference room coffee, and Bruce from sales trying to hit on you at the bar? Now you know how that paper came to be called 'butcher's paper'.

6   In other parts of Australia this meat is called devon, but it's the same thing. Why you'd name a lunch meat after a part of the world famous for rocky cliffs I have no idea. Come to think of it, why would you name a lunch meat after a bloke who sounds like he's ready to lock you up in a bunker he's meticulously and secretly carved out of the basement for the last twenty years?

Now that the gate in my mind that opened the flood of fear was known to me, my brain soon started scratching it like eczema: satisfying at first, but soon an open wound once again. I'd occasionally get pangs of fear, and when I thought about what I was afraid of, I'd again feel the blinding fear I experienced in kindergarten that day.

A few things set it off worse than others, but the number one culprit was strangers. I was terrified of anyone I didn't know. When we went to lunch at the houses of my parents' friends, they would introduce us to their kids and expect us to go and play together. I hated meeting the grownups and their children: strange kids with strange faces who smelled strange, sounded strange and talked about strange things. Eventually I learned to take the obligatory tour of their room, make all the right noises when they showed off their favourite toys[7] and then find my way back to Mum, who was usually at a dining room table talking about grownup things. She'd become embarrassed when I sat down on the floor next to her and hid my face with her dress, but eventually she just let me do it because it kept me quiet and out of the way.

Unfortunately for me this was not a solution that worked when I was old enough to go to school. Every first day at school was always the same – right up through high school. I would walk into a room that smelled of disinfectant so strongly that my eyes watered, and then a sea of strange faces would stare at me, judge me, and not want to be friends with me. Of course now I realise that they probably weren't staring, and all the

---

7   I was envious that their Lego sets always had more Lego men than mine did. But then again, their Lego men weren't still on an expedition to the centre of the earth. I guess I was lucky to have plastic companions as adventurous as mine were.

intention assigned to their look was created by my head, but at the time it was as real as anything else in my universe.

Luckily for me, Mum and Dad's passion for education was paying dividends and the fear I felt was replaced with a sense of superiority because I was not only the youngest in the class by a full year but I could also read. I spoke to adults as equals and questioned them and their points of view. Teachers tended to either leave me alone or praise me, both feelings I adored.

But some days the fear of going to school was overwhelming and I put up a hell of a fuss. Once I was so afraid to get in the car that I hatched a brilliant scheme. As we were preparing to go out the door Mum went back to the kitchen, probably to hurry my brother along or have a word to my grandmother, Dad's mum, who lived with us. I saw my chance and made a break for the sofa. I hit the floor and wriggled my way all the way under it and all the way to the back. I remember seeing Mum's feet frantically searching as she called my name and looked from room to room. She became increasingly exasperated and this must have turned into growing fear. It wasn't until I heard her call the hospital and tell them she was going to be late that I came out from my hiding spot. The worry of disappointing her was even more intense than my fear about going to school.

To complete his specialty qualification as a rheumatologist, Dad needed a placement at a hospital. He found one in Queensland at the Royal Brisbane Hospital.[8] After a year of his going back and forth between Adelaide and Brisbane, it was decided that we were all moving north.

---

8   I've often wondered – if you're a reigning monarch, do you get to wander into anything that has 'Royal' written on it and demand free stuff? Can Queen Elizabeth get a free berth on the *QEII* any time she likes? Can Prince Charles wander into the front bar of the Prince of Wales pub in St Kilda, ask for a schooner of Melbourne Bitter and then say, 'My name's on the front, love, I'll have this one on the house, thanks'?

three
brisbane

When we got to Brisbane we stayed with Mum's brother, my Uncle Jon and his wife my Auntie Sylvia,[1] who had all come out on the same boat, together with their kids, my cousins Tiera and Little Jon. They lived in the developing Brisbane area of Ferny Grove.[2] Now, it's a suburb only forty minutes from town on a bad day, with plenty of shops and a railway line. Then it was a collection of new homes and empty lots carved into the dense and steamy subtropical bush, with nothing around and apparently five days' drive from anywhere.

We arrived in the summer after the school term had ended, giving my folks plenty of time to find a place for us to live and schools for us kids to go to.

For some unknown reason, they settled upon a suburb about as far as possible as you could get from the only people

---

1 Their real names were Jonas and Birute but we grew up calling them Jon and Sylvia. I guess in Lithuania they weren't too generous handing out names either; it seems that Lithos tend to have a very small pool of acceptable words to call their offspring.

2 Brisbane is a strong believer in naming places after scenic features: Ferny Grove, Red Hill, Redcliffe, Eight Mile Plains, Kangaroo Point etc. I guess by the time Europeans had made it that far north Governor Macquarie was already tired of naming almost everything after himself, so people just gave names according to what places looked like or what went on there. They weren't very bright and sometimes named places after horrendous acts of genocide, such as Murdering Creek near Noosa, where in 1864 up to seventy Aboriginals were slaughtered by an employee of nearby Yandina station.

that we knew in the state, on the opposite side of the city in Kenmore. From then on it was always a voyage to visit our cousins. I've always been envious of people who have close relationships with their extended family, not only emotionally but geographically.

We lived at number 45 Euree Street, Kenmore, a small single-level place with a giant, ancient and dying tree in the front yard. Not long after we moved there my infant brother, who was born shortly after me, was toddlering around under this tree watched by my grandmother when a branch as big as a car fell out of the sky and landed next to him. That weekend Mum used great patience to explain to me that the tree doctor who was up a ladder in our front yard with a chainsaw clearing the dead bits of tree out of the way was a very different kind of doctor from her and Dad.

Saturday mornings in that house were always something I looked forward to. Dad had to do his grand rounds at the RBH and he'd usually take me with him. Instead of developing the fear of hospitals that many people rightly have, I soon became very comfortable there because that was the wonderful time I got to spend alone with Dad. We'd walk from bed to bed in the ward, and he'd tell me to wait in the corridor while he checked the chart of the patient, scribble something on it with his fancy fountain pen (Dad had a thing for stationery) and then we'd move on to the next patient. If we were there later, we'd sometimes go to the hospital cafeteria, which meant I got to eat a massive plate of wobbly green jelly. It was pretty excellent.

On the way home we'd make a few stops. Dad had particular tastes and there were only a few places in Brisbane where he could get the smoked meats he liked to eat and the unfiltered cigarettes he liked to smoke. He'd pull his Toyota Corona up in Toowong and I'd sit in the car listening to *The Goon Show* on the ABC while Dad made his rounds grabbing his essentials. That radio show was magical. I didn't know I was listening to two of the greatest comedians in history at the height of their powers in Spike Milligan and Peter Sellers, but I just adored losing myself in the theatre of the mind they'd paint with each scene.[3]

Before we knew it I was dressed in tiny King Gee shorts and a short-sleeved green checked shirt and was off to my first day at Kenmore South State School, or KSSS.[4] It was 1979 and I was starting Grade 1, even though I was only four years old and had already had some experience of primary school in Adelaide. Again, the horror increased as Mum walked me down the small hill to the classroom on the first day. We were 1A, the first room on the lower floor of the block, the one closest to the driveway. I put my bag into the port rack and tearfully let go of Mum's hand as I stepped into the new and strange classroom.[5] I don't know whether I was crying because I was scared or because the disinfectant was so thick in the air that it made my eyes water – possibly a bit of both. Every single day turning up to school triggered the memory of that separation fear, and so every single day I panicked when I arrived, afraid that the big dark fear would come for me again. This feeling lasted – often bad, more often horrible – for my entire school life.

---

3   Saturdays with Dad were the best, and I missed them when they were gone.

4   Acronyms are supposed to be easier on the tongue than the words they represent. In this instance, you only save one syllable by shortening things. I was thrilled to once hear Stephen Fry lament that 'WWW' became the thing to say instead of 'World Wide Web', as the acronym is actually harder to say. It's shit like this that keeps me up at night, but I'm glad it's not just me.

5   Again with the Brisbane talk: Your port was your schoolbag, or 'ya skoolbayg'. A phrase best said directly through the nose to achieve more complete comprehension by the locals.

Because I was only four at the start of the school year, after little lunch the teacher sat me in the back of the class and asked me to go through a few worksheets with her while the rest of the class got busy with some top-notch cutting and pasting busywork. I imagine she wanted to see where the South Australian education system had left me, and whether as a four-year-old I'd be able to cut it in the big leagues. She drew a picture of a Ferris wheel and asked me if the wheel was turning clockwise on the page, whether I could point to which side would be going up. She wrote the word 'up' and drew a small arrow, and then took the time to explain what the word 'up' meant, slowly repeating the word 'uuup' as she pointed to the arrow. I must have looked at her strangely because when I quickly said, 'It's the left side, isn't it?' she smiled and we continued.

By answering this and a series of increasingly complicated questions I guess I impressed her with my ability to do simple maths and read and write, because just as in Adelaide she generally left me alone. Again, I owe thanks to Mum and Dad for being so interested in helping us learn how to talk to adults, read and think about things.

As kids we tend to assume that everyone behaves as we have been taught to do. Both my parents could be called cultural elitists. They were from countries that prized education over anything else, and saw careers that were a result of such an education as taking priority over those that didn't. This thinking rubbed off on me; I felt it was normal to go to art galleries or orchestral concerts on the weekends and scoff at the people getting excited over Australian Rules football games.

So it was with no small degree of shock that on that first day in class I saw the much larger boy next to me halfway through eating his box of crayons. Not as a prank on the teacher or as a way to make his classmates laugh, but because he was still developmentally in the 'putting everything in your mouth and chewing it' phase. I felt superior even though I was younger and proud that I was smarter than he was because he couldn't do the basic maths problems I finished in a few moments. This feeling of being better than others grew as I got older, eventually turning into a toxic grandiosity and arrogance that would wreak havoc on my health, relationships and career.

Our school's principal was Mr Young. Either he was a staunch monarchist or the then-premier of Queensland Joh Bjelke-Petersen had mandated that a picture of Queen Elizabeth II be in every classroom, and that every week at assembly we sang 'God Save The Queen'. Between the gerrymandering, the police corruption and the fact that South Africa's apartheid policy was closely based on Queensland's *Aboriginal Protection Act*, Queensland under Joh was quite a nasty place.

It was at this school that I first heard jokes about Aboriginal people. I didn't know what an Aboriginal was and I can guarantee you that my joke-telling classmates were using an abbreviated form of that proper noun, but because everyone else was laughing I laughed too. That night when Mum got home from work I excitedly began to tell her the jokes that had made everyone laugh so much earlier in the day. She can't have been too happy because I don't remember telling those jokes again.[6]

Life in that house in Kenmore included a few childhood milestones, and along with the first day at primary school it

---

6   Back then I had an incredible memory for spoken interactions, be it words from a film, song lyrics or jokes – if I heard it I could remember it verbatim. These days, not so much. Sixteen years of blackout drinking tends to fuck up your hippocampus somewhat, so where obscure quotes from films used to be there's now Swiss-Cheese holes of nothing. Luckily though I've learned how to remember long scripts and other things I need for work; however, they don't stick in my head. Once I've used them, they vanish to make way for the next thing.

included the conversation about where babies come from. Dad took me into my parents' bedroom and gave me 'the talk'. Other kids' folks probably squirmed and talked in roundabout euphemisms about 'special cuddles', but because Dad was a doctor I got the full biological process explained in graphic detail. Having since compared notes with friends, Dad's was the least sexy or embarrassing version of this chat that I know of. When I tried to tell the other kids at school about the tiny follicles of hair along the fallopian tubes that moved the ovum along so that fertilisation could take place within the uterine wall, they had no idea what I was talking about. I remember one freckly kid with a runny snub nose saying, 'Don't be stupid, babies come from when mummies and daddies rub tummies!' as he rolled his eyes and then deftly served a handball into a wall.[7]

1980 rolled around and with a new decade came excitement and new ways my brain developed to freak me out. Pink Floyd had released their landmark concept album *The Wall*. The single 'Another brick in the wall (part 2)' was a massive hit, and the accompanying music video used some of the Gerald Scarfe animations made for the accompanying feature film. One Saturday morning while eating breakfast I saw this video on TV for the first time. A terrifying animated school headmaster was grabbing kids and stuffing them into the top of a meat grinder shaped like a school building. Being the

---

7   I do not have space to go into a discussion about the regional differences between handball games, but let me assure you the handball that I learned in Queensland had absolutely zero resemblance to the handball games played elsewhere. We played against a wall, like a pingpong table folded in half. Kids from southern states showed up in later grades and tried to introduce a 'four-square' version of the game which was incredibly complex. There were aces, kings and all kinds of other things. I was always wary of learning new games from people – new rules would suddenly be remembered whenever I was in the lead.

good Euros my family were, we had a meat grinder so I knew exactly what it did to animal flesh, and had been warned never to stick my fingers into it. But here was this horrifying figure with a ghastly oversized monocle winding the grinder as he pushed children into the top of it, followed by pink gooey worms of ground kids coming out of the holes at the bottom.

I was so horrified I ran to my room and hid. The terrible fear was back, and worse than before. The image of the schoolmaster grinding up children kept flashing into my head, each time flooding me with a terrible fear that turned my stomach to knots and made me tremble all over. I took a long time to calm down, mainly because I'd be curious that I was shaking, and then I'd remember why, which is when the image would flick back into my head, causing further terror. I'd bend over in pain, and then as I tried to process why I was so afraid, the image would snap back again, hitting me again with physical pain and mental anguish. This loop kept going and going and I thought it would never stop.

This was the first time in my life I remembered waking up with anxiety.

I'd wake up, notice I was feeling calm. I'd think, 'Ah, this feels nice. I didn't feel nice yesterday. Why was that again? Oh, shit!' and the whole thing would start looping and whirling and spiking me with fear again. Now my brain knew the extent of this feeling, there seemed nothing to block it. I don't remember feeling a little afraid, or slightly nervous: it was either a case of 'everything's fine' or 'the sky is falling, run!' There was nothing in between.

Not to throw my folks under the bus, at least 50 per cent of this anxiety must have been the way I came out of the womb; I was born with a mind that identified danger quickly. However, considering what both my parents went through on their journey to adulthood, I don't think it's too much of a stretch to say that if they both grew up with the sense that awful things can happen at any moment – having to leave your country, and the possibility of death at any time, the knowledge that if you stayed an oppressive military regime would utterly change your life's direction – it's easy to believe that such an outlook on the world rubbed off on us. I feel it was a case of my mirror neurons doing their job and assimilating the survival behaviours of the tribe around me. It's nobody's fault, it just happened.

Clearly someone noticed something wasn't 100 per cent OK with little Andrew, because it was around then that I was sent off to see my first psychiatrist, Dr Kerr. He was a skinny academic who had a beard that would make a hipster barista envious. I remember going to his office and playing a lot of chess or Battleship. Maybe he talked to me or engaged me during those games, but I don't remember it. Now that I pay for my own psychiatric and psychological care, I can see now that my folks were shelling out mortgage-destroying dollars so their son could play simple board games once a week with a highly educated doctor. Maybe I changed, maybe he gave me the all clear, but I do remember that I stopped seeing him after I complained to Mum that 'all he ever does is stare at his shoe'.[8] From then on it was less academic Battleship and more BMX in the afternoons for me.

---

8 As an adult I've come to be more discerning in my choice of mental health professionals. I have fired more than a few who I don't click with. But then, I had no choice. I was five after all. But I did get very good at Battleship and decimated my opponents for years afterwards with the strategy I developed in that office.

four
watching the weight

As our family grew, things were getting pretty cramped in our small home – don't forget my Czech grandmother who we called Babi[1] also lived with us. So we moved to the house where I did most of my growing up, in Moordale Street, Chapel Hill. Now it's a very fancy part of Brisbane, twenty minutes from the city on a good day, with huge blocks of land. In 1980 we lived in what was probably the first release of the land, in a split-level home that backed onto a few acres of mature bushland full of possums and scrub turkeys.

One day not long after we moved to this house, as we were being driven to school Mum stopped suddenly reversing out of the driveway and let out the kind of burp that you're pretty sure will have a follow-through. Another gastric gurgle followed, before she said, 'I suppose you kids should know, I'm having another baby.' At the time there were three of us; my big brother was nine, I was seven, and my next brother was three. In October of 1981 my youngest brother was born and we were now four boys.

As both my parents worked – Mum now as a GP, Dad in private practice as a rheumatologist – our grandmother

---

1   The 'a' sounds like the 'u' in 'up'.

Babi would look after us, and part of that meant she'd often shout curses that shook the heavens when we kids were being little bastards.[2] Her favourite was '*Sakramentský kluku, (já) se z tebe zbláznім*' which roughly translated means '*Damn boy, you make me lose my mind*' or '*Damn boy, you'll make me go mad*'. She'd often just shorten it to '*sakra*', muttered under her breath as she turned away from us and sometimes even at Mum.

With the arrival of my new brother we now needed a bigger car. No longer could Mum's Renault 16[3] cope with the whole tribe. And so it was that the great and proud Mitsubishi L300 Express van came into our lives. In later years this van would undertake cross-country journeys, ferry armies of her sons' friends around after school, help me learn to drive, transport me as I moved house countless times, drive my band and me around for hundreds of kilometres and do epic doughnuts up at the Chapel Hill reservoir car park. It had eight seats, was a four-speed column shift and because of Mum's experience working with road trauma during her time as a registrar in the

---

2 Swearing in English is actually quite boring when you think about it. We use mono-syllabic words to punctuate sentences describing our dismay, such as, 'Oh fuck, I have a flat tyre.' We don't have those long, florid multisyllabic curses that other languages have blessed their vernacular with. On my podcast once (episode 136) comedian Alice Fraser told me about her favourite curse, which I can't possibly type out without slaughtering it as it's in Arabic. However, when translated it means something close to, 'When you speak all I hear is the sound of the wind whistling through your sister's piss flaps.' That beats 'fuckwit' any day of the week.

3 I know I keep talking about this car, but it did have a big influence on the world of automotive design. It was the first-ever hatchback. Mum was a bit of an early adopter in many ways. Perhaps her medical training had taught her to stop using a legacy treatment the moment research had proven that a better one was available. This applied to her early purchase of a VHS recorder in 1977 to record *The Curiosity Show* (in her mind the only program on TV worth watching) and a microwave oven, even when our neighbours were convinced that we'd fracture the space-time continuum whenever we went to reheat a meal.

UK, she had the biggest bullbar you've ever seen welded on to the front of it.[4]

It was into this van that all of us piled that summer to take the first of many epic cross-country adventures. Our first mission was to go south 1000 kilometres to visit Dad's artist friend who lived in Bondi Beach. I don't remember much about the journey except for being incredibly excited whenever we stopped at a service station to fill up with petrol because I hoped they had a coin-operated video game. I'd beg my folks for a 20-cent piece so I could pop it in the table-top machine and try my hand at shooting space aliens (*Space Invaders*), shooting space aliens who tried to capture you (*Galaga*), or jumping over boulders *and* shooting space aliens (*Moon Patrol*). I absolutely loved playing video games. It was incredibly exciting and futuristic and all about space and adventure and nothing to do at all with board games in my shrink's office.

There were two brilliant things about that holiday to Bondi. Number one was that where the QT Hotel now stands was a series of milk bars – places where in a time before fast-food chains you could get a burger, fish and chips or a deep-fried Mars bar. The best thing for me, though, was that the space that used to have tables and chairs was crammed with stand-up video games. My brother and I would beg our parents for some money and then walk unaccompanied down Campbell Parade and across the lights at Curlewis Street to find the hallowed place where the games lived. You could hear them

---

4   Mum would often tell us stories of some of the accidents whose results she had seen. Whenever she saw an older car with a hood ornament, she'd unemotionally tell us, 'Oh, I once treated a man who was ripped apart by one of those when a car hit him and he went over the bonnet into the windscreen.' 'Was he OK?' we would ask. 'Of course not, he was open from collar to crotch, he died on the table.' This is the sort of chirpy conversation Mum would deliver on the way to school.

before you saw them – the cacophony of bleeps and bloops, the demo screens of the excitement available to you if only you slipped a 20-cent piece into the slot and pushed the '1 player' button.

I was still only seven so I couldn't really see the screen properly. There must have been a small stool for me to stand on because I remember looking down on the screen. The place was absolutely packed, mostly with boys much bigger than we were, all staring intently at the machines. Because there were so many people, a system had developed to decide who would get the next turn on the game when the dreaded 'Game Over' flashed up on the screen. You would take your poo-brown $1 note (five games) or lime-green $2 note (ten) up to the man at the counter who, with his big hands that smelled like chip batter, would give you a big stack of 20-cent coins. You'd place one coin on the tiny rail that secured the glass protecting the screen to signify that it was your turn next. If it was a popular game, five or six coins would be already lined up. To make sure no one stole your coin you'd watch with the other kids who had coins there. This served the extra purpose of helping you see other people's successes and mistakes. It allowed you to memorise the game's patterns and hopefully when it was your turn you would be able to get a little bit further than the last kid.

As I had a very good memory for audio/visual things, I could see the patterns in my mind's eye, and remembered the timing and the rhythm of the moves, memorising how the player before used the joystick and pushed the buttons.[5] I'll

5 I imagine this is what modern gamers do now with streaming channels like Twitch, but this is the olden-days version. I wouldn't be surprised if the machines we were playing on were steam-powered. These games probably ran their entire code in less space than the current EA Sports logo takes up in a jpeg file.

never forget the first time I watched someone else complete a perfect challenge stage in *Galaga*, and then when it was my turn I anticipated the game enough to be in the right place to shoot all the baddies. When I got through a perfect challenge stage I thought it was Christmas.

The second brilliant thing about that holiday was the beach. Bondi Beach in 1982 was still a pretty low socio-economic spot. It had a heroin problem so bad that used needles were regularly found on the sand, quite a few Housing Commission homes and regular brawls between the locals and visitors from the suburbs. Then there was the water quality. There was a sewerage outfall that emptied right off of the north end of the headlands under the golf course. In the right conditions, raw sewage would come into the bay, giving rise to the famous name for a floating turd, a 'Bondi cigar'.

But we were kids, so we didn't know or care about any of those things. All we wanted to do was swim in the water whenever our parents would let us. We would walk out of the apartment, down the spooky long hallway, out of the bright and heavy front door, wait for the lights on Hall Street, walk between people surrounded by seagulls hunting for their fish and chips on the grassy hill, down and across the promenade, hit the hot sand and make our way through the hundreds of people all with their towels out on our way to the water. I can still smell the coconut tanning oil,[6] the plumes of cigarette smoke,[7] and hear the sound of fifty different AM radios all blaring out different stations, filling the air with a mix of pop music, strange radio ads and horse-racing calls.

---

6   This was the early 1980s – no one gave a shit about skin cancer.
7   This was the early 1980s – no one gave a shit about lung cancer.

We'd be coming from the south side of the beach, which was and still is a topless beach. Seeing bare boobs made me giggle and feel a little funny in the tummy.[8] I giggled because 'boobs' is a funny word, but the feeling in the tummy was something I hadn't really felt before. Sexuality emerges differently in different people and at different times. For me it was pretty early. I knew that if I looked at or thought about the boobs for too long, I'd start to feel blood rush to my penis and be faced with the horror of having a stiffy on the beach. From the safety of the water I'd sometimes notice boys (probably men) standing up and talking to the girls who were lying on their towels, propped up on their elbows with their bare chests in the sun. I was astonished that these guys weren't wrestling with uncontrollable erections, how they somehow managed to casually talk to these women (who were often in pairs) without their bodies betraying what was going on in their minds. Bear in mind I was only seven, and thought that everyone had a hair-trigger erection reaction like me so it wasn't until way later (alas, much later) that I understood grander concepts of arousal, flirting and courtship.

Once we were in the water, I couldn't care about the boobs any more. I just loved being in the ocean. I loved the power of the waves that would knock me off my feet, I loved jumping into the wave face and having it smash me, roll me around, bounce me off the bottom, fill my bodily cavities with water and sand and push me up out onto the shore again. I would jump up and run as fast as I could back into the water to

---

8   They weren't like boobs now, boobs that are expected to stand to attention at all
     times. I guess everyone was OK with the fact that boobs vanished into armpits when
     women lay down. The technological advances that allowed breast implants were
     still pretty primitive and if they did exist were well out of the price range of most
     people – so boobs were just boobs, in all different shapes and sizes.

smash myself into the face of the next big wave I could find. The sleep I would have after a day spent doing this was the kind where it feels like one moment it's night, then you blink and suddenly it's day. I yearn for sleep like that now.

This was the summer that I first learned to bodysurf. I wasn't yet brave enough to go out where I couldn't touch the bottom, so I'd go as far as I could and push off towards the shore when the wave came. It took me a few goes to get the timing right, but when I got the hang of it I just couldn't get enough. The incredible power of the ocean was now carrying me faster than I could ever swim, racing towards the shallows past all the people standing up to their waists, then the people standing up to their knees, when finally my hands would touch the sand and I'd turn around and run back out to catch another wave. I learned by copying others diving under the waves that you didn't have to get smashed, and this immense power could pass right over you. If you timed it right you'd emerge on the other side just fine and look back to see the carnage of people cleaned up by the wave just surfacing to get their bearings again. Much later in life I rediscovered my love of bodysurfing, but then it was just stoke in its purest form, even though I was afraid of the surfers because they looked like the mean boys at the milk bar who wouldn't wait their turn on the *Galaga* machine. It made me feel so incredibly good to be in the water, to be lifted up and carried by this power so much greater than anything I'd ever known, past all of these other people to the shore and then doing it all over again. I was never afraid when I was being held by the ocean.

When we got back from that holiday we moved schools for a better education and headed to Our Lady of the Rosary on the corner of Kenmore Road and Moggill Road. I was in Grade 3 for the second time – repeating because I was the youngest kid in the class, and the smallest – and again faced with the horror of a new school and new strange people.

By this point things between Mum and Dad had started to get pretty bad. With three adults and four kids in the house, there was a lot going on. Dad had bought the rheumatology practice of a retiring colleague and it was taking a while to get off the ground. Because we had moved to Queensland and she had young kids, Mum couldn't dedicate the time to starting her own anaesthetist practice, so she had retrained as a GP. It is no mean feat to go from a specialisation into general medicine. Added to that was her mothering being constantly under question by my grandmother, and the stress in the house was intense. The days when people weren't yelling at each other became fewer and further between.

The relationship between my parents and Babi was a constant source of stress in the house. I was utterly terrified every time I heard any of them being mean or sarcastic because within about thirty seconds the fighting would begin, the horrible words would start flying around the room and I'd be completely petrified. It would become hard to breathe and my stomach would tie itself in knots. Somehow I always interpreted arguments between the adults to mean that the world would probably end if they didn't stop fighting.

During this time I discovered that eating could make the fear in my stomach go away. I was pretty good at making sandwiches and snacks, but living with a European grandmother who survived World War II can really mess you up. She was in constant fear of strange things like the lights being on at night wasting electricity, but her greatest fear was hunger. It was the enemy. She was only happy if we were eating, almost as if she was rubbing dirt in Hitler's face every time she fed me another gravy-soaked dumpling. There were no light meals around the Günsberg house, nothing remotely appropriate for a Brisbane summer's day. It was meat, meat and more meat, with a side of gravy and lard spread thickly on black bread. Meals were washed down with strong green cordial that I drank so fast I'd sometimes vomit straight afterwards. I couldn't get the food inside me quickly enough.

Hunger brought the fear that I might feel bad and I would do anything to avoid it. I'd come home from school hungry but instead of just a snack I'd make myself a gigantic sandwich. And not just a regular sandwich either – hand-sliced black bread, smeared with thick homemade plum jam from one of Dad's Czech friends, thickly sliced camembert cheese piled on top and then another slice of black bread. The thing was so huge I could barely get it in my mouth. Two hours later at dinner I'd eat to bursting again, piling the food in my mouth as fast as I could.

It must have been pretty obvious that I was ballooning because one day Mum told me that on Thursday night she and I were going somewhere special together. I loved the idea of this, just me and Mum, away from everyone else. We drove to the office tower above Westfield Indooroopilly and she led me down a sterile hall to a room where strangers were all sitting in rows on stackable chairs. After we had filled out some forms, Mum stood on a scale next to the desk and wrote down a number in a column on a piece of paper she was given with her name on it. Then the lady at the desk gave me a similar piece of paper and asked if I would also step on the scale. It was 1982, I was eight years old, I weighed 48.8 kilograms: 107 pounds in the old measurement. I was obese. We took a seat near the back and a nice lady walked to the front, the room went quiet and she said, 'Welcome to Weight Watchers.'

Mum had probably explained to me what this was all about, and because she was super-awesome (and probably trying to lose some weight herself after my last brother was born) she'd decided to lose it with me. She took it very seriously, and got all the recipes she could get her hands on, made special portions for just the two of us, and we shared the pangs of hunger and the headaches of sugar withdrawal. We'd go every week, stand on the scales, and write the ever-decreasing numbers in the columns on the progress sheet that we kept on the fridge. While I was scared to be in there (I was the only kid), it was still pretty OK because I was there with Mum.

Two decades later when I attended my first 12-step fellowship meetings, I instantly recognised the format and feeling: they were very similar to Weight Watchers meetings (except that my adult meetings were full of alcoholics). Both were filled with people dealing with a common struggle, sharing their stories of experience, strength and hope, sharing what works and doesn't work, and keeping each other accountable.

After a few months of eating very special meals every day Mum and I both reached our goal weight. She was smiling more and more, wearing nice newer clothes and by all definitions a skinny woman. We had both worked very hard to get there and for a while we were both very happy. However, the way we were eating wasn't sustainable. The feeding machine that was my grandmother was still around, and while the program had given us great tools in knowing *how* to lose the weight I must have been too young to understand *why* I was eating the way I was. It wasn't long before I was discovering that the special Weight Watchers ice-cream blocks, if microwaved for ten seconds, tasted delicious in between two pieces of white bread toast with thick jam. The fear of hunger was back and my old habits returned to settle in for a long haul. It wasn't long before I eclipsed my previous peak weight, and the body shame set in.

five
how to make everything better

I was really lucky, not only in winning the genetic and demographic lottery (I was born white, male and middle-class in a safe and prosperous country), but in knowing really early what I wanted to do with my life.

At primary school, every Friday each class would take in turns to perform a song or a skit at the whole-school assembly. It was at one of these assemblies that I first stood on stage in front of a crowd. I remember standing in the wings waiting to come on. I could see the first few rows of kids staring, mouths agape (they were five years old so that's understandable), and feeling the butterflies in my stomach. It wasn't uncontrollable fear, just a tension that was needing a release.

I heard my cue line and walked out just as we'd rehearsed, and saw for the first time a few hundred staring faces all focused on me. They were silently waiting for me to do something, because all the action was leading towards whatever it was that my character was going to say. It might have been just a moment but it felt like an aeon – and all of a sudden the constant fear that circled over me like a hungry wedge-tailed eagle went away. My head was quiet for the first time in as long as I could remember. It might have been the slight pause, but when I delivered the line (whatever it was) I saw every staring face change expression to one of surprise, and pretty much everyone laughed. It was a sound and sight that sent a bolt through me, a reaction that made my spine tingle and every colour seem more vivid. I walked back offstage and was overcome with desire for more of whatever it was I had just felt. That was probably the first high I ever got, and I knew I wanted more of it, much more of it, I wanted to lie under a waterfall of it with my mouth open, swallowing as much of that feeling as I could until I burst.

From that day onwards I did everything I could to try and get that feeling again. I tried to make a show out of almost everything – from getting out of Mum's car to crossing a road; I'd overact my movements, putting unnecessary flair on every gesture, and then look to see if anyone would react. I'd talk too loudly in lifts or small spaces, making bad jokes or laughing too hard and then out of the corner of my eye check to see if a stranger had noticed or reacted in any way. It wasn't until 2006 when I was diagnosed with social anxiety that I recognised why I was doing this. Because I was afraid of strangers, specifically what they might have been thinking about me, my logic was that I would at least try to be in control of their judgment by making sure they noticed me. Pretty intense stuff for a kid.

Being on stage also meant that the noise in my head, the constant buzzing of fears, the flashing of images that knotted my stomach – that all went away. As an adult I know why I pursued my media career with such passionate zeal. It was the only thing that made the fear retreat. While being on stage or on camera is absolutely terrifying for most of the population, for me – someone with anxiety – it means peace. I know my anxiety comes from a lack of control over my world, an inability to protect myself from the unknown, that all-encompassing fear is right here inside my head ready to be unleashed at any moment given the right trigger, but when I'm on stage or on camera, I'm the one in control. I'm the one that's talking and everyone else is quiet. I get to say what happens next, and I know what happens next is going to happen no matter what because that's how stage productions and television shows work. In 2011 when I was on CBS doing *Live To Dance* I was live across America, coast to coast to ten million viewers; Harey my floor manager would count me in from five seconds then give me the cue to go – and for that one minute where I would look down the barrel of the lens and speak to the millions of people watching at home and the hundreds in the studio, in my head there was nothing but absolute serenity.

Anyone who has lived in Brisbane will know that it can get hot and sticky. In a time before easily affordable split-system air conditioners, the best anyone could do was a ceiling fan. The next best thing was to own a swimming pool. In our street there were a couple of houses with pools, but it took a treacherous journey across their bindi-infested lawn to get to the cool waters.[1]

One hot day just before Christmas when I was nine I asked Mum if I could go a few doors down the street for a swim. I

---

1 Not the famous daughter of Steve Irwin, the bindi is a small plant fashioned perfectly by nature to pierce the soft underside of children's feet. Covered on all sides by needle-sharp barbs, bindis dig deep into the sensitive flesh of your soles and hurt like nothing else. We would get very adept at picking our way from patch of grass to patch of grass, like Indiana Jones skilfully tiptoeing his way through a booby-trapped crypt.

knew the boys who lived in the house, and their mum had cleared me to jump in.

Pools in Queensland are the greatest thing ever. Bomb dives were a fine art to be perfected (my cannonball was good, but my can-opener was epic), and swimming laps underwater was absolutely my favourite thing in the world. I loved moving in a three-dimensional space, and wished I could stay under there forever.

Before long one of the boys who lived at the house came out carrying an old-style snorkel mask with a big oval viewing port and a heavy rubber strap. We were taking turns using it, swimming back and forth doing laps underwater. I can't quite remember how we ended up in the shallow end of the pool but he and I were wrestling or fooling around and he was being quite rough. He was bigger than I was and clearly enjoying the power advantage that he had. My memory is very patchy around what followed, but the game went from wrestling each other, to daring each other to do things, to him telling me to put on the mask, go underwater and put his penis in my mouth, then he would do the same thing to me.

I don't know why I did it, because at that point any kind of sexual arousal was so overpowering my body reacted the same way it did when I saw the boobs on Bondi Beach and I got an erection. This was super confusing because everything felt very bad and wrong and awful and mean but my body was filling my brain with chemicals that were supposed to be associated with feelings that were nice and lovely and warm and fuzzy. All this felt awful and wrong but it seemed like a continuation of the escalating game between him and me. The mask went on, I went underwater and I felt his dick push up against my soft palate. He kept it in there for as long as I could hold my breath. When I got back up, I felt just horrible.

He took the mask off me and then he went under the water. I pulled my penis out, and he put it into his mouth and bit down hard. I pushed him away, very upset that he hadn't done what he said he would. He promised that he wouldn't do it again, then gave the mask back to me and told me that it was my turn. I didn't know that I could refuse, my body was so full of arousal chemicals but at the same time disgust and fear. Down I went again, putting his penis in my mouth. Again I felt him push inside my mouth, this time so far I felt it touch the back of my throat, and I gagged and came up for air spluttering.

His mum must have seen something strange going on, because when I surfaced I remember her suddenly being at the side of the pool and saying in a very grave voice, 'That's enough swimming for one day, Andrew. Time to head home.'

As I write this now, I still feel the horrible shame in my stomach. It must have happened in the days just before Christmas, because I remember sitting on the living room floor, my new shiny presents recently unwrapped on the carpet in front of me and I couldn't even smile, my head flooded with the repetitive loop of guilt, shame and disgust. At the time, I never told anyone about this.

My mind replayed the feeling of his penis in my mouth every ten to twenty seconds day after day for weeks, followed by the shock of dread running through my body. Strangely, I felt the sensation still in my mouth, as if the incident were happening there and then, like my brain didn't need the other person there to provide me with the feeling of contact. However, it didn't feel like flesh, it felt like I had a thick turd in my mouth, physically feeling that bits of that poo were stuck to the roof of my mouth. At night when I brushed my teeth I would turn the toothbrush upside down and brush my soft palate, trying to make the awful repetitive sensation go away, but nothing worked. From then on, any kind of sexual arousal triggered a combined feeling of shame and guilt that stayed with me for years.

It took a very long time before I would feel close to normal again, and ever afterwards the warm and exciting feeling triggered in my body when a pretty woman smiled at me, kissed me or touched me in an affectionate way instantly flashed me back to this moment, flooding my body with the familiarly awful feelings and sensations instead of warm deliciousness.

When I first became sexually active in my late teens, I remember experiencing sex as an observer instead of as a participant. I would feel as if I was watching what was happening rather than being in my body, because being in my body and experiencing the rush of arousal was a horrible and dangerous feeling, and it was safer to disassociate with myself.

I'm still working through this with my therapist more than thirty years later.

That summer our Mitsubishi van once again headed south, this time all the way to visit our cousins in Adelaide. In a time before dual carriageway highways, massive twenty-four-hour truck stops with adjoining KFC and McDonald's stores, we drove almost directly south-west across the wide brown land. I'm so grateful that my folks took us on that trip. Australia is such a vast and beautiful country, and so many people barely see a tiny percentage of it, preferring to head overseas. Why,

I wondered, would anyone live out in these incredibly remote one-car towns, with a combination post-office/service station/ grocery store on one side of the street and the pub on the other? There was hardly even TV out there, only the ABC in grainy black and white.

Having doctors for parents means that you get very used to discussions about blood and pus, with being in hospitals and with talking about death. Part of becoming a doctor involves taking the Hippocratic Oath, a long-winded promise that has roots all the way back to Hippocrates somewhere in the fifth century BCE. It basically says you'll help people whenever they need help and not use your doctoring powers for evil. Because my parents were bound by this oath and mobile phones were yet to be invented, we used to stop at a lot of car accidents. It was the early 1980s, and lower safety standards in the older cars still on the road, plus a culture of drink driving, meant that we saw some horrible scenes when we were still kids. More than once on the way back from the beach on a weekend I remember Mum telling us to 'just lie down on the back seats, boys', so we wouldn't see what they were getting out to help with. They would come back to the car with grim faces and say, 'It's OK, kids, there's nothing we can do', and we'd head home silently to have dinner.

On this particular cross-country trip we were somewhere south of Moree in central New South Wales, a part of Australia where it's so flat that mirages like giant pools of water appear on the road towards the horizon. As we drove around an unusual bend in this otherwise straight two-lane highway I heard a loud rumble from outside the car. A few seconds later we came upon a semi-trailer stopped in the middle of nowhere. The truck driver walked down to our car and said with a clearly distraught face, 'There's been a terrible, terrible accident.' Mum didn't pause and said, 'Well, we're doctors.'

The truckie directed us onto the shoulder of the road. We drove across the dirt, past all the cars stopped in front of the truck, and saw a brand-new light-brown Toyota Tarago, slightly angled so that its back left wheel was off the road, with a red XE Ford Falcon lying ninety-degrees to it across the oncoming lane. It was clear that the Falcon had crossed the centre line and hit the snub-nosed Tarago head on. With both cars travelling at more than 100 kilometres per hour, the impact had been catastrophic.

Mum and Dad leapt out and went to work. I heard Mum ask if anyone had sent for help, and the truck driver said, 'Yeah, we sent one car in each direction looking for a phone, but we are a hundred kays from anywhere here.' That would mean an hour to get to a phone, then maybe at least another hour before an ambulance could come. Cars started to pile up behind the truck and people were walking past our van to get a look at what was happening. It was clearly very bad, as we could see their faces went ashen when they saw the accident, and they turned to walk back to their cars quickly.

Mum and Dad had left in such a rush that they had left their car doors open and after a while curiosity got the better of us. My brother and I quietly opened the side door of the van and walked around the side of the Tarago, which also had the side door open. The kids who had been in the van that crashed were standing around, distraught; it looked like they had been on a holiday adventure just like us. We walked behind the van and around the side where we saw the driver's door open and Mum leaning almost all the way into the car. She was covered in blood. We walked a bit further around and I saw the driver

– a slim and handsome young father with a 1980s moustache. He was awake but grey-faced, and he had the steering wheel of the van inside his chest. Mum saw us and shouted for us to get back to the van and lie down on the seats.

The western plains of New South Wales are isolated, with horizons that go forever in each direction. When the highway is at a standstill it's a very quiet place. All we could hear as we lay on the seats of the van was the quiet sobbing of the family and the stern but reverently quiet voices of those gathered around the van. No one was yelling.

Suddenly a man in a uniform jumped into the driver's seat of our van. He asked where our parents were and we said, 'They're helping with the accident.' He started the van; as he turned to place his left hand on the passenger seat to reverse one-handed, looking over his shoulder in the old-school way, I saw the epaulettes and the badge on his sleeve indicating he was with the ambulance. He told us he needed to get his ambulance closer to the accident and Mum and Dad would be back soon enough. A while later Dad got into the driver's seat. 'Your mother is going with the ambulance,' he said. 'We'll follow her back to the hospital.'

As we set off, our little Mitsubishi struggled to keep up as the panel-van ambulance absolutely flew down the road, creeping away over the horizon. Dad said we'd find the hospital in Moree as it couldn't be that big a town. A few minutes later we passed the ambulance stopped on the side of the highway. I heard Dad sigh and tell us we'd see Mum when we got to town.

We arrived in Moree and found a single-level brown brick motel to stay in. A long while later we heard a knock at the door and there was Mum, with a policeman. She was wearing the same skirt as before but with a long-sleeved business shirt that was way too big for her; the blood-covered t-shirt was nowhere to be seen. She and Dad and the policeman all spoke in hushed voices for a while. The policeman told us that the highway asphalt had sunk down to cover a drainage pipe underneath, much as a heavy blanket would cover a hiding cat. This formed a pronounced hump in the road that was mostly harmless if seen in time – but the Falcon had hit the hump at top speed and become airborne. On landing the driver had overcorrected and ploughed straight into the Tarago.

When he left I asked Mum what happened to the man. 'He died, I'm afraid,' she said. 'He went into cardiac arrest on the way and we tried to help him, but he'd lost too much blood.' I fell asleep that night watching Mum write out in longhand her statement for the police on a legal pad they had picked up on the way back from the hospital.

I think all of us had nightmares that night. That family could have been our family – they had been just a few cars in front of us.

The next day we made a second attempt to drive south. At the site of the accident nothing could be seen, but about a hundred metres past where we had parked, there it was – the drainage pipe running underneath the highway from one side of the road to the other. It must have been a metre in diameter and when the road was built would have sat another metre under the road surface. Years of floods had eroded the fill between the asphalt and the concrete pipe and the asphalt had slowly moulded itself over it. The Tarago driver never stood a chance.

Years later Mum told me what she had seen. We must have arrived just after it happened, she said, because everyone was still in the car screaming. She said she took one look at the driver and knew he was going to die. She felt his chest where the steering wheel had pierced his ribcage, but couldn't see anything because blood was pouring out of him. In her hand went, up under his ribcage, and her fingers found his abdominal aorta, the main artery from the heart to the abdomen. It was ruptured and spurting like a garden hose, so she pinched it shut with her thumb and forefinger. When I saw her she had her right hand inside this man's chest, holding his leaking artery shut with her bare hands – no wonder she was covered in blood. Mum held that man's aorta closed for at least two hours until the ambulance showed up, and she stayed like that while they cut him out of the car. She went with them in the ambulance because without surgery there was no way to stitch that artery closed again.

I will always love that in the middle of the bush, miles from help and in the face of certain defeat, my mother walked straight up to this dying stranger and stuck her hand under his ribcage and into his chest to keep him alive until an ambulance came. She didn't hesitate. If it hadn't been for her, that family would have seen their dad die in a few minutes and then have had to sit there for two more hours while someone came to cut his body out of the van.

They still lost their dad, and a woman lost her husband. The kids were about the same age we were, so I don't know if any of them would be aware that this book even exists. But if you're reading this, please know that we all cried for you that night.

*

The fear and panic that lived inside me was now finding easier and easier ways to come to the surface. My first full-blown panic attack happened in front of my entire Grade 6 class. I was meant to deliver a project I'd been doing on the American inventor[2] Thomas Edison. It was exciting to research this man because I was always very curious about how things worked, and from what I'd read about him he was also a very curious person. The project was a big biography of him, presented on a large piece of heavy construction cardboard. I'd written the whole thing out in running writing, a huge essay in tiny font covering both sides of the cardboard around my crudely drawn light bulb and phonograph.

Two of my classmates held the cardboard which I'd stayed up late the night before finishing, and I was supposed to deliver an oral presentation for my assessment. We took our place in front of the blackboard. I looked down at some palm cards that I'd put a few sparse notes on, and off I went. This should have been a breeze because I was standing in front of people and talking while they were quiet, which was my favourite thing to do. I got through the first paragraph all right but then started to forget what came next.

I looked at my palm cards, which were bullet points at best, and had a complete blank. My hands started to shake, then my knees, then my voice. All of these reactions were pretty normal for someone who's delivering an unprepared speech for an assessment – par for the course. But then came the feeling that the fear would come again, and no sooner did I think of it than it was there. I stepped back, right into the blackboard, turned and put my shaking right hand on the chalk tray while I tried

---

2   Or patent thief and racist. When you haven't got Wikipedia, you have to take what sources you can, and they're often dodgy.

to steady myself as I was rapidly losing balance, and the world was beginning to close in on me.

'Would you like to take a moment and get a drink of water?' my teacher kindly asked. I said I would, and as I ran out of the classroom down the stairs to the bubblers, the tears started to flow. I was in a full-blown panic, unable to snap out of it. Down at the water fountain I tried to breathe normally but the sobbing/fear gasps were too overwhelming. After about five minutes, I heard my teacher's voice from above me asking whether I was ready to come back up. She was leaning over the railing of the balcony outside the classroom, looking down on this round kid hunched over the water bubbler, his body spasming in tears and terror.

'No, I'm not,' was all I could muster.

Some people may read this and think, 'Ah, grow a spine, pal, it's just a primary school oral exam.' Fair enough. But by now my brain had an incredibly quick shortcut straight past reason and rational responses, and I went from zero to catastrophe in the blink of an eye.

The teacher sent one of the boys from the class to stand with me until I started feeling better. To his credit the guy stood there, even though he must have been pretty confused, and told me that it was going to be OK. It took a really long time for me to stop crying because my brain went back to the trigger moment in front of the class about every eight to ten seconds and I'd feel my stomach drop to my feet again. This went on for hours.

However, there was a positive side. Graciously, my teacher allowed me a few more days to finish the project, and I was to present the piece on the following Monday. Wanting to avoid a repeat of what had happened, I was highly motivated to learn the words this time. I spent the whole weekend reading, re-reading and making more apt palm cards for myself, and when Monday rolled around I delivered that project as if it was a top ten TED talk.

It was the first time I remember working on something so hard that I didn't notice the passage of time. When my brain gets stuck in that 'fear loop' it can be devastating. However, when I can use the same looping engine and focus it on something positive such as learning something or finishing a project, I'm like the Terminator.[3] I absolutely positively will not stop until it is done. Unfortunately for me, I had to be motivated to do such hard work, and I put that kind of focus only into things I was interested in. This would prove to be detrimental to the next phase of my schooling career.

---

3   *The Terminator* was a sci-fi film made by James Cameron in the 1980s. It was the absolute breakout film for Arnold Schwarzenegger, and is still really bloody good to watch. *Terminator 2* always bothered me because John Connor was too old when the film took place; he should have still been only nine. Sorry. It's still a pretty ace film.

testing times

Like many others, my parents' marriage, wasn't 'great' one day and 'finished' the next. It was a long, slow drag along the bottom, like an oil tanker running aground onto a pristine coral reef in very slow motion, taking years instead of seconds. Mum and Dad had money worries compounded with arguing patterns that they just couldn't seem to break out of. Sometimes I'd almost be able to repeat their arguments word for word, they were so trapped by their habitual behaviour.

Knowing what I do now about how early childhood affects your adult view of the world, they never stood a chance. Throw in a meddling, live-in mother-in-law and the marriage was probably over before it started.

In the year before I started high school my parents divorced. I was twelve. My Czech grandmother had moved to a one-bedroom flat not far away the year before and Dad moved out of my parents' bedroom, but none of it had made any difference.

Once Dad had moved out of the house altogether it was a lot quieter, and I didn't worry so much about coming home: Dad was one of those people who could not let things lie, and I never knew how he would respond. Once you threw in Mum's reactions, the two of them were a tinderbox just waiting to fire up into an argument. It was nice to have at least that anxiety gone, because the flood of fear from starting at a new school was right around the corner.

In 1987 I was sent off to St Joseph's College, Gregory Terrace, the all-boys Christian Brothers school on the edge of Brisbane's CBD. I'm sure everyone remembers their first day of high school – that shrinking feeling from having been among the biggest kids in primary school to being jostled around the hallways by grown men who towered over you in uniforms that looked too small. Some of the guys in my high school were repeating Year 12,[1] which made them eighteen, so they weren't boys, they were men. Men in shorts and school ties. Men who drove cars to school and smoked and drank and had girlfriends. They had beard stubble and loud, deep voices. Some of the kids in my class had hit puberty already and were just gigantic. I wasn't the only fat kid in my year, but I was the only one in my class. On the first day at school not only was I grappling with the terror of all of those strangers, but because it was summer I was going to be naked in front of them as we got changed for swimming class.

On day one of high school we had physical education. This was my greatest fear, for these were the days when a teacher was allowed to call a kid 'fat' and yell at him for being so. The class took place at the Olympic-sized pool a short walk from the school. The change rooms were enormous and frightening, just long benches with no cubicles and nowhere to hide.

As soon as I got my shirt off the teasing started: howls of cruel laughter and name calling from the bigger kids, even people pinching my stomach as if they'd never seen someone like me before. I was fucking mortified. I didn't quite realise

---

1   Which we called Year 13.

that this would happen twice a week until I was in Year 11 and PE was no longer compulsory.

I absolutely dreaded going to school. The nerves I'd get the night before were intense, and always worst on Sunday evenings. As the dusk enveloped our home and the birds finished their last calls of the day, I felt nothing but fear about the day to come. Unfortunately for me, this fear led to more eating, which led to me getting fatter, which led to more teasing.

It was a vicious circle. And just when I didn't think it could get any worse, it did. Way worse. As puberty started to hit, my hormones got a bit confused and I began to develop breasts. Little buds started to form under my nipples around the age of thirteen and by the time I was back from summer holidays to start Year 9 I had actual boobs growing on my chest. They were very painful and when I felt them they were about the size of a big squash ball. Because I was so fat, they looked as if they belonged on a woman and not on me. Over the summer I had gone to Adelaide to visit relatives and worn a t-shirt to go swimming because I was so ashamed of them. After a while in the ocean my nipples started to hurt. I looked down to see why I was in pain and saw they were bleeding. The t-shirt was rubbing the delicate skin completely raw. This wasn't in the pamphlet about puberty we'd been given in Grade 6. I thought I was becoming a woman.

I put on a bunch of weight quickly over the summer break, and when you're a teenager you can change shape in a matter of weeks. During the first PE session for Year 9 when I took my shirt off one of the big guys screamed, 'Look! Günsberg's got tits!' and ran at me grabbing my chest and squeezing my chest lumps while the whole class howled with laughter.

That night in tears I told Mum what was happening and asked whether there was anything we could do. Mum was an absolute champion and booked me in to see a few doctors. The first specialist we saw diagnosed me with gynecomastia, a hormonal imbalance not uncommon in teenage boys. He told me, while my case was more pronounced, not to worry because it would probably sort itself out by the time I was eighteen. Eighteen? Fuck that. I needed this gone now. I hated my body, I hated what was happening to me.

Mum was kind enough to then take me to a plastic surgeon. He told me he would be able to remove both lumps but he was still reluctant because it's a condition that corrects itself eventually. I broke down in tears in his office telling him how horrible it was to be at school. He took pity on me and said we'd sort it out. A few weeks later I went in for the surgery and had both lumps removed. The left one grew back a few months later and I had to go in again, but it too was taken out.

This surgery had two wonderfully positive results. One, I no longer had boobs that jiggled under my school shirt when I walked. Two, I was able to get out of a whole term of PE while I healed. Having your school notes signed by your mum who's also a medical doctor definitely has its benefits.

When you're a fat kid, the teasing is pretty relentless. Like most fat kids I tried to get ahead of it and be self-deprecating. I had seen the film *The Goonies*, with the fat kid Chunk making his friends laugh by wobbling his tummy around. I started to do this on the pool deck as a way of pre-empting the bullies and trying to have some power over how exposed I felt.

There weren't really any positive role models for me. One afternoon a few years earlier I had watched the kid's TV show *Simon Townsend's Wonder World*, broadcasting legend

Jonathan Coleman's first TV gig. Jono was a big guy and he had a superhero character, a man in a cape and mask that helped people, called Flash Flab. I was so happy to see that a fat person was doing good things that I got a pair of scissors and an old pillowcase and made my own costume. Later that afternoon I could be seen riding my BMX bike up and down the street, wearing a cape, an approximation of a Zorro mask (a headband with eyes cut out of it), and an old t-shirt with 'FF' on the front. It was the first time I'd felt that I wasn't a complete piece of shit for being so fat.

Unfortunately for me that feeling didn't last long. Through my teenage years at St Joseph's I was relentlessly bullied because of my size, and often responded in anger (fear comes out as anger). This made me an odd kid to be around, I'm sure.

My eating was out of control. Mum was flat out working six days a week to earn enough money for us kids to stay at our fancy school so she'd often just cook up a vat – not a large pot, but a vat – of bolognese sauce on a Sunday that we'd just eat throughout the week. She'd showed us how to cook spaghetti, so often I'd just come home and pull some spaghetti from the night before out of the fridge, slop on some of the bolognese sauce and nuke it so I could mindlessly eat something while I watched *Degrassi Jnr High* and avoid my homework. Then I'd eat another meal at dinner – usually more spaghetti and sauce.

When the spag bol ran out we'd order pizza, which always came with a bottle of Coca Cola. I really got the taste for Coke, and because Mum was utterly exhausted and couldn't argue with us any more she relaxed the 'no soft drinks in the fridge' rule and started buying Coke at grocery time. The summer I was sixteen, I was drinking up to three litres of this stuff a day. I was understandably edgy, pimply and blimp-like.

In Year 12 I was so ashamed of my body that I even asked my then-girlfriend if she'd mind me keeping my t-shirt on if we ever had sex. Bless her heart, she didn't mind and for years I'd wear that t-shirt around, proudly telling everyone that it was the t-shirt I lost my virginity in.

Somewhere around the end of my senior year of high school I weighed myself for the first time in what seemed like years. I was 112 kilograms.[2]

My shame about my body and my eating had reached new lows, so I did what any good food addict would do: I ate. I felt disgusting and worthless and because I felt disgusting and worthless I'd eat, which made me feel more disgusting and more worthless. A nasty cycle.

To try and offset this feeling of worthlessness, I chased down opportunities to perform as often as I could. Having been learning guitar since I was eight, I had now switched to playing bass which meant I was able to be in three separate school bands at once. Add to this our own teenage garage band, and I was managing to get on stage at least a few times a month.

Again, being on stage made everything better. I performed in choirs, barbershop groups and eventually that rite of passage, the high-school musical. We were an all-boys' school so we paired up with All Hallows girls' school a few kilometres away to put on a show once a year. On the backstage crew for two years, I auditioned for and got roles in Grade 11 and Grade 12.

I just adored being a part of these productions. As we were a rugby school, some of the other guys in my grade would tease

2   That's 246 pounds if you're American.

me about being a sissy and not playing footy on the weekends. But I was spending my weekday afternoons pressed up against cute and fun All Hallow's girls in cramped backstage areas, which were ripe with the whiff of male and female teenage arousal hormones, while theirs were spent with their heads pressed up against another bloke's arse in a rugby scrum. I know for sure what I was more interested in.

I probably should have studied more subjects that would have helped me get into university, but I was so focused on performance that I spent all my time singing, playing piano, and becoming the best bass player I could possibly be. It was the only thing that brought me real joy in those years, the knowledge that once I got on stage everything was going to be all right.

As Year 12 was coming to a close at the end of 1991 I tried to line myself up for the hope of university study. The dream was to study acting so that every single night I could do what I had done on stage at the age of nine. I had very little concept about bringing a character to life or living the truth of a character or anything I've since learned actual actors do. But I put the forms in anyway and waited to see whether I'd get an audition. I applied for two drama courses, one at Queensland University of Technology Kelvin Grove and another at the University of Southern Queensland up in Toowoomba. I was rejected for QUT but had high hopes for USQ, the school you went to if you didn't get into the big one: the National Academy of Dramatic Art in Sydney.

The USQ audition was held at the Queensland Performing Arts Centre, right on the river. I was instructed to arrive at a certain time, and I walked into what looked like one of those big rooms that Bond villains train their armies in: a whole room of people all dressed in leotards and dance wear, all doing stretches and leaps and limbering up. In my Canterbury rugby shorts and my lucky 'virginity' t-shirt, I felt completely out of place.

There was a movement requirement as part of the audition, in addition to a compulsory monologue and one of my own selection. Having zero dance experience at that stage I was very intimidated by seeing all these people who had clearly been dancing their whole lives, while I had simply hit up Ms Anderson our drama teacher at school two weeks before and asked her to choreograph a routine for me. Out of the goodness of her heart she had done that in her spare time. It was a two-minute piece set to 'The Jet Song' from *West Side Story*. I practised and practised on a vacant block of land near our house, taking the battery-operated tape deck that I'd recorded my earliest radio plays on, and popping in a cassette of piano music Ms Anderson had given me. I thought I was ready to go.

I waited in the big room for my name to be called. Then I was led through the twists and turns of the backstage area and came out into a rehearsal studio, a black space lit from above. Behind the table at one end sat a large man in a standard older-theatre-guy wide-necked t-shirt and a younger guy who looked like an assistant, busy shuffling papers until he found my application and handed it over to the boss.

'OK, let's start with your monologue,' hissed the older man. I wasn't ready for his abruptness so I took a moment, found my place in the centre of the space, breathed and began. Using all the speech and drama training I could remember, channelling every moment of stage time from the school musicals I'd been a part of, I poured everything into that monologue.

For about five lines.

'That's fine, thanks,' he interrupted. 'Do you have a movement piece?'

'You don't want the other monologue?' I asked.

'Just the movement piece, thanks.'

The person who had walked me in hit 'play' on the tape deck before I'd got into my starting position. I gave it everything, putting as much oomph as I could into what I was now finding an enjoyable expression of my body. I was down onto the floor facing away from the desk and getting set for the big spring up from the prone position to a dazzling spin move when the tape stopped.

'That's enough, thanks,' snapped the older theatre guy. I stood there doing the breathless-after-a-dance thing dancers do and stared at him, perplexed. I had done all the things they had asked me to do. Why did he look so upset?

'What kinds of roles do you think you'd be cast for?' he asked me. Ignoring the sibilance in his speech that could have peeled paint,[3] I saw my chance. This was it! The question I'd been waiting for, this was where I could tell him that all my life I'd wanted to be on stage, nothing felt like it and it was all that I wanted to do and I'd do just about anything to have the chance to be on stage and act. I breathed in ready to start my rehearsed answer when he continued.

'You really are kidding yourself if you think anyone would take you seriously as a lead, as fat as you are. There are just no leading roles for people like you, I mean you'd never be cast as a love interest or anything. You might get a role in a comedy being that fat, but you'd never be taken seriously. There's really no point considering you.'

---

3   This guy wasn't doing the small-town theatre professor stereotype any favours.

I heard a door open behind me, and the person who showed me in said, 'This way,' and handed me my cassette. That was it. My dreams dashed, everything I thought I wanted, every possibility of my future that I'd imagined vanished in about three minutes.[4]

---

4   A little over ten years later, when we were making *Australian Idol,* I felt a lot of compassion for people who got a rough audition.

roadie

I hadn't done so well in high school, mainly because I didn't try. Since Grade 1 I'd been quicker off the mark and ahead of my classmates, so I never really had to try to get good grades. This led to a laziness that I was never able to shake as I got into high school, when the work got harder and required more application and self-motivated learning outside of school hours. All the way through Year 10, I was getting 75–85 per cent in most exams after only a cursory cram session the night before. I felt very smart because with a quick look at a blackboard and a critical thought question in my head I could grasp almost all the concepts we were being taught. Textbooks were for the other boys who played rugby and pronounced their 'th' sounds with a 'ff'. Oh, how I looked down upon them.

Unfortunately for me, by the time Years 11 and 12 came around, the more challenging subject matter required things called 'learning' and 'study', which we were supposed to have spent the previous four years learning how to do. Of course I had no idea how to do either of these things, and the boys I'd previously felt incredibly superior to were utterly eclipsing me in 'maffs'.

My brilliant ego ignored my woeful first term Year 11 marks in Maths 1, and scoffed at my kind teacher's offer of transferring to the more basic Maths in Society,[1] which I found frankly offensive and degrading to my intelligence. Despite Mum's best efforts of organising a tutor for me, maths eluded me completely. I would sit there gazing at the blackboard as differentiation of quadratic equations was explained time and again to me, the white dusty numbers floating around in front of my eyes in a confusion-induced loss of focus.

With my ego stretching its legs and having an early go at running the show, I didn't stoop to doing any meaningful work or study through Year 11 or 12, so it was no great surprise when I was at the very bottom of the scores for getting into university. My third preference after drama courses at QUT and USQ was an all-encompassing Arts degree at Griffith University, a leafy campus in the south of Brisbane that smelled of weed and eucalyptus.

In the dark ages before the internet we had to wait for the newspaper[2] which printed university place acceptance notices on a nervous day in January. Published for the whole of Queensland to see in the *Courier Mail*[3] on that day in 1992 – was not my name among the list of those accepted for university places. I found all of my friends' names, I saw all of the courses that they got into, but my name was most definitely not there.

To say I sank into despair would be an understatement. I just went numb. I was home alone at the time, with no clue

1   Maths in Society, aka Vege Maths, Maths for Rowers, Maths for Footballers, Maths in the Beer Garden, Maths in Space.

2   A large, paper-based communications device consisting of words and pictures, which was delivered to our home by a man in a station wagon. He had an incredible right-arm-over-the-roof throw that would land a shrink-wrapped newspaper on our front lawn by 4am every day.

3   Then a broadsheet that in those days screamed far less about the perils of anything that wasn't white, male and straight.

what to do next – so I opened the fridge, made some food (even though I wasn't hungry), and turned the TV on as I sank into a beanbag.

Some time during the Channel 7 midday movie the phone rang. I sprang into action and picked it up to hear my high-school friend Shane Barrett on the other end. Shane's hot cousin Kristie had a cover band that was playing four to five gigs a week, and they were looking for someone to run the lighting rig and help loading in and out of the clubs. Shane wondered whether I would be interested. I didn't know it at the time, but that phone call changed the course of my life.

Shane gave me the number for David, the guitar player from the band who ran things, and I called him up. Of course I had no idea how to run a light show, no driver's licence, no experience at all with nightclubs, but this didn't stop me from lying through my teeth and convincing David that I could do the gig and was happy to do any kind of work in the industry. He was paying $40 a show, and I said 'yes' before I even knew what that meant.

Forty dollars in 1992 was equivalent to $72 in 2016. Here's what I'd be doing for that money. Arrive at David's house thirty minutes away either by bus or with a lift from Mum sometime around 1pm; load the PA, lighting rig and all the instruments from the lock-up under his home into the shitbox Econovan; drive with David from his house into the city where the club was; find the bar manager and get the loading dock unlocked;[4] unload everything into the club; take everything out of the

---

[4] It helped if you got to know the bar managers, as they'd be happier to unlock the gates and shuffle cars around to let you get a start on the load-in, otherwise you'd have to wait until they had finished up their bar-stacking routine for the day and you'd be sitting on the street in the blistering heat waiting for the beer truck to move. My favourite bar manager worked at a nightclub called Mary Street. It was, surprisingly, on Mary Street in Brisbane. His name was JJ and later he would give me the biggest career break of my life.

road cases; set up the PA and lighting rig, running the cables from the stage back to the front of house area; get everything set up and working for the band to do a sound check; tidy everything away and secure the gear so that the stage looked neat, with no leads or cables anywhere for punters to trip over or steal; secure the stage and instruments after sound check and make everything look clean for when the venue doors opened; head home for a shower and dinner around 5pm; take an 8:15pm bus back to the club for 9pm; make everything set for the gig to begin at 9:30.

At the gig, when the first forty-five-minute set began, followed by a forty-five-minute break where the DJ played, I had to watch the stage and chase away drunken punters from the drum kit; repeat for four or five sets; when the band wrapped, start to pull everything back down, rolling hundreds of metres of leads, trying to work around utterly blotto patrons; waiting for the DJ to play the last song at 3am; when the house lights went on, pull the vomit-soaked multicore cable off the floor of the club and roll it up; wait for security to get everyone out of the loading dock;[5] get the Econovan back in there; change back into shorts and a t-shirt for the load-out; get everything from the stage back into the van, keeping a constant inventory so I'd see whether an opportunistic drunken patron tried to steal a three-phase power lead for kicks; do one final scan of the stage and backstage area for anything at all that might have been left behind;[6] find the least-dangerous cab queue to wait for a $10 taxi to take me home around 4:30am; be back at David's house at 1pm the next day to do it all again.

---

5   It was a dark place, convenient for nookie between men and women who couldn't wait to get home.
6   AKA the idiot check.

I don't really want to figure out the hourly rate, nor do I want to think too much about the lack of occupational health and safety training or insurance or compo. I especially don't want to think about the three years of doing this job four to five nights a week that left me with permanent hearing damage and two hernias. I do want to think about what I was learning. Yes, I was probably earning $3 an hour, but this job was preparing me for my career in radio and television, unlike anything else. This job was teaching me what sacrifices were needed to make a show, what work went into making a show that paying customers wanted to see, how personalities inside a band worked (or didn't), how the business of show business worked, how you got paid, how you dealt with it when you didn't get paid, and how the amount of work and effort and rehearsal and preparation and attention to detail were directly proportional to the quality of the gig and the enjoyment of the audience.

They were *monster* days, and they gave me the gift of not being afraid of hard physical work or long hours. I write this twenty-five years later, and while I don't lift heavy things outside of a gym any more I am still unflinchingly saying 'yes' to jobs that involve fourteen-hour days because that's what it takes, and that's what it's always taken.

If I want to get on with whatever task has been bothering me a little, all I have to do is remember the smell of a Brisbane nightclub during the day, without the odorous mask of cigarette smoke – the ghastly smell of rotting carpet, sodden with spilled rum and Coke, stale beer and the overwhelming acidic pang of vomit. I just have to remember what it was like to sweat for a few hours of heavy lifting and breathing that wretched stink, and I am more than motivated. If you've never had a roadie job, I suggest you do something similar for a few months, so you'll work as hard as you've ever worked never to do it again.

The first band I worked for was a sequencer-based live version of what it might be like if a DJ played a mega mix of the greatest disco songs of the last twenty years. A drummer, keyboard player and guitarist played on top of a heavily programmed backing track, and two beautiful women sang and danced choreographed routines.

It was a tight-knit performance, and unfortunately the band were a few years ahead of their time. They were playing what would go on to explode as 'retro' in only a year or two – but in 1992 punters still wanted to hear Cold Chisel and Australian Crawl, not the brilliantly arranged live mash-ups of Prince into Grand Master Flash into Chic that these guys were playing.

With stars in their eyes the band moved to Sydney, but I'd garnered enough about the emotional dynamics of what was happening in the band[7] and I didn't feel confident that they'd last too long under the pressures of moving to the big smoke. And so I willingly leapt into the waters of unemployment.

Being unemployed sucks. I hated being on the dole, I hated taking the money, and I hated not doing anything for the money. I felt useless, worthless and ashamed every time I put my form in, and humiliated every time I was told I had to go and apply for jobs that weren't anywhere near what I wanted to do if I wanted to keep my unemployment payments coming

---

7   This was my first exposure to Rule No. 1: Never sleep with anyone in the band.
    One of the beautiful singers and our very handsome keyboard player started
    sleeping together, and before you knew it the whole thing went pear-shaped. For
    other examples of Rule No. 1 see Fleetwood Mac, Abba, The Eurythmics, The
    Smashing Pumpkins. It's the sure-fire way to break up your band no matter how
    successful you are.

in. Access to unemployment payments has become far more difficult since I was on the dole, yet as shitty as it was I am very grateful to have had those unemployment benefits to tide me over until the next job to take me in the direction I was going.

Living at home with Mum, I found myself slipping into uselessness as each day went by. After a few weeks of this I started to notice my brain turning to jelly.

There was an ad on TV at the time with a male character saying, 'I didn't want to have to get ready for a job, so I just got ready for whatever might come along.' This really resonated with me, and I got inspired to go for a walk outside. But when you're a fat kid, walking is the enemy. Walking makes your thighs rub together. And in tropical Queensland, that sweaty raw skin quickly gets fungal and you end up with a whole world of nasty in your trousers. It was hellish, and made me plan my days to minimise the amount of walking I'd be doing wherever possible. So instead, I made myself a sandwich and waited for *Oprah* to start.

But I wanted to lose weight, and realised I really needed to trick myself if I was going to get anything physical done. So I told the lazy part of my brain, 'I'm just going to check the mail.' It was about a twelve-metre walk down the hill to the mailbox, and then twelve excruciating metres back up the hill to the front door. 'Just putting some shoes on,' I'd say to my lazy brain; I didn't want to alert it to my actual plan. I plodded down the hill and when I got to the mailbox I just kept walking. I walked down my street and then left around a street that formed a six-hundred-metre loop back to our street, and then back to my house, where I picked up the mail and went inside. I had to show the lazy part of my brain that yes, we had just checked the mail.

On the third day of doing this I told the lazy part of my brain, 'Just going for a walk around the block,' but instead of turning left I kept going. It was 1800 metres of walking, very hilly, and quite a challenge. However, in the end I'd 'just gone to get the mail'.

I started to walk further and further. I had nowhere to go and nothing to do, so I'd just walk and explore the extended neighbourhood. I didn't have a Walkman so I'd just walk and think. I hadn't really put together why I was walking for so long, but I did notice that the more I walked, the more I felt like walking. I looked forward to my walks, and slept better for them.

When I set out for what was a now-daily walk a few weeks later, something powerful within me rose up and I just *had* to run – there was no way that I could resist the urge to do so. If I didn't run I felt that I was going to burst. So I hurled myself forward, as fast as I could down the street, feeling the wind in my hair, my chest aching, my legs screaming as I launched myself ever forward with every plodding stride. When I could finally run no more I turned around to see how far I'd come, and it was probably about forty metres. Happy with what I'd done, I walked for another two hours.

Within a month of incrementally increasing my running distance every day I ran the full 600 metres around the block. I was probably getting skinnier but that wasn't the goal. I wanted to get ready for whatever was next, that was it. When I ran I felt strong, I felt in control, and afterwards I felt calm. It was as if I'd discovered some secret sauce that made everything OK.

The dole office wanted me to go and get a sandwich prep job, but I knew I'd never meet the right people or get the right breaks if I was spending sixty hours a week slicing salads and stacking cold cuts. I might have failed high school, I might not have got into uni, but I knew I was smart – albeit lazy when I was not motivated by what was being taught in school. When I was motivated I could go from never having set up a PA or lighting rig to knowing every cable, connector and problem that could happen with the whole front-of-house system, and devising a more efficient way of working it in only a matter of days.

Driving was the other skill I needed. I had already failed my first driving test, so when I heard that my friend David Hutchinson had great success with his instructor Nick I gave him a call. Nick picked me up in his Toyota Corolla, a proper driving instructor's car with the second set of pedals in the foot well of the passenger seat that allowed the instructor to hit the brakes in case his young students panicked. It wasn't long before I discovered that Nick was the keyboard player in a cover band and he found out I'd been working as a lighting roadie for a band that had just broken up. Within a few weeks (and with a driver's licence) I started working for Nick.

This band was very different. They were all men, and the youngest was a full ten years older than me: I was barely eighteen. They were absolutely tradesmen of the stage, pumping out the pub-rock classics that the punters wanted to sing along to, five sets a night, five nights a week. Their work ethic was as blue-collar as it gets: they'd go on, plug in, rock out, pack down and then do it all again night after night. They were seasoned road warriors with a 300-song repertoire of songs that would make any beer garden erupt into classic choruses, inspiring the thirsty punters to buy two more beers before the next song to lube up their singing voices, which would make the bar managers happy. We worked all over south-east Queensland, driving the ploddingly old truck, north to Bundaberg, west to Roma and south to Lismore. Even though I was a jumpy fat kid who still didn't know how to look strangers in the eye, they took me under their wing and taught me the ways of the travelling musician.

The first band had had a strict 'no drinking' policy before a gig. These guys had a strict 'drink everything' policy. The first band were all about 'the craft of the performance', these guys were all about 'the craft of the perfect drink rider'.

My former high-school counsellor had kept in touch via my two younger brothers who were still at school. She genuinely wanted to see every kid that went through that school achieve success in Year 10. She had helped me get work experience at a recording studio, something I'd flourished doing. She knew how dedicated I was to music, musicals, and playing in all of the bands at school. She had helped me compile my spectacularly failed applications to the Conservatorium of Music, QUT and USQ drama. Yet even though she had another whole class of kids to concern herself with, she asked me to come in to talk about what I was doing. She had heard about a contemporary music course running at the local Technical and Further Education college. It was basically learning how to run a band as a business, not unlike what I was helping this cover band do. I jumped at the chance. There were two arms to the course, sound engineering and performance, and I applied to the performance strand of the course.

On the day of the audition I rolled in wearing footy shorts and a VB[8] polo shirt, the only collared shirt I owned at the time. I plugged in the crappy bass I'd bought with cash from a music store in Cairns on tour a few months before and played along to the song they'd asked me to learn for the audition. Then the musical director of the course got behind the keyboard and asked me to play along with him. The years and years of playing with my friends, jamming on songs we knew and riffs we'd made up, practising scales and familiarity with the instrument, all paid off. Not only could I keep up with the complex chords he was jamming on but I was able to offer counter-harmonies that he could play off, taking the music in a different direction – the wordless communication between two musicians that gives playing together its allure and magic. I can't remember how long we played for, but I gave it stacks. I pulled all the faces when we hit the good notes together and occasionally yelped out a 'yeah' like I'd heard on jazz records when a particular chord sounded juicy.

It worked.[9] Inside I felt they had taken pity on me and were doing me a favour.[10] Even when I reminded myself that out of 1500 people who had auditioned I was one of only nineteen who had been accepted into the performance arm of the

8   An Australian beer, Victoria Bitter. They were set on an aggressive infiltration into XXXX territory up in Queensland, and VB was suddenly everywhere.

9   Here's a piece of advice that you can take to the bank – if you completely fail high school, go and do a TAFE (or whatever is the equivalent where you live) course in something that you're *really, really* good at. It does wonders for your self-esteem, and if you work hard (which shouldn't be difficult because you're doing something that you love) you can use the marks from that course to leapfrog your way into a university course that you'd otherwise never have been accepted into with your toilet-paper high-school grades.

10 This is known as 'imposter syndrome' and it plagued me throughout my life and career.

course, I still thought they felt sorry for me and my stupid footy shorts and VB shirt.

On the first day of the course in a getting-to-know-each-other exercise, the lecturers divided up the performance side of the course into bands. As one of only three bass players I played in three or four different combinations of musicians with different singers each time. After a year of being a roadie for other people's stage adventures, I stood on stage and everything started to feel good again. The rumbling of a high-end bass amplifier pushing air behind me resonating in my chest, the great feeling of locking in with a drummer on a groove you've both found, the eye contact and body language musicians use to change arrangements mid-flight, and most of all the feeling of the stage lights warming the skin on my face, all of this erupted within me and I was hit with an overwhelming revelation: *This is the thing I'm actually really good at. I want to do this as much as possible.*

From then on the roadie job was just a way to make beer money. I no longer wanted to build myself up into some super-high-end lighting director illuminating rock stars who filled arenas. I wanted to *be* the rock star who filled the arena. That's what I'd always wanted to be from the first day I'd picked up a guitar at the age of eight. So I immersed myself in everything the course had to offer. There was something so nourishing about waking up every day and being surrounded by people all moving in the same direction. It was a complete revelation and the effect on me was profound. I had found my people.

It was so different to any educational experience I had had up to that point. I couldn't learn enough fast enough about what we were studying. I sat under that waterfall of knowledge with my head back and my mouth open and I gorged myself on as much work as I could get. Obsessional tendencies can be handy when it comes to acquiring knowledge you are interested in. We worked five days a week during the very rock'n'roll hours of 10am to 4pm. Every day involved playing in some way and every day felt like it was a gig, and of course we wanted to keep the vibe going once class was done for the day.

Almost every day after class a core group of us would head to the charming beer garden of the nearby Plough Inn and order a few jugs of beer to share, and the drinking would begin. None of us really had anywhere to go so we'd often stay there until seven or eight some nights just hammering down the beers. Kids like me who'd spent their teens not really knowing anyone else to talk to about the complex interplay between bassist Ray Brown and vibraphone player Milt Jackson on the classic *Blues on Bach* record suddenly had permission to rant and rave and shout and sing and scream and laugh with each other, all fuelled by the intoxicating amber ale. We didn't drink like this on special occasions, but every day. I didn't know it was binge drinking. It was just drinking, the kind I'd done on weekends with friends around the barbecue, the kind you start so early that you need a nap late in the afternoon so that you can get through the evening session of more drinking.

I was still living with Mum, who was paying my minimal TAFE fees, and had received a pay rise[11] from the band I was working with, so I now had a few hundred bucks a week of disposable income to piss up against a wall. I'd get so plastered

---

11 I was now earning the princely sum of $50 a gig, and Nick paid me in cash. I'll never forget the first week I worked for him. We were loading in to the Mansfield Tavern, an ancient rock barn left over from the 1980s that still had a neon light show in the ceiling. Nick walked over to me, pulled out a wad of $100 notes and slapped two of them in my hand, plus another $50 to make up the five gigs that week. It blew my mind.

that I'd sometimes fall asleep on the bus on the way home and then stumble back from the next bus stop after mine trying as hard as I could not to look utterly shitfaced when I walked in the door. My younger brothers were still living at home so I can't imagine what they saw when I opened the front door. Most of the time I'd just walk in the house and go straight to bed.

What I'm describing probably sounds pretty standard to most first-year tertiary students. From what I gather, most other people de-escalated their drinking from this point as their lives and careers kicked into gear. For me, however, this wasn't even first gear – this was me clipping in my seat belt and releasing the parking brake.

As the year of intense musical nerdery continued I was beginning to define myself more and more as a musician, and I wanted to explore more and more aspects of what it was to be a bass player. So I saved up the money I was making and bought a beautiful Maton JB4 fretless bass. To this day that guitar is the most beautiful instrument I've ever touched. It had active EMG pickups, a custom truss-rod access, and it cried when you played it.[12] Because it was a fretless instrument, pitch was of vital importance – there were no markers on the neck to show you where the notes were, so it was all ear, baby. When you were sharp, it hurt – when you were flat, you got the stink-eye from your band mates; but when you were on the note, oh honey, nothing sounded like it.

This being the early 1990s, we were still swapping cassette tapes with each other of music that we liked and wanted other people to like too. It was at college that a drummer named

---

12 Years later this beautiful guitar was stolen from the loading dock of a gig we'd just played at the Woolloongabba Hotel, so if you or anyone you know has a Maton JB4 with a custom carved truss-rod cover and the serial number S93, let me know – maybe we can work something out.

Mick slipped me a home-made compilation of the greatest songs from Parliament-Funkadelic on one side and some jams from Tower of Power on the other. I'd been into funk for a while, namely the more jazzy styles of Herbie Hancock whose album *Head Hunters* was a massive influence on me. But when I heard P-Funk, I think my head exploded. The sound of a band made up of about twenty people, all dressed as interplanetary space creatures, jamming 'on the one' for ten to twenty minutes a song? I was sold. And as for Tower of Power, I'd never heard such intricate, driving funk pushing the beat at semiquavers accented by the tightest horn section ever to stalk the earth.

I was diving head first into being the most accomplished bass player that I could be. I'd stay up late just workshopping scales on that fretless, playing songs over and over, getting the muscle memory perfect. I would listen to that tape Mick gave me, try to figure out the notes and then play the song over and over. I would dive so deep into practice that I would completely lose time and look up hours later with a sore neck, hungry because I'd missed dinner. I was beginning to understand that I was capable of incredibly intense focus which would result in a fast track to mastery if I spent long enough on it. For any bass nerds reading, I'm proud to say that I was able to flawlessly play 'A Portrait of Tracy' by Jaco Pastourius[13] for about three days before a weekend of work wiped the focus and muscle memory from my hands. Nowadays I would have YouTubed myself playing it to prove that it happened. Then I just sat in my bedroom in astonishment as the final harmonics rang out, amazed that I'd pulled it off.

---

13 This piece of music is essentially the 'Rachmaninov 3' of fretless bass. It's the 'Eruption' of fretless bass. It's the 'Nessun dorma' of fretless bass. It's the high-bar which you must pass over in order to reach the upper reaches of musical accomplishment.

So at the end of 1993, graduating with honours in most of my subjects, with a fancy-pants instrument to set me apart from the pack and my hair and shorts now at the appropriate length for a serious musician, I was ready for the doors of stardom to open up and to take me on a ride to fame-town.

I put my name on a musicians' contact service and went back to doing roadie work; I tried out for a few bands but nothing much happened. Auditioning for bands meant turning up to a rehearsal studio or a house that was full of strangers, and I was terrified of strangers. I'd stiffly play my way through the audition songs which were always covers – I'd play them by ear or follow by looking at the guitar player's left hand, and then scurry home after the audition was done. They would call up and offer me the job which I'd then turn down, saying it was because musically it wasn't where I wanted to go, which was only part of the reason, but the real reason is that I was terrified of having to talk to strangers or be around strangers or even smell strangers.[14]

One phone call I got was from a nice guy called Oliver. He had got my number from the college I'd been to and they'd recommended me as a bass player to work with in the band he had with his brother Daniel. We talked a bit about the musical direction he was going in and it sounded very much like pop music and not the fretless-funk/Frank Zappa strangeness that I wanted to play. I told him thanks but no thanks and we left it at that. Years later I figured out that the Daniel in the band was Daniel Jones and the band he eventually put together out of this band was Savage Garden.

---

14 I was completely freaked out by the way other people smelled back then. I wrote this footnote in the economy cabin of a packed plane to Adelaide while the snoozing man next to me let out nap farts and I'm proud of how far I've come.

A few days before my twenty-first birthday I got a call from a guy I was at school with, who was in a band made up of musicians from the grade below me. His parents were saying he couldn't be in the band if they were going to support him through university, and he asked if I would like to audition to replace him as the new bass player. They were called Feeble's Junky,[15] and they played very funky grunge music a la Soundgarden and Jane's Addiction. I was handed a cassette with a few songs on it and told to learn the bass lines. Learning by ear and drilling down on technique until it was automatic muscle memory paid off and when the audition came around, they chose me.

I was a year older than they were, but also took this band very seriously. I insisted that we rehearse every night of the week until we were a tight unit. I was obsessively controlling about a lot of things, really quite a prick sometimes. We worked very hard and got very good, and soon enough were playing bigger and bigger gigs. We wrote songs that had odd time signatures, we smoked a lot of weed, had a lot of fun and when we played the pretty girls danced. This had a great effect on our shows: pretty girls dancing acts as some kind of lure to guys.

This band consumed my life; it was all that I wanted to do. Gigs on Fridays and Saturdays meant that I could no longer be a roadie for the cover band, and I gratefully bowed out of the job that had given me so much. This meant that all I did now was play in a band that only played original songs. In other words, I was back on the dole.

---

15 Named after the epic Peter Jackson film *Meet The Feebles*. I *loved* this film. *Lord of The Rings* Peter Jackson made some brilliant horror before he did those pictures. Check out *Braindead*.

When we played a good show I would be buzzing for days from the rush of being on stage – still my favourite drug. When we played a bad gig, I'd insist that we rehearsed and rehearsed each night until the next show so that we'd avoid such a mistake again. I could be a real punisher, I'm sorry to say.

The high-school fantasy I had once had about being on stage and getting the girl had now morphed into something even bigger. If we played a good enough gig, then someone would sign us, then we would get a record deal and then we would play even bigger gigs and soon enough *boom* – Madison Square Garden. I was pinning the hopes and expectations for my entire life and career on this band. It was a completely unfair amount of pressure to put on these guys, but that's how I approached it, and every missed rehearsal or botched gig I took as a personal attack.

We recorded two EPs which I am still very proud of, and for a while there was a lot of heat from Sony Music. They were sniffing around the Brisbane band scene, which had just produced the breakout signing of Powderfinger to a major label.[16] Sony were hunting for their Australian band that could ride this exciting new post hair-metal style of music called grunge. Sony execs turned up to our gigs a few times, and they'd stand in the back without moving. They stood out among the long-hairs because they looked like someone's dad had shown up to the gig, and they watched us with the level of comprehension of a dog being shown a card trick. I'm sure these guys knew what they were doing, though, because years later I discovered that there were three bands they were

---

16 Interestingly, a common course of action at the time was to show gig income and expenses as proof of work for the Department of Social Security, and then get put on a special job-hunting program to bring you to a point where you could be signed by a major label. Bands like Powderfinger were able to use this with great success.

looking closely at, and we were one of them. Eventually they signed three kids from Newcastle called silverchair. We had played with them a few months before, and I remember the same Sony guys sniffing around backstage. When I heard that the band had inked the deal, I was distraught. They were living my dream! How dare they! It took a long time for me to get over that sense of entitlement.

loudmouth

By now I'd moved out of home – Mum was getting a bit fed up with my coming home at 4am, and the daily drinking. I moved into a place in Swann Road, Taringa, with my high-school friend Damian Barbeler. He was the leader of my very first high-school band, and is now a very successful Australian composer. Damian was studying composition at the Queensland Conservatorium of Music (AKA 'the Con') and introduced me to some of his Con mates who were doing the audio engineering course. I soon made good friends with them and often joined them for the all-night sessions at the very well-appointed recording studio that Con students could access between 10pm and 6am.

Already quite accustomed to late-night work from the road crew job, I just loved spending hours in that studio watching these guys experiment with songs, sounds and all other manner of musically nerdy things. It was an early lesson in 'no matter how out-there your idea is, if you deliver it with skill and commitment it just might work'. One night they pushed together the three grand pianos in the main hall of the Con, only putting microphones on the Steinway, holding open the sustain pedal so the strings would vibrate in empathy with other sounds in the same frequency and then singing or playing somewhere else in the hall to just record only the sound of that empathy. It was a very convoluted way of achieving a harmonic reverb with what would now be a simple digital plug-in, but the hours spent doing such things left me with a ceaseless desire to experiment, always to see what else might be possible with the equipment available.

But after paying for rent, beer and petrol, there wasn't much left over. Mum had taken great pains to show me how to cook at least a few basic dishes, yet I found out quickly that I couldn't afford to eat meat every day as I had done when I lived with her. One small piece of meat about the size of my palm was all I could afford in any week, and I cooked that meat with all the care and spice I could muster. For the rest of my week I lived on creatively cooked packets of two-minute noodles or a simple handful of pasta mixed with some home-brand sauce from a jar. No longer able to afford a steady diet of take-away burgers and fries, I lived on rice and frozen veggies, and found that I was feeling altogether lighter, both physically and mentally.

Two mates from high school, Michael Duce and Luke Heggie, invited me to come training with them in the park in the evenings. They were doing sprint training to stay fit and have a bit of fun. We'd go to Moore Park on Russell Terrace, not far from where we lived and do hill sprints, intervals and other things they'd learned in their time doing track and field at high school. Working out with these two changed the way I looked at exercise. It was no longer something that an angry man with a beard and a whistle was yelling at me to do – it was something fun I was doing with my friends. I would get so excited when it came time to go train with them, and would be buzzing for hours afterwards.

The weight absolutely fell off my body.[1] After only a few months of walking, then running, then doing sprint training my body had transformed. I estimate that I lost around twenty kilos in around three months. One night I went with friends to a Brisbane night spot Alice's Rock Cafe.[2] I was at the bar, standing shoulder to shoulder with one of the rugby guys who used to bully me in the PE change rooms. He looked straight at me without recognising me at all.

Sam our drummer hooked me up with a part-time job at the local supermarket delivering groceries to pensioners. On Wednesday, Thursday and Friday afternoons I'd load up the band van with groceries and deliver them all over the west of Brisbane. Around 97 per cent of my customers were single women pensioners in their eighties, living alone and on a fixed income at home or in one of the area's many nursing homes. I guessed I was the only person who ever came to see them because they'd always ensnare me in conversation. Sometimes I'd even take five minutes and indulge in a cup of tea while they boasted to me about their grandkids.

At first I had no idea about a delivery system or even planning out a route: I just tore up and down the twisting hilly roads of Kenmore, Bellbowrie and Brookfield trying to get the deliveries done before dinner time. The stress of making sure people had food to eat really got to me, and it was the first time that what was going on between my ears was affecting

---

1   Bear in mind that I was nineteen and my metabolism was very different. These days all it takes is a big family dinner on the weekend and my perfectly tailored suits aren't so perfectly tailored any more. More than once my stylist has had to move a button to the left to save me from a suit jacket that looks as if I have an invisible apron string tied around my waist.

2   It was wall to wall with pop culture memorabilia and American licence plates, had a food menu consisting of burgers and thick shakes, and pretty much looked *exactly* like a Hard Rock™ cafe. I don't know if you could get away with that kind of IP infringement now.

my work. I became irritable and full of road rage, shouting at other drivers to get out of my way, swerving all over the road and generally driving like a dangerous idiot.

One particularly busy afternoon it all became too much. Heading directly into the setting sun, my whole body was tight with stress. I was worried about the ten more deliveries I had to make, worried about the frozen foods rapidly becoming mushy in the afternoon heat, how much this run was going to cost me in petrol, making it back before the supermarket closed for the evening, my band, and on top of all the worry I was unspeakably angry about how every other driver on the road just didn't get the fuck out of my fucking way, what the fuck were they doing going so slowly …

And on this sunny and warm Brisbane afternoon, for the first time in my life I fantasised about how easy it would be to make all the stress go away. The thought crossed my mind like a cool drink on a hot day, as effortlessly as the exhale after a yawn. I thought, 'If I just flick the wheel a little I'll go right into that tree over the guardrail, and all this will go away. I might end up in hospital, but at least I'll have a rest for a few days and not have to worry about anything for a while.'

When the magnitude of what I was considering washed over me I was horrified. I'd given myself an incredible scare because the idea of hurting myself seemed so effortlessly close and made so much sense. I now realised that the most dangerous thing I could encounter wasn't a burglar or a violent drunken idiot or a home invader. *I* was now the most dangerous thing in my life, and that scared the shit out of me.

After that incident, I spent ten minutes before each grocery run plotting out my route. And of course when I took the time to plan where I was going, I used about a quarter of the petrol and was done in a little over an hour. The job got a lot more relaxing but the paradox of working part-time while on the dole was difficult to deal with. Working nine or ten hours a week to bring in $80–$100 meant that I'd get between $100 and $120 less every week from unemployment benefits. I could earn more money by sitting at home letting my brain turn to porridge than I could out on the road paying for petrol and the wear and tear on my car ten hours a week. But I didn't mind because I wasn't just earning money, I was earning some dignity back.

However, I knew I couldn't keep going like this. I needed a job I wanted to do, something to pour my soul into. The band was a long way from making any money, so while I still committed to gigging or rehearsing almost every night, I committed everything else I had in me to finding that job.

Since I was a kid I had worshipped the radio. It was our lifeline to the outside world. With no internet and only a few music magazines that made it to Brisbane, we only had the radio to bring new music and news of the bands we liked. I hung off every word the DJs said, made tapes of my favourite programs and dreamed of one day getting behind the mic myself.

In Adelaide Dad had made friends with a fascinating Czech announcer at the ABC named Jaroslav Kovaricek. Jaroslav hosted a ground-breaking ambient music program called *Dreamtime*. In his gloriously viscous voice he would gently announce luscious auditory adventures and strange soundscapes, always with the tag line 'meditation and dreaming in stereo'.[3] Dad took us to visit Jaroslav at the ABC studios in Adelaide in the late 1970s and I was fascinated by the quiet studio booths, the wonderful sounds that came out of the speaker and all the special-looking equipment.

Years later Dad had a short-lived weekly show on radio 4EB in Brisbane where he played Czech music, spoke in Czech and read news from any Czech newspapers he could get his hands on: the EB in the call sign stood for 'ethnic broadcasting'. Dad had a beautifully soothing speaking voice when he wanted to use it, and I'm sure other Czech people around Brisbane felt a little closer to home when Miša Günsberg's dulcet tones came over the airwaves to back announce the latest hit from Antonín Dvořák.

Being in a band was brilliant, living out of home was also nice, but I was still sponging money off Mum, who was subsidising my rent. Now I was beholden to Mum as well as the government. I never related to people on current affairs shows who loved being on the dole, people who liked taking money they believed was owed to them to go surfing or smoke bongs. I felt shame in taking the money and I couldn't wait to replace that with a sense of pride when I finally got a job doing something I loved.

---

3   I believe I have Jaroslav to thank for introducing my dad to the experimental music in our record collection. When my friends were playing their parents' records, they put on Abba, the Beatles and maybe some Cold Chisel. I on the other hand was putting the needle on Karl Stockhausen's *Musique Concrète*, Pierre Henry's *Tibetan Book of the Dead* and John Cage's landmark *4'33"*. Dad had *4'33"* on vinyl. It was 4 minutes and 33 seconds of silence which could be played on any instrument or any size orchestra and was written to demonstrate that the sounds around us are as musical in their very being as anything that could be composed. On the record all you heard besides the delightful pops and scratches were the sounds of turning pages of the sheet music, as *4'33"* was played in three movements – 33", 2'40" and 1'20". Of course silence doesn't exist in the world unless you put yourself in an anechoic chamber as Cage did, but I wouldn't recommend it. Being completely deprived of auditory input can cause intense auditory hallucinations and even cause you to lose balance after only a few minutes.

For the first time a thought came into my head, calmer and clearer than all of the other noise going on there. It was, 'I should write letters to the radio stations, then I'll get a job there that I will enjoy.' And so, like a Manchurian Candidate spurred into action by an embedded trigger word, I began to put together applications for jobs that hadn't been (or never are) advertised.

Using recent studio photographs done by a friend, I went to the copy store and collaged a few pictures on sheets of A3 paper, then cut out and recopied them to form the basis of a letter of application.[4] I then called up the radio stations in Brisbane, got the name and address of the person who received job applications and went to work. Sitting on the floor of my apartment, Nikko pen in hand, I spent hours writing letters to each of these people in my excited, angular, son-of-a-doctor handwriting. The letters went something like this – and you should read this in your best overly-excited-young-adult-presenting-an-afternoon-kids'-TV-show voice:

Dear Lisa,

My name is Andrew and I would do anything to work for you.

All I have ever done in my life is music, and all I want to do is be around music. I've listened to your station since I was a kid and it's been a dream to work there since then.

At the moment I'm playing bass in a band called Feeble's Junky. We're touring a bit and are about to record an album – but I still want to do more in the music industry.

---

4   Life was very different before Photoshop and Canva.

Now I understand that jobs don't open up every day, that's OK – all I really want to do is be around what you're doing there. I have a job delivering groceries at the moment so I have enough money to live off, but if there's anything you need doing around the station, please give me a call. I'm very good at making coffee, I brew a superb cup of tea (just ask my mum), I can change tricky light bulbs and I'll even catch pesky spiders and let them go outside if you need. Whatever you need doing, I'm your guy.

Can't wait to hear from you, have a rad day.

xx

I walked down to the post office, bought a few stamps, some large envelopes that I covered in a bunch of bright stickers like the ones that kids like to put on their cupboards and sent all the letters on their way, giving it over to the universe for the next step of my adventure.[5]

A few weeks later I started to get letters back in the mail. Not everyone wrote back, but those who did were very encouraging. Triple M Brisbane encouraged me to keep going, to keep checking with them to see if there were any jobs coming, but no, there was nothing at the moment. One letter came from Lisa Barp, the head of promotions at B105, what was then Brisbane's number one FM station, saying she loved my letter and asking if I would like to come in for an interview for a job as promo driver.

---

5   In the days before internet banking, Mum taught me that if you wrote nice things on the outside of the envelope or even stuck gold stars or stickers on it, the mail carrier would look at it longer, and because of that they'd leave it on the top of the pile, which would mean it would get handled first when it was delivered. She'd sometimes sit there at our dining-room table writing cheques and I'd help her stick shiny gold stars on the envelopes so that the late bills would be hopefully given priority by a bored mailroom employee and we wouldn't get our power shut off.

I was elated. I called them immediately and lined up a time to go in. When the day came I turned up looking like the keyboard player in Joe Cocker's band from the 1970s. I wore checked pyjama pants, a t-shirt with buttons down the front all undone and an ill-fitting sports jacket. My hair was a resplendent mane that reached my belt line. It flowed behind me as I bounded into the interview room and I flicked it out of the way dramatically as I zealously greeted everyone there. The three people at the round table were Lisa, Valerie who was assistant promo director, and a guy I vaguely recognised named Jamie Brammah. Then it all clicked – Jamie was JJ, the bar manager from one of the clubs I used to work at. JJ who was all hustle and smiles. JJ who I used to chat with when I was loading the band in. JJ who'd seen the photo I sent in and said to his boss, 'Hey, I recognise that guy – he'd be great. Let's get him in for an interview.'

This was a massive moment in my life. Despite the enormous amount of money and sacrifice my parents had put into my education, I'd never figured out how the world actually worked. I had been told that if you wanted a job you looked in the newspaper and found the job you wanted, then you called up and asked about the job and then the people with the job gave it to you. It's difficult to imagine, I'm sure, but I really had no concept of training, connections, references, momentum or anything. I thought it was all a system that worked like cogwheels in a machine. For the first time I was able to see that everyone you meet in your career will always be in your career, and the way you leave them feeling about you will be what makes or breaks you when you work with them again. I guess I'd impressed JJ on those stinking hot load-in days, because after the interview I got the job, working in promotions at B105.

This meant driving around a big fancy Nissan 4x4 that had the on-air name of a Black Thunder. They had a hot-rod flame-job up the side and the biggest esky you've ever seen in the back, chock to the brim with icy cold cans of Coke. The job was to go out to a prominent street corner in the city somewhere (usually where the ratings were low) and call in to the station to encourage people to come and see us, so they could get their hands on some swag.[6] The idea was that people driving by would remember our station when they filled their radio survey books and just tick 'B105' even if they'd never listened because it was a familiar brand to them. I didn't care why, all I knew was that I had to do the first week free as a trial, and then I'd get paid $8 an hour before tax.

The problem was that my working hours were netting me more money than the allowable threshold to keep collecting unemployment cheques but not enough to live on. So for the first six weeks of working there, I was earning less money working nearly full-time than I had been on the dole. I had to move back in with Mum because I could no longer afford rent. However, this time I didn't care because it felt amazing to be doing a job that was fun, was about music, and was as close to being on stage all the time as I could get. I was working as hard as I possibly could to make the most of the opportunity that was now presenting itself, and that was enough for Mum to let me move back home.

Once a few trial runs had been heard and approved by the program director Rob Logan, I was ready to get on air for the first time. However, before I could make my radio debut, I needed the most important piece of equipment a nineties FM

---

6   Swag. Free stuff. Usually with gaudy sponsor logos all over them. I believe SWAG is an acronym for Stuff We All Get.

radio promo driver could possibly have – a radio nickname. In what was probably a hangover from the CB radio culture when FM radio first began in the 1970s, drivers of the promo trucks were expected to have a cool-sounding nickname to identify them on air.

If you were lucky you got to pick your name yourself, if you were unlucky it was picked for you – and the name usually had a basis in some aspect of your job or character. I worked with Hotplate Harry (a chef who cooked up meals for hundreds in a mobile kitchen called The Rock Cafe), Spinderella (a delightful young actress from North Queensland), and Black Betty (because it was Queensland in the 1990s you could call a brown lady Black Betty, and we were all expected to be cool with it).

JJ was searching for a name for me when he saw the hair-wrap I'd had put into my mane of locks a few months prior. My hair was so long it landed somewhere down past my nipples. A glow-in-the-dark spider was woven into it, so that when I stood on stage flinging my hair around there was a spider flying around in there as well. JJ took one look at that thing and said, 'You're Spiderman. Better yet, Spidey.' And that was that. For the next four years, no one outside the family ever called me Andrew.

I didn't realise it at the time but this job was the best radio training I could have asked for. Everything I'd go on to perfect later in my career started from those first few weeks of training with JJ. Brevity, branding, labelling, resetting and tagging – all the elements of a perfect radio talk break started to take shape in those promotional crosses.

I was taught to write down what I was going to say (usually on the back of a station bumper sticker that we'd later give out).

We'd call into the studio on a mobile phone the size of a shoebox, and when the DJ was rolling tape and recording us we'd put on our best impression of a DJ voice and hit them with the details: 'Yeah thanks, Craig, you can catch the B105 Black Thunders on the south side at Beenleigh Tavern. We're just off the freeway in the car park under the big sign giving out icy cold cans of Coke, and the Video Ezy movie of the week *Hot Shots 2*. The first person to tell me the name of the lead character's real dad will walk away with that brand-new VHS tape. So come and see me, Moondog, Spinderella and Black Betty at the Beenleigh Tavern car park right now and keep listening to find out when we're near you later today – until then, this is Spidey with the B105 Black Thunders on Brisbane's B105.' I put everything into crafting those crosses. I'd sometimes work all day just to get those eighteen seconds on the radio absolutely perfect. Cutting a syllable here, crafting a hook there, maybe sliding a cheeky joke into the verbal interplay. I absolutely loved it.

I didn't quite realise until a few weeks in that being on the street team was a pathway to getting on air. I heard that a few of the guys were doing panel shifts, sitting in the studio on a weekend and pushing 'play' on gigantic twelve-inch reel-to-reel tapes holding the pre-packaged network shows that filled the airwaves on Saturday and Sunday afternoons. To do those shifts you had to know how to make the tape machines work, how to fire the commercial breaks when the segments ended, and basically how to run the studio. Once you were able to show that you could be trusted not to put the station off air, you might get a weekend 'mid–dawn': the midnight to dawn shift, either from midnight or 1am until 6am.

You'd then tape what you said on air and hope the program director would listen to it. If Rob liked what he heard, he might shrug his shoulders and let you do another shift. If he really liked what he heard, he might call you into his office and tell you that this or that part was absolute shit and if you ever wanted to make something of yourself you'd change this, change that, slow down, stop yelling and tidy up that fucking sloppy panelling.

All of this I learned while driving around Brisbane from suburb to suburb, constantly followed by what the station called 'loyal listeners' but what we called 'prize pigs' (self-explanatory) or 'nuff nuffs' (because they could never get enough free stuff).

When I called into the station to do the cross I got that hit of dopamine that only performing could give me. Like the addict I'd later become, I did everything in my power to secure another fix, and then a steady and reliable supply of gear. Soon JJ asked me to do nearly all of the on-air crosses when I was out with the team. After only a few weeks I got promoted to be the exclusive street guy for the nightly countdown show. That meant five shifts a week from 5pm to 9pm where I'd go out and do street giveaways and stunts for the nightly countdown show. I said yes straight away.

My self-centred decision forced the boys in the band to push rehearsals back until after I finished work so we wouldn't start until 9:30pm and would often finish after midnight. It was a shitty move on my part, but I say this with complete honesty – I had absolutely zero concept of how my actions might affect others. As far as I could see, this was a work opportunity too good to pass up and I was going to take it.

On the two nights of the week when I didn't have to race off to a late rehearsal I would wrap up my Thunder shift and wander upstairs to the studio. These were the days before

Southern Cross Austereo bought the Triple M network, so we were still in a full-blown radio war. I loved being up with the on-air team of Stuey and Zoe, watching Stuey Paton drive the panel like he was expertly playing a piano. He had started a few years earlier in the same job that I was in, but driving the Thunders down in Melbourne. And now here he was – running the number one night show on the number one station in Brisbane and driving a gold BMW coupe. Stuey probably hated the job because he was in a town that didn't even know what AFL was, but I thought he was incredible.

When 10pm rolled around Stuey and Zoe would be out of the studio before the final song had even finished playing, and the late-night host Clare Blake would be there to take over. Clare was a petite woman in her early thirties, smart, beautiful and with a sharply cynical sense of humour that could strip the skin off a normal human being. Another transplant from Fox FM in Melbourne, she'd wound up on the late-night shift in Brisbane – the cul de sac of Australian radio. It was a lonely shift and I didn't want to really be anywhere else than on stage or in that studio, so on nights that the band wasn't rehearsing I would hang out in the studio with Clare, talking about radio, her career, her travels, her boyfriend and what the hell I was going to do with my life.

I'd watch her hands like a hawk to figure out how she ran the panel, asking all kinds of questions about what all of the buttons did. To her undying credit Clare patiently explained to me how everything worked, what she was about to do in a particular talk break, do the break, and then explain afterwards why she'd done something different when the caller had gone in an unexpected direction. Clare showed me how to answer the phones and produce up a caller so that you could record them saying something that would make great radio. She taught me how to amp up a caller so their energy was high when they got on air, how to hear their story through and then get them to tell it again but quicker, how to suggest points in the story that could use embellishing or accentuating.

On Thursday nights she ran a relationship call-in show where people would ring up to either praise or damn their partner; in the 1990s you could get away with doing phone topics based on song titles. Seventies rock legend Meatloaf had just released a new album and the lead single was 'I Would Do Anything for Love (But I Won't Do That)'. One night Clare went with the phone question, 'You would do anything for love – but you won't do what? 223 0055 call us now.'

The phones lit up like a Christmas tree. After the second talk break Clare asked me, 'How's line three?'

'He's got a fun story. John is his name, you could go into it by asking him what he's done for his wife but she won't do for him.' I gave her the line heavy with sexual innuendo, but he was only talking about recording her favourite shows when she was at work. 'Ha! I love it,' she said. 'Put some cans [headphones] on and come in on the break with me, you can bring him in and do the line.' My heart raced as she hit 'record' on the Otari quarter-inch reel-to-reel machine, and introduced the first caller.

'It's Brisbane's B105 Clare Blake with you tonight. I've got Spidey from the Hot 30 in with me ..., Jenny from Redbank Plains, what won't you do?' Jenny told a great story about how she'd do anything except deal with her mother-in-law after a bottle of wine. When the laughter subsided and we'd moved on to the next beat, Clare gave me the eye that said we needed to move on to John.

'Tell us, John, when you ask even nicely, even when you've been a good husband and done that 'special' thing that she likes – your wife won't do what?'

John said, 'She won't record the footy for me. I'm on nights so I record *Oprah* for her all the time, but when I'm working and I ask her to record the footy, she won't.' John delivered his punchline just as he and I had rehearsed it off air, and the laugh we got out of Clare was perfect.

The next day during the meeting when all the announcers gathered around the boardroom table to talk about that weekend's promotions, new music that was coming up and to complain about other people smoking in the studio, Rob Logan played the tape of what Clare and I had done the night before. I don't exactly know why he did it – he might have wanted to just showcase the fun interplay between Clare, myself and the caller – or he might have wanted to show what a twenty-year-old kid who was driving Thunders and hanging out in the studio for free was doing while they were asleep. Either way the next night that I went in I found Clare on the other side of the desk.

'You're panelling tonight,' she said. She talked me through the exact order of the buttons to push, the right way to cue up a tape to play back a caller and even how to splice edit the quarter-inch tape.[7] I was terrified, and incredibly excited, but I concentrated and it worked.

The following Tuesday Clare greeted me with some brilliant news – she had a corporate gig that Friday night, she'd talked

_____

7   Back then I used a Chinagraph pencil to mark the tape, a razor blade and a splicing block to cut the tape using a small piece of special tape to splice the tape back together. I'm very glad I learned to edit on a reel-to-reel: once you have had to edit an entire interview in this laborious way you're far more efficient when you first record it. This was the radio equivalent to shooting on film; you are conservative with your input so you can be efficient with your output. It was a perfect way to learn to do interviews.

to Rob our boss and vouched for me, and if I wanted to I could do the 10pm–2am late-night show that Friday night. Less than six weeks after I had started as a Black Thunder driver, I was pulling my first on-air shift.

To say I'd fallen into the job was an insult to people who have fallen into things. Yet here I was, twenty years old at the number one station in the city making my radio debut, and it wasn't even midnight yet. The shift was terrible and I was so nervous I vomited after it was done – but when the microphone was on, it was everything I ever wanted to do. The noise in my head stopped, and I somehow managed to not put the station off air, say 'fuck' or set the building on fire – I was chalking it up as a win.

The following week Rob Logan called me into his office and went over the tape of the shift with me. 'You've got something, mate. You've got to slow down, stop fucking yelling, hook more, tease less, be more natural and generally not be as shit – but you've got something. I'll put you on a few more casual mid–dawns and we'll see how you go.' It was the most incredible break I'd had up until that point. It meant that about once a month I'd do the announcing on the overnight shift which on the weekends were midnight to 6am.

My evenings with Clare had become an unpaid training ground, my enthusiasm to learn was utterly unquenchable and I'd jump at anything that Clare taught me how to do, sometimes staying back after she'd left at 2am to practise on the machines until I knew how to work them perfectly. I owe my entire radio career to Clare.

Word got around the station that I was now on the roster and one of the other Thunder drivers, known as Outback Jack (he was from western Queensland), was far from happy. He'd been there longer than I had, and as far as he was concerned by getting on air before him I'd jumped the queue. The next free night I had from the band I walked in to the studio for my regular late-night hang with Clare to find Outback Jack sitting in the announcer's chair looking like a naughty schoolboy. He wouldn't make eye contact and informed me, 'See ya, mate, it's my night with Clare.' I turned and left, knowing that our times to hang out were over.[8]

Over the next few months I began to do one, then two overnight shifts a fortnight. They paid $25 an hour, and the extra $125 a week in my bank account (plus not having to pay rent living at home) meant that I could now drink fancy drinks after gigs when I went out to the club.

At the same time, now knowing how fragile a career in radio could be, I had enrolled in a business course at the Queensland University of Technology. I honestly had no idea what a business course was. It was just the course that I could get into with my now-improved tertiary entrance grades thanks to that year in TAFE. I looked at the course handbook and truly didn't even understand what the course would teach or what kind of job I'd be trying to get on the other side of it. I just knew that friends of mine had done the course, and they seemed to enjoy it – so I thought it might be

8   Clare still works in radio in Brisbane and I truly don't have enough words in this book to thank her for what she did for me. Whatever you want to do with your life, whatever career you wish to pursue, I hope that you too find someone like Clare who can take you by the hand and show you the ropes with kindness and humour, someone who can kindly answer all of your stupid questions, someone who can instil in you a solid work ethic and skills for handling the uncertainty of an uncertain industry that can act as a foundation on which you can build an almighty empire. I'm still just bolting the frame onto the foundation that Clare helped me build, but you get the idea. I wouldn't have even known that I was able or even allowed to build something until Clare believed in me and told me that it was possible.

a good idea. When it came to choosing a major, I ticked the box marked 'Communications' because I was already in radio and I thought that the two were related. They're not related in the slightest, and I still can't believe I was so utterly ignorant of how the university machine worked or how career paths are formed out of a degree.

Come February 1995 I started at QUT Gardens Point Campus. From the beginning I was completely out of my depth. I simply didn't know *how* to learn. I didn't know how to study, how to take notes, or how to write an essay. I didn't know how lectures, tutorials or assessments worked. I just wandered around the campus looking at everyone else who seemed to have their shit incredibly together, wondering when they all acquired this knowledge and how I had managed to miss it. I soon realised that my new-found university ambitions would be over before they'd even begun.

It was 1995 and Feeble's were running hot; we were playing most weekends and building a solid following. While the band was gaining momentum and we were writing and rehearsing new material, I was picking up more and more overnight shifts mid-week. With my new university schedule two to three times a week, my day went something like this:

9:30am Wake up and head into QUT
11:00am Lecture on writing skills
12:00pm Go and grab something to eat and sleep on the
  Kidney Lawn
1:00pm Sit in the tutorial wondering what the hell I was
  doing there and why everyone else in the room seemed to
  know what was going on
2:00pm Head into the radio station and prep for the night's shift

4:00pm Head down to the studio to panel Martin/Molloy

6:00pm Go downstairs, pack the truck for the night show's Thunder drops and head out

9:00pm Finish work and head to the rehearsal room

9:30pm Rehearse with the band

11:30pm Head back to the station with my sleeping bag and crash on the audio booth floor

01:30am The late-night jock and radio legend John Peters wakes me up and I start pulling my CDs to play for my shift.[9]

02:00am Start my shift bringing the better music variety from the '70s, '80s and '90s to the late-night inhabitants of Brisbane

05:0am While still on air, pull the CDs for the breakfast shift

06:00am Get off air, spend ten minutes putting all my CDs away and head home

06:45am Crash in bed and set an alarm to do it all again

I managed about six weeks of this before I knew something had to give. The band was killing it, the crowds were getting larger and larger, the songs we were writing were more and more fun, and we were loving it. Rob Logan was by now

---

9 Before digital storage of music, we had to manually play every song off a CD. This meant picking through a colossal library of music to get the songs we wanted. At fourteen or fifteen songs an hour, balancing the CDs for a six-hour shift was an art form – whoever designed CD cases clearly thought, 'What's the least stackable, most fragile casing we can possibly come up with for this format of music?' On more than one occasion I'd be trying to make it back to the studio before the current song faded out when the giant stack of CD cases I was carrying fell and clattered all over the floor. Cases shattered and shiny discs rolled in every direction. With the song still fading and the dreaded dead air waiting on the other side, you had no option but to step over the chaos, run to the studio and push the button to fire the next song and buy yourself three more minutes, and then head back to just grab everything and take it back to the studio, where you'd spend the rest of your shift trying to put everything back in the right cases.

giving me almost weekly airchecks, ripping my shifts to shreds and giving me points to work on for the next week, where he'd offer the same amount of devastating criticism, but also just enough encouragement that I could make a career out of this if I put the work in. University remained a mystery. I'd gone because I thought I should go. However, after six weeks I'd have to start paying fees. And so, with a great deal of relief and not a lot of ceremony, I dropped out of university.

As I strolled out of the enrolment office after informing them I was leaving on that last day, feeling the sun on my face and the smell of the adjoining botanical gardens in my nose, the relief was immense. I felt good about quitting. My academic career to this point had been filled with enormous shame at underperformance, but now that I had a chance at a career I seemed to have a natural aptitude for, there was nothing else I wanted to do.

The early success I'd had, the raw talent that Clare and Rob had recognised in me, buoyed my confidence. So when I saw in the weekly music press that the music channel Red TV (later to become Channel [v]) on the new cable subscription service called Galaxy (later to become Foxtel), was hiring, I jumped at the chance to have a shot as an on-camera presenter. I'd seen some press on their flagship host Jabba and thought I should do that job too, so I wrote the sort of letter that had got me my radio job and jumped on my super-long skateboard to pop it in the mailbox.

I was so excited and sure the job was mine that on the way home from the mailbox I took a route that led me down bigger and bigger hills than I'd ever skated down before. With my ego running the show and my adrenaline high, I pushed off the top of a gigantic slope in the newly developed back streets of Chapel Hill. As I approached terminal velocity, a terrifying attack of speed wobbles hit me. Fearing that I'd lose control altogether I had the genius idea of saving the situation by jumping off the skateboard. I'd never before timed myself when it came to running speed, but it became quite clear that I could in fact not go from a stationary position on my skateboard to running at around 40 kilometres an hour. I managed two flat-footed sole-slapping steps before the momentum of my upper body overtook the deceleration of my lower body and I went head over heels a few times before ending up on my back, my bare flesh skidding down the hot summer tarmac. Realising I was in the middle of the road, I crawled onto one of the perfectly manicured lawns off to the side in case any cars came by.

To give you an idea of the size of my ego and sense of self-importance, the intense pain I felt from slapping my head into the road and the agony of shearing the upper layers of skin from my right hip to my right shoulder blade were absolutely nothing in comparison to the shame and embarrassment I felt surge through my body. I was 100 per cent certain that every stay-at-home mum in the street was glued to her front window laughing hysterically at my fall. Alone, I started to laugh too. Not because I found it funny (I was in fact terribly hurt and in a lot of pain) but because I thought that if I laughed these people would think that I was laughing at myself too, and go back to their *Oprah* and infomercials. It was a clear moment of the desire to control others' imagined perceptions of me overriding any kind of self care.

The letter I had posted before the accident worked; I got a call later that week telling me I had an audition in a few days at a casting office in the Valley. Not wanting to mess with the formula, I wore the same outlandish outfit I'd worn to the B105 interview, including the purple jacket over a long-sleeved t-shirt. This helped because I had not sought out any proper medical attention after my skating accident. I hadn't wanted to worry Mum, and I was too ashamed to admit to her that her fully grown son was still stupid enough to fall off things, and my entire back was still a weepy mess of scabs that would soak through my t-shirt by the end of the day.

As I walked into the room I saw a few people on one side, where a small camera and tripod were set up, and on the other was John Coghill, the drummer from Powderfinger. The audition called for me to address the camera directly and talk about why I wanted the job, and then I was to interview a musician, who was John. I had my hair out in full mane mode and kept shifting around because my scabs would weep and stick to my shirt and would start to hurt. I thought I did a pretty good job, and it helped that I had met John a few times. I probably went pretty nerdy and very 'in' with my questions, showing off that I was in a band too and I was *so* important because I knew people that he knew too. When the camera switched off, with a massive flick of my hair I left the room and headed to work.

The next morning the landline phone in our house rang, and I ran all the way down the hall to get it. On the other end was a man with an American accent who introduced himself as being from Red TV. He said he loved my tape, loved what I did with the interview and wanted to offer me the job. I was absolutely over the moon. He did however have one condition – he said I'd have to cut my hair.

I was so proud of my appearance, so caught up in vanity that even though this was a job I wanted very badly I said,

'If that's the case, then, no.' I was turning down what would have been a massive break in my career, an access all areas pass to the entertainment world – and a TV career at my feet, but if it meant cutting my precious, luscious, resplendent hair I didn't want it. This turned out to be a good decision, because no sooner had I turned down the gig than I heard a familiar Australian voice scream, 'Gotcha!'

The voice belonged to Jamie Dunn, the hero of the station's breakfast team. There was no job, just on-air humiliation. One of the people at the audition had been a young entertainment reporter for the *Courier-Mail*. She had absolutely slaughtered me in an article that morning and in hindsight she was probably aptly describing the hubris she'd seen on display. I was utterly humiliated, doubly so because with my radio opportunities just opening up I could hardly refuse to let them air the prank call the next day on the breakfast show. The nuff nuffs teased me for months after that about not cutting my hair.

Keeping a regular daytime schedule of work and two or three times a week needing to be awake enough to sound great on radio really throws your body into a strange place. You can't tell when you can or need to sleep, hunger becomes a distant memory because your mealtimes are all messed up, and you can't even begin to think about a regular pooping schedule. Not to mention that by the time you're able to sleep it's nearly 7am and already 36°C. So I turned to sedatives to help me get just a few hours in a row of quality rest. I would start with some Jack Daniels when I got home around 6:45am but when that didn't do the trick I'd smoke a cone or two of pot to try to relax my body enough to sleep. So on at least three mornings a week I was drinking and using just to get to sleep, which then left me groggy waking up so I'd smash coffee to get back up to operating speed. Then later in the day when I had a chance to sleep again I couldn't, so it was more whisky and weed. I probably don't need to tell you that these are not great lifestyle choices.

Things on the street team were pretty tight. We were a band of brothers and sisters out there on the road every day, getting $8 an hour to be clawed at by toothless punters who seemed to believe that if they didn't get a bumper sticker they would fuckin' punch someone. We all worked so much that we became our own social circle, catching up on weekends for drinks and dinners.

One of the women on the team and I became particularly close. Her name was Cymone and she spoke with a slight American accent, having just returned from La Crosse, Wisconsin, where she had been studying acting. From far north Queensland, she was a talented actress. She'd also returned with a fiancé, an African-American man some years older than her. Since she was off the market, we were able to develop a friendship that never stepped past that boundary.

After about nine months of working together on the street team she had worked her way up to producing the night show I was working on. She would answer the phones and run all the business of the show off air, including scheduling interviews, fulfilling competition promises and keeping everything moving. Our relationship started to get closer and closer until one memorable night.

Through the station we'd got tickets to a rave, and with a few people from work we went along. It was in the seedy part of Brisbane called Fortitude Valley, in an underground club with dark and slippery side rooms where different kinds of music were playing. I was only drinking that night, and as we were not fuelled by the same amounts of amphetamines that were propelling the rest of the crowd to climax at the drop of the sixty-four-bar snare roll, soon enough it was time to go home.

I had moved out of home again into a house that smelled like cat litter and bong water way out in the sticks of Brookfield that I shared with my drummer Sam, his girlfriend and our stoner mate Bob who worked in a second-hand record store. It was a great house, but a prohibitively expensive cab ride away from the city. Cymone lived nearby and assured me that I could sleep on her couch and not to worry about going back out to the bush. When we got to her house, however, her 'couch' was a tiny two-seater bamboo-framed piece of furniture that looked as if it had been lifted from a Gold Coast apartment block.

When I told her I couldn't sleep on that, she replied, 'I guess you'll have to share my bed.' I was a little confused because I thought she had a fiancé. It turned out that the tyranny of distance had put an end to that relationship, and before you know it, we were together. After the second night I stayed over I never left. It wasn't long before I moved all my stuff out of the Brookfield house and into the bedroom of her apartment in Kangaroo Point. It was a former brothel just two streets away from the Gabba cricket ground, with a sink in the bedroom. Occasionally we'd have lost old men wander down from the nearby Pineapple Hotel and knock on the door, their distant drunken memories telling them that 'third house on the left' was a good time. Once I piled all my crap into her house there wasn't any room for us, so we pulled the mattress out of the bedroom, lay it on the living-room floor, and the bedroom became the storage room.

Cymone and I were now officially live-in boyfriend and girlfriend.

I was twenty-one years old, and I was so happy.

I was in a band that was having more and more exciting gigs, I was getting high every day, excitedly losing myself in music or films with more enthusiasm than I could ever muster when I was straight, and thanks to my new girlfriend and mid–dawn shifts every weekend, I was getting regular sex and regular pay for the first time in my life.

Cymone and I were both working very hard and I'd often go six or seven weeks without having a day off, but it was OK because I just loved the work and life was exciting and new. I loved being with Cymone and the world she was showing me. She really had to take me by the hand and teach me how to treat her, though, and I can't thank her enough for that. I didn't know about holding her hand in public, introducing her to people when we met; I was a total dolt when it came to such things. I had very, very few social skills and Cymone was kind enough to give me my first lessons in how to live as an adult.

I was also really enjoying the stoned adventures I'd have whenever I wasn't working. When I got a precious twenty-four hours when I wasn't on air in some way I loved having a skewed perspective on a city I'd spent so much time exploring and that now I was seeing as if for the first time. I'd wake up and smoke a cone before I even had my cereal, then spend the day in a stoned haze, observing the world through a prism of THC.

As radio got more exciting I put less energy into the band. The momentum of radio was increasing; the new program director Brian Ford also heard something in me and was being equally encouraging but twice as brutal every time we went over a shift together. Cymone and I would even sometimes get on air to fill in across holiday breaks during *The Hot 30*, and those shows were so much fun. There really is nothing like live radio, it's the most nimble form of broadcasting there is, and when you're on a show that's firing on all cylinders there's nothing to top it. Radio was still satisfying my unquenchable craving for that feeling that I got when I was on stage. It scratched that itch just enough to make less and less appealing the idea of getting back in a HiAce van and schlepping up the coast 1500 kilometres to a gig in Mackay that no one went to.

The daily weed smoking brought its share of paranoia, but now I had someone around to ask if there were actually cops knocking at the door it made things a little more bearable. I'd still smoke until I got terrified, but then the next time I'd go to smoke I would somehow forget that getting terrified was a part of this experience and go ahead and get stoned anyway. I only remembered the fun giggly parts, not the horrible frightening parts that happened almost every time I smoked, yet I still persisted.

The trick with keeping a job as a freelancer in radio is to make yourself indispensable. They can't fire you if they can't run the station without you, can they? The problem was that both Cymone and I had pushed into this strategy, and now we were together, organising time away at the same time was difficult. However, with sympathetic bosses we managed to wrangle a weekend together and we jumped into her ancient Rover hatchback and headed south to the hippy outpost of Byron Bay.[10]

---

10 I fitted in well with the fire-twirlers down there because at the time I had taken to dyeing my beard and eyebrows different colours. It made for fun times on stage with the band. If only the people listening to the radio for their favourite Bryan Adams song knew that a long-hair with a blue beard was the one telling them about him coming up after the ad break.

We ate and drank and swam, and life was magical. Cymone had a family friend, Bill, who lived inland in Mullumbimby. She and I popped over to his house one afternoon and he shared stories of how he knew Cymone's mum back in the day, and how fun it was to see Cymone all grown up. Bill was about thirty years older than we were, and had another mate and his family over that afternoon. Bill and his friend were rolling and smoking joints that looked more like cigars than cigarettes, and greedy little me must have been salivating at the sight of the weed getting passed back and forth.

'You want a smoke, mate? Let me roll you one,' said Bill. The joint they were smoking looked like it would get me higher than I'd ever been, and I was champing at the bit to try it. After about thirty-two seconds of deft one-handed spliff rolling, Bill handed me a joint that looked about as thick and long as a barbecue lighting match wrapped in Tally-Ho papers. He must have sensed my disappointment because he said, 'Just be careful with that.' The joint was so skinny I had a hard time lighting it, but eventually I took a puff of what was without doubt the most potent weed I'd ever smoked. Time itself seemed to slow down and the pitch of everyone's voices dropped about an octave. Not wanting to seem a wuss in front of Cymone's people, I took a few more enthusiastic hits on this skinny little blunt, doing my best Snoop Dogg impression as I held the smoke in.

Soon it was time to go, and as we walked downstairs the panic began. It wasn't like the regular weed panic where I knew I was high and that eventually the weed would wear off and I'd laugh about it all later on. No, there was no tether back to reality and this panic was all-encompassing and completely terrifying. The bottom dropped out of the world, there was no future. Everything was going to end and I felt the full horror of death approaching right there in that peaceful and verdant Mullumbimby driveway. It felt as if I was the only one who knew that the world was ending. That I was alone in this waking nightmare only reinforced how utterly terrifying this panic was.

I tried as hard as I could to keep it together, but Bill's wife caught my eye. She was an older hippy-type woman still wearing the Stevie Nicks-inspired flowing drapery that follows you around after you've passed by. 'Are you OK?' she asked.

'N ... no ...' was the best I could come up with.

Bill saw instantly what was going on. He calmly said, 'How about you guys don't leave just yet? Hang back for a bit, come back upstairs for a while.' I was too afraid to tell Cymone what was happening, but soon enough I had to. I was so utterly terrified about the world ending and I asked whether Cymone could hold my hand to make death less lonely for all of us.

In a few moments Bill emerged from the kitchen with a freshly quartered orange straight from the fridge. 'Here you go, mate, this should sort you out,' he said. As I bit into the orange and felt the first citrusy tang of cold juice pierce my claggy cotton-mouthed palate, the terror started to lift.

It took about an hour and a lot of talking down from the ledge by everyone there, but eventually I felt OK enough to go home. Unfortunately for me, the *Necronomicon*[11] now lay open in my mind and it would never, ever close again. Now my brain knew how to access this acute experience of terror, it would automatically go there at even the slightest trigger.

---

11 It's a book often referred to in horror literature as a portal to the underworld. If you ever want to resurrect a demon, this is your go-to tome. It's the book that the kids looking for kicks in the cabin in the woods discover in *Evil Dead* – and once they open it demons come to visit a living hell upon them. If you ever find a copy, don't open it.

We returned to Brisbane and went back to work. I was now the full-time overnight announcer. The radio term for this is 'floater': you do the five overnight shifts and one breakfast shift per week as a regular thing, and move up the schedule when one of the other announcers has a break. The best I got was filling in on *The Hot 30* with Cymone while the regular team were on holidays, but then it would be back to mid–dawns. When I got the full-time job, the morning announcer Craig Bruce congratulated me with a piece of advice, 'Mate, stoked you got the gig – you've been working really hard towards getting that. Just remember, your heart is supposed to race with excitement every time you turn on the microphone. The moment that stops happening, get out of the chair and let someone else have a go.' These words were a little lost on me at the time, but as my career has grown, they've helped me know when to hold 'em and when to fold 'em.[12]

I was drawing attention from other departments in the station too. Having heard me do the voiceover on a few promo spots for *The Hot 30*, our commercial audio director Daryl Missen came to grab me one day, asking for my voice on an ad. Whatever I'd done in the booth had impressed Daryl enough to ask me to come back a few days later, this time to read a few different scripts for some radio ads. I wasn't being paid but I was getting priceless instruction in the art of delivering a voiceover script from one of the best audio directors in the country. Daryl taught me the difference between a hard sell and a soft sell and everything in between. We struck up a great friendship, and he was kind enough to take on the role of mentoring my career moves – he was the first one to put the

---

12 For more on this concept, see Kenny Rogers' 'The Gambler'.

idea into my head that I'd be capable of doing a job outside Brisbane. He constantly encouraged me to get better and push for more airchecks, more time on air, and to send my tapes to as many stations as I could.

In a time before the internet, overnight radio was a rare form of human-to-human contact for many people in the city. Overnight television was test-patterns and infomercials, so the only actual sign that you weren't alone in the world was sometimes turning on the radio and hearing someone talking. I loved having the opportunity to speak with so many different people in my job. I had the wonderful privilege of being able to talk with people from different backgrounds all over the city, living lives I'd never come close to experiencing, all in the course of a regular shift. On any given night I'd speak with a baker trying to win a bet with his apprentice about the year a song was released, a nurse manning the ER desk where a man had come in with a very creative reason why his penis had got caught in a vacuum cleaner, some mates celebrating the birth of another friend's child, a nineteen-year-old woman spending the first night alone with her new baby, and a swathe of people who wanted someone to talk to because they couldn't think of a reason to keep going.

One regular called Colin would call most nights. He lived alone, was unemployed, and his mental health situation meant he wasn't about to find a job in a hurry. He hadn't called for about a week when he showed up one night on line three, slurring. I asked what was going on, and he told me he was done. Something was clearly wrong but he wasn't saying what. I kept him on the line and after about ten minutes he told me he'd taken every pill in the house because he didn't want to live any longer. I could hear his speech getting more and more slurred, his ability to form sentences diminishing rapidly. After I had asked him about ten times, 'What pills did you take, Colin?' he finally told me the names and dosages. I put him on hold and called the ambulance.

'Yeah, that will kill him if he doesn't get help,' the kind operator said. 'Can you get us an address? If you do that we can get the cops to go in and bust the door down, because this phone call is enough for us to show that there was a concerned person making contact.'

I quickly picked up Colin's line again. He'd already fallen asleep on the other end of the phone but I managed to get him to start talking again. I just kept asking him for his address and eventually he stopped resisting and answered by rote, as if he'd just been pulled over. I hung up, called the ambulance again, and that was it. A few hours later the driver called me back to say that they'd busted the door down, found him already unconscious and that he was now in hospital getting help.

About six weeks later Colin called again, sheepishly apologetic for what he'd done and telling me he'd since been in the critical care psych ward for a month. At the time I was glad he was alive and I was able to help, but I was also angry that someone would deliberately take enough pills to kill himself and call a stranger so that person could helplessly listen to him die on the other end of the phone. Now I'm just left with being grateful that I was there for him. I'm especially grateful that I put that action into the karma bank of the universe, because in a few years' time I'd be the one making desperate calls in the middle of the night.

My relationship to alcohol was not yet a daily dalliance, but I was definitely working on the operating system that if I wasn't working that day I should probably get wasted. This was especially true when it came time for the annual summer music festival the Big Day Out. I had been to my first one on the Gold Coast in 1994 and soon it was a day I looked forward to from the moment the lineup was announced. The Big Day Out was always a great day full of excitement. Years later at Channel [v], the promoter Ken West told me it wasn't about finding the most interesting bands he could put together on the one stage – he only used the bands to bring the most interesting people together in the crowd. He did a good job because on these days I'd see people from all sections of society, fans from all genres of music all coming together for a hot, sweaty boogie.

1995/96 was the first summer Cymone and I spent together, and because Rage Against the Machine were playing we acquired tickets for the big show from Rocking Horse Records the moment that they were released.

Planning ahead for the drinking meant that I booked a room at the Pink Poodle Motel on the main drag of Surfers Paradise so we could stay the night and not have to worry about driving home after the day's boozefest.

On the day of the festival I was obsessed with getting there early enough to see the opening acts, saying I wanted to get maximum exposure to the music I'd paid to see. Because I walked in the door and went straight to the beer tent, I probably also wanted to spend as much time drinking as I possibly could.

Cymone and I had just escaped the incredible heat of the aptly named Boiler Room where we'd watched an early performance of the Prodigy – Keith was still just a dancer, not yet the twisted fire starter we came to know in later years. I got a refreshing beverage from the beer tent and we wandered over to the main stage to watch legendary band TISM perform tracks from their latest surprise hit album. Somewhere between singing along to 'Greg! The Stop Sign!!' and '(He'll Never Be An) Ol' Man River' a thought came into my head, as clear as the words you're reading on this page right now.

It went exactly like this: 'This is fun, but I really wish the Beastie Boys were here. I'd love to see them play again. I love their album *Ill Communication*. In fact, I'd love to not only see them play again, I'd love to meet them one day. I know! I'll finally get that job at that TV station Red, and when the Beastie Boys release their new album – which won't be long now – they'll probably tour Australia. Then when they tour, I'll get to interview them. Yeah, that will work.' Looking back, either the universe sent me a message or a higher power spoke to me, I still don't know what to call it. It took a while, but that message changed my life.

Meanwhile, I had plenty to be getting on with. I'm sure you've heard the phrase 'the harder you work, the luckier you get'. Being motivated to do the hard work necessary to keep the band afloat was getting harder and harder. So, like any long-term relationship that was waning, we tried to spice things up and begin experimenting. We put together an acoustic set, which put the fire under our arses, and we started having a lot of success. The shows were great, and while it was tough lugging my double bass around with me, it was great to pull out on stage and it sounded spectacular.

Then Dave Atkins, formerly of the Brisbane tech/funk/metal group Pangaea, rang me. I was a massive fan of Pangaea and tried to control my fan-boy side while working with Dave who had produced Feeble's first EP *Panticlerevgator*.[13] He was lining up a gig at the Livid Festival where he would play drums, I'd play double bass and DJ Katch would be on the decks scratching in hooks. The idea was to just get up and jam and see what happened. We ended up not playing that day but the idea stuck with him. A few months later Dave called again and asked whether I'd be interested in coming down and jamming with him, Katch, another producer called Blunted Stylus and a few Brisbane rappers. That weekend was the first rehearsal of what went on to become Resin Dogs.

Gigs with Resin Dogs were just incredible. We'd play at Ric's Cafe in Brunswick Street and the walls would be just crawling with people, and that's no exaggeration. Ric's had a small counter that ran around the wall so that you could eat while sitting up against it – and security had to eventually give up pulling people down from there where they had climbed to find some space to dance.

The gigs got bigger and bigger, and we'd play shows at the legendary Brisbane venue the Zoo which were total sell outs. It was everything that I had hoped Feeble's would have been. Packed houses, people dancing, so much fun. It was a total dream – to be standing on stage with one of my musical heroes, laying down bass lines that made people dance, locking in to Dave's hi-hat and kick, marvelling at DJ Katch's incredible turntable skill and loving everything the rappers were doing. It was brilliant.

---

13 Panticlerevgator is the name of a card game we used to play. It's the same as 'battle snap' where instead of just saying 'snap', the moment someone says 'panticlerevgator' it's all in to try and wrestle as many cards as possible from every other person playing. The melee stops when someone gets a new card down in the middle. We actually recorded us playing a game of this and it appears as a hidden track on the first EP we did. It was a very violent game.

One night I played a massive gig at the Zoo with Resin Dogs, got off stage and sped across town to play a gig with Feeble's in front of about twenty people of whom we knew eighteen. For me it was the beginning of the end.

With Feeble's playing fewer and fewer gigs, I was going out to nightclubs more often. Cymone and I would go dancing with friends from work, and as the radio gig got bigger we were invited to more and more parties. It was at one of these after parties that one of the people I worked with handed me a small ball of Tally-Ho rolling papers. We were about six hours into a drinking session that didn't show any signs of slowing down and I asked, 'What is this?'

'Just some speed,' he said. I was already drunk and thought, 'Fuck it', so I put the pill in my mouth and swigged it right down. Within five minutes I'd gone from being a slurry drunk to being sharp as a tack. Actually, whatever you use to sharpen a sharp tack, I was that sharp. Everything was crisp and fine, every sound was piercingly clear and I had instant recall of every detail of the situation around me. While this was interesting, I was not happy with my newly found sobriety. This was an after party. I was supposed to be getting smashed. So I began to order booze by the bottle over the bar and before the night was out I'd drunk an entire magnum of sparkling wine.

I had failed to consider that the next day I had scheduled in a precious and expensive studio recording session with Resin Dogs. The speed had let me drink nearly triple what I'd usually be able to handle and now it had worn off I was left with a hangover that still gives me shivers to recall. The whole band were there – Dave, Katch and all the rappers had assembled on this special day. Studio time was expensive and hard to come by and I'd shown up utterly useless.

The engineer Geoff sensed that I needed a bit of time so rather than lay the bass tracks down first he told the other guys to put down what they had. By mid-afternoon there was nothing left to record but me, so soon he and I were in an airless soundproof booth, with him inhaling the toxic gases from my lungs as we struggled to mic the double bass to find the most authentic sound. The playback started and everyone was on the other side of the double-walled glass window watching, waiting to hear the brilliant bass line that would tie the whole track together. Instead what they got was terribly played and woefully out-of-tune junk. That week Dave called and said they were booking a Resin Dogs gig in a fortnight and they were going to try another bass player.

He was Chris Bosley, an incredible player, a human metronome of a musician. I see now why they replaced the drunken and unreliable long-hair they had brought on, but at the time I was utterly wounded that I'd been kicked out of the band. How dare they replace me! My ego was telling me I was the greatest bass player that ever lived, but the reality is that I was now more interested in getting wasted and striking rock poses on stage than I was laying down serious funk for the people to dance to.

I'd blown too many gigs in a row with sloppy playing and that drug-fucked recording session was the last straw.

Resin Dogs went on to be incredibly successful, touring Australia and the world. Dave and Katch continued to work together running the successful label Hydrofunk Records. They are bloody good at what they do and deserve all their success.

It was only a few short weeks after I was booted from Resin Dogs that Feeble's decided to call it a day. We went out on a high and played one final show at our regular haunt Crash 'n' Burn on the corner of Mary and Edward streets in Brisbane. We invited everyone we knew and even filmed the final moments of us as a band. It was a fun show, but now it was all over I had no idea what to do next.

What I did do was more and more speed. It gave me a rush that felt like being on stage but without all the pesky songwriting, rehearsing and hauling around of heavy equipment. Every time I drank I'd go harder and harder, as if all I needed was another shot, another line, and then everything would be OK. Of course that never happened, and soon enough I'd be on the ground outside a venue somewhere, vomit chunks caught in my hair, with Cymone clearing the matted filth out of my airway and gently asking me, 'Maybe you want to have a think about why you do this to yourself. Do you really need to do this every time?' I dismissed her compassionate and loving gesture. As far as I was concerned, she didn't understand that the party hadn't yet started and if I could only hold on for a few more hours something magical would happen, the fairy dust would sprinkle over everyone, I would have arrived and everything would be OK.

nine
a wider world, or maybe not

The thing about radio jobs in a metropolitan market is that you pretty much have to wait for someone to die before you'll get a chance at a gig when the sun is up. There were announcers on air who were in their sixties, but because their voices still sounded as they had done in their heyday it didn't matter[1] how they looked. Try as I might to impress my now third program director Rex Morris, I just couldn't get a shot at a day gig in Brisbane.

It was June 1998 and I was at a dead end. During one of our regular talks I told Dad about how tough it was to get a break and he suggested I come with him to have a look at the world a bit. Dad was still working as a specialist in Brisbane and living with his de facto and her son. He had a big rheumatology conference coming up in Geneva in Switzerland and suggested I come with him, after which we'd go and visit Prague for the first time since he escaped. Mum bought me the plane ticket, and Dad helped with some of the other expenses while we were away.

I asked my boss for a month off work. Luckily he agreed, and in September 1998 Dad and I set off. While he was at

---

1 This is not the case now, and anyone who's been stuck behind a city bus will tell you that radio announcers now have to look half decent, because with the advent of social media marketing you are on camera as much as you are on the mic – so 'a good face for radio' is a thing of the past. Unless you're Howard Stern, but he's the king of all media so I guess he can get away with it.

his conference I'd arranged to spend a few days in London to catch up with my friend Luke Heggie. Luke was working in the west of England and he came to pick me up from Heathrow and drive me out there. We then spent a few days with mates in London he had met as a lift operator in Whistler, Canada. I never had a chance to go backpacking; those few nights sleeping on the floor of a Camden flat packed to the rafters with travelling Aussies was the closest I'd get.

Travelling is important to do. It's only when you look back on where you've come from that you get a true perspective on what is happening in your home life. Of course, London was big and exciting and all things at all times. There were dozens of languages being spoken around us on the Tube and everywhere we saw faces from all over the world. The world's possibilities were opening up before my eyes.

Once Dad's conference was over we headed off to Zurich to spend a few days with relatives who had escaped when the Russians had cracked down on Prague in 1968, and then Dad and I were off to the Czech Republic.

On the plane to Prague from Zurich, Dad got more and more nervous. By the time we got to immigration in Prague airport he seemed terrified that he was on some sort of secret list of people who had escaped and must now be punished. However, the bored, mulleted guard spoke to Dad in English – he had a British passport – stamped our passports and we were in.

We spent two weeks visiting people Dad hadn't seen since his escape. Most days would begin with a few pints of Staropramen, a glorious pilsner that would line the stomach and fortify Dad for the emotional day ahead. Dad met former high-school friends, lecturers and neighbours. Every single one of them instantly absolved him from the immense guilt he felt about having to abandon his life and country in the middle of the night. I had bought a video camera to document the trip, and I filmed a few of these conversations.

Dad's former professor at the university where he studied medicine said that when the Russian tanks rolled in to crush the Prague Spring he had been the editor of the most important medical journal in Czechoslovakia. Once the communists really cracked down he had been forced to become the typesetter of the paper, working the printing presses in the basement until the Velvet Revolution in 1989. He told Dad, 'You absolutely did the right thing. Look at what happened to me. You had the chance to go to another country, start a new life and bring a whole family into the world.'

As we walked away from his house, I filmed Dad and his face had changed. The face of anguish I had known my entire life was no longer there. He said he felt as if 'big rocks have been lifted from my shoulders'.

We celebrated with a few shots of slivovice and some more beer.

I'd never really known my dad until that trip. To me he had been a guy who spoke differently than all my friends' parents, ate stinky sausages and rock-hard black bread, listened to strange classical music and looked at the world as if tanks would come down the street and break up the party at any moment. That wasn't too surprising, considering what Prague had been like when he was there before. The trauma of displacement should never be underestimated: it affected Dad's entire life. But now, in a city full to the brim with stinky sausages, strange classical music and thousands of other people who also remembered what it was like to have tanks roll down the street, suddenly Dad made sense.

Now I knew why his eyes always lit up when he saw the ocean: Czechoslovakia is a landlocked country and its capital, Prague, sits on a river that only does two things: flow or freeze. All this made me think of a holiday we had when I was only five and Mum and Dad took us to Lady Elliot Island to see the Great Barrier Reef.[2] There's a resort there now, but in 1979 there was an airstrip, about four small shacks, a lighthouse, the lighthouse keeper's cottage and nothing else. For people who liked the finer things in life my parents sure liked to rough it from time to time.

We flew north from Brisbane, crammed into the back of a tiny plane no bigger than a minivan and after a few hours aloft, the pilot even let Dad fly for a while. I was completely freaked out by this because Dad was an incredible doctor, but not the most handy or dexterous person on the planet, and I worried he might accidentally sneeze and put us all in the drink.[3] Thankfully we made it, and soon were over the impossible blue of the South Pacific, surrounded on all sides by an ocean filled with tropical fish, manta rays and glorious coral reefs.

One afternoon we got word that a cyclone was coming through and it was very important that we all stay inside. When the storm finally hit, the thin steel reinforcements of our shack shook as the strongest gusts hit its outside walls. In

2   While the memory often embellishes things, making them bigger and more colourful, I know for a fact that the Great Barrier Reef no longer looks as it did in 1979: less and less like it every day. If you do just one thing from reading this book, get yourself to a still-healthy part of the reef and see it before it's too late, because once it's gone it's never coming back.

3   I do take after him in this way. Many beautiful sets of six bowls or four glasses have been reduced to odd numbers when they leave my hands.

the face of peril Dad was apt to let out a nervous giggle and watch with excited curiosity, and this night was no different. I woke up a few times whenever the big gusts hit. Every time, I saw Dad in the same spot – by the front louvres, watching the casuarina trees bend sideways in the wind, smoking quietly in the glow of the lone hurricane lamp, and I could tell that he was exulting in the sight.

That European trip getting to know Dad was important in other ways. After a month away in Europe, Brisbane seemed like a very, very small town. I arrived home at 6am and was back on air at 1am that night. When I rolled in around 12:50am to pull my CDs, the late-night jock unleashed a tirade on me, accusing me of not taking my job seriously by turning up so late, saying I was a lazy announcer, that there were better people who hadn't got the job and I should feel lucky to have it. Before the trip I would have taken his abuse very personally and felt that he was in a position of authority over me and that I should heed his words and do what he said. But now I'd seen a glimpse of how big the world could actually be and what possibility lay beyond my city of Brisbane, I saw his anger as petty schoolboy bullying. The world was way bigger than Brisbane radio and I wanted to get out there.

Cymone and I started hustling for gigs wherever we could. We sent our tapes to whomever would listen – both our solo shifts (Cymone was also doing mid–dawns), as well as a tape of us hosting the night show together. A radio consultant named Dave Charles, originally from Canada, kept his ear to the ground for any new jobs coming up.

When Dave called and said that there might be a job on the Gold Coast opening up in the breakfast shift, I didn't even think about the implications for my relationship or for

Cymone. I just called the program director and arranged to meet him. I was getting pretty good at the in-room hustle and thought I did a terrific job of impressing him. When he asked me to come down for a second chat I pushed Cymone as my co-host. I called him every week.

One Tuesday I was called into the B105 general manager's office. My program director Rex Morriss just came straight out with it: 'Stuey from the night show is going to the Gold Coast to do breakfast, and starting Monday I want you to do nights.' I'd be hosting the show with Zoe Sheridan, Stuey's former co-host. So Stuey had got the job I wanted. I was terribly disappointed but also thrilled. I was finally going to have a marquee show, the nightly countdown between 7pm and 10pm. I'd been working six- and seven-day weeks for the last four years for this opportunity. Big pop music was just making a massive comeback, the Spice Girls were unstoppable, Hanson were an absolute phenomenon and the Backstreet Boys were cranking out hit after hit. It was an exciting time to be in music.

At that meeting, there was a contract on the table which I signed without even looking at the terms or the dollar figure. When I shared the news with Cymone, we were over the moon.

The next day I savoured the sweet taste of victory, calling my parents and brothers and letting them know the great news, enjoying the excitement of planning the next step of my future with Cymone. To make ends meet, we had taken a job being part-time live-in nannies to two girls aged eleven and fourteen. Cymone took care of getting them off to school and I did the dinner and off-to-bed part.

That Friday, as I got set for what was going to be my last mid–dawn ever, I got a call from Rex's assistant asking me to come in for a meeting with Rex and the general manager.

I explained that the kids had just got home from school and I had to get dinner on, but I was told it was urgent. I piled the girls into the back seat of my bright orange 1977 Sunbird and drove into town. Thankfully Cymone was already at work producing the night show, so I could leave the kids with her while I went upstairs to the GM's office. I walked in to find them both sitting there, but this time it was a far different mood in the room.

'We've got some bad news,' he said. 'Zoe's taken a job doing the day shift in Sydney. The national bosses have decided not to do a local night show, and they're going to take Ugly Phil and Jackie O off the satellite from 2Day FM instead.'

The ground swam beneath me as I walked back down to the studio. Stuey and Zoe were still on air, and when they saw me their faces said that they knew I'd been told. I could barely tell Cymone as I gathered the girls and took them back to the car. It was now absolute peak hour on the South-East Freeway heading back to where we lived, and the girls were hungry and tired. As I sat motionless in what was supposed to be a 100-kilometre-an-hour zone, the girls started to complain loudly that they were hungry. I was so overwhelmed with the situation I just sat there and dropped the clutch in and out as we edged forward one car space at a time, and as their wailing grew louder I retreated further and further into myself.

Normally I would have gone to bed at the same time as the girls to try and catch a few hours' rest between nine and twelve, but this night I couldn't get a wink. When Cymone came home we hugged and I didn't speak a word. I got back in my car and drove to what was supposed to be my last ever mid–dawn shift, and here I was again, trapped in the endless cycle of broken sleep, too much instant coffee and Bryan Adams ballads.

My shift began at 1am and I was supposed to do a talk break after the second song, but I was too heartbroken to speak. I just sat there for five hours and didn't say one word, just played the music and the commercials and stared at the wall. Around 4am the morning crew came in, and Ian Skippen was first through the door (as he always is and always has been). His first words were, 'I'm so sorry, mate. I really am.' It seemed that Rex had told everyone but me that I hadn't got the gig. Jamie Dunn was also very kind that morning, as was Robin Bailey. They all commiserated with me, and understood why I didn't say a word all the way up to the 5:55am 'the crew is up next' talk break.

I took the situation very personally, but I just kept going. One thing I have going for me is that I often don't know when to stop. Sometimes that's a bad thing, but in times like this it looks like resilience. The truth was I just didn't know what else to do but to keep showing up for the mid–dawn shift, keep trying to get better on air and keep sending tapes to Dave Charles. I certainly didn't know to look at the contract I'd signed, or any termination clauses in there – I was still a long way off actually reading contracts or even hiring lawyers to negotiate for me.

I kept at the overnight shift and one day a few months later I got a call from Phil Dowse, the program director at SA-FM. He said he'd heard my tape and was wondering whether I'd be interested in a job doing afternoons in Adelaide. It was a much smaller market than Brisbane in a city a long way away, but it was a job in the daytime and a chance to move up. I called Daryl Missen, my friend and mentor who had since moved to Sydney, and asked him what I should do.

'Take the gig!' he yelled down the phone. 'You'll be in Sydney within a year.' His confidence in me was all I needed, so I called back Phil from SA-FM to take him up on his offer. At that stage, leaving Brisbane for a new job seemed as normal a thing to do as opening a fridge door looking for something to eat.

I said I'd come only if he paid to move me there and found a job for my girlfriend Cymone too. In hindsight this looks like incredible cheek, but I didn't think of that. Amazingly, he said he would pay to move me and would do his best to get a job for Cymone as soon as he could. And so on 8 December 1998 I left my girlfriend, my family, all my friends and the only city I'd called home to go to Adelaide, a city I hardly knew.

On the day I arrived I put on my Walkman and AKG headphones and rode my long and dangerous skateboard across the park that divides the CBD of Adelaide from the surrounding suburbs to meet with the assistant program director, former B105 daytime announcer Craig Bruce. He talked me through the gig, told me how excited he was that I was there, and we made big plans about the coming months.

It was during this conversation that my best known stage name was born. I'd never been known by my birth name really, only nicknames. As a kid, I had been known as Günz (rhymes with shins). As a roadie the band called me Game Boy due to my Nintendo addiction, though I never realised they'd sometimes not pronounce the 'm'. When I got to B105, JJ called me Spidey, even on the mid–dawn roster sheets. Here was my chance to finally be called by my own name.

'So, Spidey – what are you going to call yourself on air?' asked Craig.

'Well, I was hoping to use my real name.'

'Of course – Andrew is a great FM name – what's your surname?'

'Günsberg.'

There was the sound of air being sharply inhaled through gritted teeth.

'Yeah ... this *is* Adelaide,' he said. 'I don't know how Günsberg's going to go down. How about Andrew G?' And so Andrew G came into being.

1998 had been a bad year for SA-FM. The former giant of FM in Adelaide wasn't even in the top five stations any more, and the company had had enough – we were gearing up for a full-blown, old-school radio ratings war.[4] But Craig had big plans for my career and wanted to develop me on and off the mic. To start with he asked me to write some promos for the station, so I got my first ever work desk and even a computer I could use in the afternoons. I felt ever so important.

I was introduced to the street team with whom I'd be heading out every day so that I could get a vibe of the people of Adelaide. They were like the street team in Brisbane but a little less hungry to climb the radio ladder. One of them recognised that I'd only just landed and asked whether I was 'sorted'. I told him I was dry, and he reached into his pocket and produced a sticky green bud of weed that I almost got high from just sniffing. After raiding the now-dormant CD collection from when SA-FM was a rock station, I made a few hasty cassette copies for my Walkman and skated home.[5]

---

4   Before consolidation of the market, Australian radio was far more cut-throat. Now you can adjust the male-skewed station's programming to make sure the female-skewed station that you also own gets a better survey result. But back then, it was pistols at dawn. Programming, counter-programming, secret information exchange and headhunting and then mothballing of key on-air personalities all happened, and all in an effort to get those precious ratings points. If you win the ratings, you set the rate card for advertising. Radio in the 1990s was a battleground and I *loved* the competition.
5   Yes, I participated in music piracy.

That night I had my first experience with Adelaide hydroponic weed. While the jaw-dropping musical complexity of Frank Zappa's album *Joe's Garage* played in my ears, I sucked back on that nasty smoke and proceeded to get more high than I'd care to have been. The inevitable panic was worse than normal and it took a walk down Rundle Street to grab a kebab with the lot to alleviate it. Of course I didn't let this adverse side effect stop me, quite the contrary – I seemed to be sure that I'd be able to work past those moments of panic if only I smoked *more*.

I fell into a cycle of smoking weed every night, moistening my cotton mouth with at least a six-pack of Cooper's Green and then the next day to spark myself up for work, punching incredibly potent coffee for a few hours to shake off the haze. This would of course make me terribly anxious and I would attack the first drink and cone of the day earlier and earlier once I got home, with a fervour that could best be described as rabid.

As Cymone wasn't there to temper my intake, I let fly. I'd only really ever drunk in binges before, but I was now settling in to a proper daily cycle of self-destruction. If I had been odd around people before, now that I was around other humans in a morning-after weed and booze haze or a pent-up ball of anxiety, work became a challenge.

With absolutely zero experience of corporate life I had no idea about meeting protocol or the delicacy needed to criticise the ideas of a superior in front of a co-worker. During one promotions meeting the team who had mostly been there since the station was number one (and also on the long slide down the ratings) started pitching ideas about getting back some public vibe for the once-proud station. My promotions director, a very pretty woman in her late thirties, said, 'Let's do sticker spotting again.'[6] Without missing a beat I shut her down in front of the whole team: 'Nah, sticker spotting is so boring and so eighties.'

I thought I was just stating a fact – surely everyone could see that doing an old idea would make us seem old and boring? We were moments away from becoming the 'All-New SA-FM', we had to think of something fresh and innovative. I was completely unaware that I had just committed an incredible faux pas, had disrespected the promotions director who had been working there for nearly twenty years, and stunned the room into silence. I just thought they were being quiet because they were thinking up more ideas.

Just before lunch that day my program director Phil Dowse – a kind and wise man who would be the world champion in a Michael McDonald look-alike competition – took me aside and gently said, 'Mate, I love your passion for getting us to number one – you've got great ideas, and I'm so excited to have you here. How about in future you just come straight to me with any of your ideas, OK?' Oh. Right. I finally realised what he was on about. I'd seen the promotions director emerge from Phil's office a few minutes earlier, slicing me in two with her angry gaze.

As well as being kind and very wise, Phil was a take-no-prisoners old-school radio warrior. He carried out the most ruthless tactic I've seen to this day in order to win a few points of a survey. He heard one of our opposition breakfast DJs talking about how much he enjoyed a glass or two of South Australia's finest red wine with dinner every night. So Phil immediately

---

6   This was a massive craze when bumper stickers were a massive craze. The idea was that you'd have the sticker on your car, and if a member of the street team saw you and pulled you over, you'd win a prize of some description. It already hadn't happened for years by the time I had started.

and anonymously signed him up to a 'wine of the week' subscription, where he would be sent a dozen assorted bottles of Barossa beauties every week, delivered straight to his doorstep. Sure enough, within two weeks this particular DJ was sounding more and more dusty in the mornings, giving our team an hour's head start on the valuable breakfast audience. While now I would object to exploiting another's issues with alcohol for corporate gain, at the time it was a complete baller move.

I was starting to learn that everyone else had a superhero ability to tell how other people were feeling without their having to say it out loud. I knew I'd done something wrong in that meeting, but I never felt the emotion that came with it. I began to keep a mental list of things I should and shouldn't do. I would do certain things not because I felt they were right, but because I'd seen other people do those things and it seemed to make people around them happier. I was beginning to realise that my ability to feel empathy or read an emotional situation was almost non-existent compared to other people's. So I began to learn pattern behaviours to act out whenever certain trigger parameters were met.

After ten long weeks as a bachelor, Cymone arrived in Adelaide. True to his word, Phil my boss paid for her to fly down with our two cats to start a new life in Adelaide. She and I shared a house on Campbell Road, Unley, right across the road from the Arkaba Hotel. Her job was as a producer on the breakfast show while I was on the day shift doing noon to 3pm, but I was usually in the office writing until well after five.

By the time I'd ridden my bicycle home she would be winding down for bed (breakfast radio people go to sleep around 7pm) and we'd enjoy an early meal together before she turned in. It was a new routine for us, but I sure didn't feel we were going to follow it forever. I hadn't really got used to the pace of Adelaide – not after the full-force volume of an international city like London.

Cymone and I were quite an anomaly. At the time Adelaide had negative population growth. People couldn't believe we had left Queensland to come down here, a place where even major intersections had no street signs because everyone had always lived there and just knew where, for instance, Portrush Road was.

Adelaide sure wasn't full of the excitement and opportunity I had hoped leaving Brisbane would bring.[7] Sure, the cost of living was incredibly cheap and everywhere was twenty

---

7   While we lived there, that's when the Snowtown murders were taking place in a town just north of us. While I'd never been shoved in a barrel of acid in a bank vault, I saw my share of strangeness. I was quite bored before Cymone arrived so I'd put some posters up around town saying that I could play theremin (the first ever electronic instrument, which I'd built from a kit and had played a little in Brisbane with a band called Full Fathom 5 just before I left). One day my phone rang and it was a guy named Charlie. He asked me to come up to the house and play for a while. When he said 'house', he meant 'converted silver mine' out of Adelaide. His house was the former worker's entrance and shed – and he even had the former access tunnel at the end of his cavernous living room. If you took a torch and headed down the tiny and claustrophobic tunnel about 300 metres into a mountain, you'd find a shrine to Elvis Presley waiting for you in the eerily silent darkness. Charlie asked me to set up in the corner of his massive living room, which he informed me often hosted performance art, musical performances and even plays. I asked what he'd like me to play, and he said he wanted me to make music that snakes wanted to dance to. Soon after I arrived, a photo shoot started setting up in another corner of the living room, and a very well-built male model just took all his clothes off and started posing on the prop couch for a female photographer. 'Are you cool with this, mate?' asked Charlie, referring to the soft-core art-porn unfolding before us. 'Yeah, of course,' I responded, just going with the incredible oddness of it all. While I made the swooping and aching singing noises so associated with the instrument, the photographer produced a three-metre-long python that writhed with the model on the couch, the photographer shooting off frames where the animal was covering the model's penis. I'm positive the snake was reacting to the music I was making – but then again, I was pretty fucking stoned playing theremin in the corner of an eccentric artist's living room while a naked man writhed with a python on a couch in front of me. It was a pretty great, and pretty strange way to spend a Wednesday afternoon. Charlie and I kept in touch over the years. He's a good guy.

minutes from everywhere else, but I could not see myself staying there. In fact I *had* to get out.

The universe must have known I was ready because one Friday I got a call from my former B105 audio director Daryl Missen. Since moving to Sydney Daryl had been audio director at the newly formed pay TV giant Foxtel and his message was simple and clear. 'Nathan Harvey has just left Channel [v]. Send them a tape as soon as you can.'[8]

The small camcorder I had bought to document my journey back to Prague with Dad had come with me to Adelaide. I'd used it to make short video postcards I'd dub off onto the SA-FM boardroom VHS machine and send back to Cymone in the intra-company overnight bag as a way of staying in touch with her. That weekend I wrote out a script and set about driving my HZ Kingswood Sedan around some of the more picturesque parts of Adelaide, using them as backdrops to deliver my earnest pitch for the job down the lens of the camera. I'd had a lot of practice talking down the barrel by this point, purely from the short films I'd been making, so I managed to sound like someone who knew what he was doing. From my Powell Sidewalk surfer skateboard I talked about how much I love music, how much I love broadcasting, and how curious I was about the exciting music that was being made right now that we hadn't heard yet. Just as Mum had taught me, I covered the VHS tape with bright and shiny kids' stickers and put it in an envelope with another letter, handwritten in Nikko pen. At this point I'd started to obsess about documenting my life, so I even filmed myself posting the letter to Sydney.

---

8   Nathan Harvey was one of the hosts of the daily music video request show on Channel [v], *By Demand*. I'd seen the show before at Cymone's parents' house.

Two weeks later on a Monday I got a call. Jacquie Riddell the creative director at Channel [v] liked my tape and wanted me to fly over to talk about the job as soon as possible. The next day at 5:30pm, I yawned and rubbed my eyes at my desk saying, 'Oh boy, I'm stuffed. See you tomorrow, everyone,' to no one in particular because people emptied out of that office a lot earlier than they had at B105. I strolled down to my car and quietly pulled out of the car park. At the second set of lights from the station I hit the gas and broke all speed limits to get to Adelaide airport to make the 6pm cut off for the 6:30pm flight to Sydney. Running through security, I just made the plane, tried to catch a little sleep on the flight and then when I got to Sydney told the cab driver not to spare the horses, and to get me to Foxtel by 9pm.

At the meeting with Jacquie, I was so nervous and edgy that I babbled like a brook and knocked over just about everything in the office. Afterwards, I crashed for a few hours, then got up at 4am to get to the airport by 5am for the 6am flight, which got me back to Adelaide just in time to run back to my Kingswood in the airport car park, hoon through peak-hour traffic back to SA-FM and then casually stroll through the front door yawning, 'Oh, good morning!' to the receptionist as I arrived.

Nothing happened for a few days and I thought I'd blown it. I'd seen the mountain of VHS tapes on Jacquie's desk. My sense of self was still so low, my feeling of worthlessness so potent, and I honestly felt that Jacquie had granted me an interview out of pity. With my poor performance at the interview constantly on my mind, it was hard to focus on work.

Part of my radio job meant driving to workplaces around Adelaide to record people announcing songs for the 'workplace lunch break countdown' I ran every day. I was heading out to a distant part of the city in a station car to record one of these shows when Jacquie called. She couldn't have rung at a worse time. I was late, flustered, lost, trying to read the street directory with one hand while talking on the phone with the other, and when a cop pulled up next to me, I rudely ended the call and pretty much hung up on her.

Realising that I might have just blown the gig altogether I got on the phone a few hours later and sent Jacquie a bunch of native flowers with a note saying I was sorry I'd hung up on her, looking forward to talking to her whenever she had the chance. The phone didn't ring for three long days and I was certain that was it.

But she finally called back to ask me to come out to Sydney again to meet the big boss and my potential co-host to see if we'd get along. It was another skin-of-the-teeth mission to get the last flight out, and when I was rushing to get to the Darling Harbour restaurant for the meeting, my phone rang and it was Craig Bruce from Adelaide. I answered, still in the heaving crowds of Darling Harbour.

'Oh hey, mate, are you out?'

'Umm … yeah, just getting some dinner.'

'Oh, great! Where are you?'

'Ah … Glenelg.'

He bought it and asked me whether I'd be interested in accompanying some listeners on a trip as part of a prize he was thinking about. I agreed to everything he said, trying to hustle him off the phone before one of the nearby ferries could let off its horn to signal a departure from the dock – Glenelg most definitely does not have ferries.

When I finally got upstairs to the restaurant I realised that this was the big final hurdle. At the table were Jacquie

Riddell, her boss and general manager of Channel [v], Barry Chapman, and a woman named Paula McGrath. She was a few years older than me, and I had worked with her briefly at B105 as a Black Thunder driver for a few months. Turns out she was the co-host Jacquie was talking about. When we worked at B105 together, I'd recognised Paula as someone who knew what she wanted out of her career and was prepared do whatever it took to get it in the quickest way possible.

Distant alarm bells were ringing in my mind due to my previous experience, but they were drowned out by the sound of Barry Chapman talking about his exciting project of building a studio in a public street, and that he was looking for a team that could anchor a live show out of that studio every day of the week.

We stayed late at dinner which left me with only about two hours' sleep to do the dash back to Adelaide, but the following afternoon I got a call from Barry and Jacquie. They offered me the job. Barry faxed me an offer letter for $55,000 a year. It was twice as much as I was being paid in Adelaide. I couldn't believe I would be making that much to do something I loved so much I'd have done it for free.

Once I had the letter of offer in my hands I wrote out my letter of resignation and walked down to the office of the general manager at SA-FM. She couldn't believe I wanted to leave. She kept asking whether she could offer me anything more – more money, no weekend shifts, fewer hours – anything at all. But there was nothing there for me.

After I told my big boss I was leaving, I had to tell the man who had helped me get the job in the first place. I sat in the office that I now shared with Craig Bruce and told him I had just resigned and I was leaving radio to go to work in music television. Craig's initial reaction was to scream, 'Fuck! *Fuck!*' and kick me in the shins hard with each expletive. He had put so much effort into getting me there, had so many plans for me, and I understand why he reacted like that. I had a nasty bruise from where he kicked me, but I would have been pissed off too.

My final month at SA-FM flew by. The ratings that came out in my last week there put the station less than 0.1 per cent off the number one position – a long way to have come in such a short time. It was nice to leave on a high.

the big smoke

O n 11 April 1999, just four months and two days after leaving my mid–dawn job in Brisbane, I was living in Sydney and hosting live national television.

Daryl had been right after all.

The first show wasn't the greatest and I looked stiff and scared on camera, but I could see how much possibility for exciting change lay within the format of the show. On that first day, too, I met people I would continue to work with throughout my entire TV career. Producers, camera operators, lighting and audio operators: they were so many extraordinarily talented men and women and I am lucky to still work with so many of them to this day. Among the most notable people I met on that very first day was a young work experience kid named Carla Mico. She was still in high school and doing some intern work in the makeup department. It was her first day too, and though I didn't know it then, Carla and I would go on to have a working relationship that would change the course of my life.

That first day on TV also revealed a lot about what I could expect in the next few years. For one thing I had absolutely zero idea how to handle a strong-willed woman like Paula, who was used to always getting her own way and had an uncanny ability to corral others to make that happen. Secondly, an old laptop on set had an IRC chatroom client running. I asked my director whether we could show the live chat on the TV because I wanted to talk to the people at home and have them see their reactions when I asked them about the video they'd just watched. In a few minutes we became the first people in Australia to broadcast a live internet relay chatroom across the country reacting to a host asking the room questions. We were creating truly interactive television in the early morning of the internet age.

That first night we all went out to celebrate the first show with drinks at one of the bars in the nearby casino. Barry was buying and my producer Tim Daley taught me a valuable lesson that night – don't stop drinking before Barry closes the tab. While Barry was indeed putting them away, I was going 2:1 up against him at the bar. That night I went to bed worried that I'd drunk too much in front of my new boss and new team, and I woke up with intense remorse and guilt about going so hard the night before.

Cymone and I were in a big city neither of us knew, so she found a place for us to live that was within walking distance of the Foxtel building. It was in an apartment block at the end of Saunders Street, Pyrmont, with a balcony overlooking the winding bicycle path off the newly built Anzac Bridge. Now it's all fancy down that end of the city, but we lived with the ten-to-a-room international students who filled the rest of the building and the constant noise from the enormous construction site that would become the building where Nova FM is now.[1]

---

1   Network Ten is at 1 Saunders Street, Pyrmont, and at night we would get a kick out of watching the big studio lights fade down at the same time they did on the television when Sandra Sully signed off on the late-night news.

Those first few weeks at Foxtel were so exciting. We were a team of young, hungry, creative people plugged into the very core of the Australian music industry. None of us could believe that *this* was what we got paid to do every day. Everything felt so right. It felt like I was on a path that had been set up by the universe to be free of struggle and just full of excitement and opportunity.

I knew this to be absolutely true when six weeks after I started working at Channel [v] I met and interviewed my idols the Beastie Boys about their new album *Hello Nasty* – exactly as I had imagined three years earlier while watching TISM at the Big Day Out. Unfortunately for me, it was an absolutely terrible interview – I was so starstruck at meeting some of my musical heroes that I switched into full music-nerd mode and started asking them about samplers and scratch routines and all kinds of other things that precisely zero people were interested in. I got a *lot* better at interviewing people because of that experience. However, it was a truly incredible moment of reality meeting up with a visualisation in precisely the way that I had imagined it.

My walk to work was great; every morning something different was going on. This was a thriving part of the city and my route would take me past the fish markets, through the casino and past the super-yacht marina, to arrive at Foxtel's magnificent headquarters at Wharf 8 Pyrmont. Sydney Harbour was still accepting container ships and it was pretty great seeing the bustling, working harbour every day. Walking home, however, took me past any number of open pubs, and it was not uncommon for me to stop off and wind down with a beer.

This happened more and more often as I struggled against the cliquey culture within the team I was working with. I had thought this place would work like B105, where success was achieved through merit, enrolling others in great ideas and compromise within a team. But in my team I was experiencing intimidation and secret behind-the-back cliquey deals that shut me out of opportunities. While Barry definitely provided great leadership, I didn't know how to access or utilise his skills or wisdom. I didn't have any tools to deal with this situation so I reacted with what I knew. And that was anger, stonewalling, and drinking very heavily. Not a great way to handle things.

I'd started to notice that Paula would disappear in the middle of the day for an hour or two at a time, and later during the live show we'd throw to an interview of a big star she had recorded earlier that day. I just accepted this the first few times, but after a while I started to demand that the interviews go live and that we both be involved. Once we moved the show out to our newly completed outdoor studio at Fox Studios (where excitingly they had just filmed *The Matrix* and were currently filming *Star Wars*) things got even worse. I dealt with it by simply drinking more and more, which was easier as there was now a bar right across the street.

When I started having constant nightmares I called my dad and told him I was incredibly stressed and I just wasn't coping. He was able to write me a referral to a psychiatrist at the big end of town, and I went to see him.

I had previously had my first brush with Australia's mental health system when I was nineteen, and teen hang-ups about sex led to me attending a sexual health clinic for an HIV test after every guilt-ridden adventure. One of the clinicians there noticed the frequency of my visits and, presuming that I did not have a fetish for blood tests, sensed something was amiss. She helped me make an appointment at the Queensland

Department of Mental Health Outpatient Clinic in Fortitude Valley, where I met my first proper adult therapists: Simon, a handsome Asian guy only a few years older than I was; and his colleague Marie, who I worked with for over a year to become a mostly functioning adult.[2]

This time, the doctor my dad referred me to suggested that I drink less coffee and alcohol, and consider going on antidepressants. I flatly refused, having seen the numbing and addictive effect that prescription meds had had on both my parents. Rather than taking medication to support my brain while I learned how to deal with new and challenging emotional states, I decided I could just simply drink more beer and that would make things OK. Yeah, right, great decision.

Now I had my stress-coping 'strategy' dialled in, I'm sure you'll understand that I don't remember my first year in Sydney too well. I am sure, however, that I was awful to work with, sullen and sulking whenever I didn't get my way. All this did was reinforce the clique I felt was against me and even justify their actions, which now makes perfect sense. I didn't know how to make friends, and when I saw friendships form around me and heard people refer to good times they'd had outside work I saw it as a personal attack, convinced that everyone was out to push me out of this job I had worked so hard to get. Of course that wasn't the case, I was completely

---

2   Looking back, I am absolutely certain that I owe my life and career to these two people. But what really astounds me is that, because this happened in Australia, all of this was freely provided by the state. Simon and Marie not only saved me from becoming an angry, jumpy loner who was too afraid to leave the house or even look at people, but they were *employed by the government* to do so. I was on an ever-tightening spiral of paranoia and, later in life when I lived in the United States, I couldn't help but think of what would have happened to me if I had grown up in a country where those services weren't freely available. I think of them every time I pay my taxes – because every day, somewhere in Australia, someone like them is helping someone like me.

inventing all of it, but I reacted as if it was real and therefore it would reinforce my irrational fears – sometimes to the point where they would turn into reality and therefore justify my behaviour. I was creating a loop of fear and anguish to live within. I don't recommend this.

When you add the effect that me being on TV had on other people in public places, things were getting strange pretty fast. I always feared what other people were thinking of me when they looked at me, given my irrational and ego-filled belief that they were constantly paying attention to me. Unfortunately, now that I was on television, albeit cable television, every now and then people actually *were* staring at me. It was first noticed by my younger brother when he came down to Sydney to visit me. Once he confirmed that I wasn't imagining it, it felt like I'd slipped backwards down one of the super-steep water slides at Wet 'n Wild and there was no splashdown pool in sight. Walking through public places would never be the same again.

But I told myself this was basically OK, because there was always beer, the great insulator. But at the 2000 Big Day Out on the Gold Coast I needed more than beer to get me past the staring eyes. Attending the festival as a punter to party with Cymone and my former bandmates was a foolish idea. The whole Channel [v] team was there covering the marquee interviews backstage with the network's superstar Jabba. We were out in punter land and I'd started drinking very heavily very early to provide some emotional padding to every spike of fear that shot through me when someone I didn't know shouted out 'AndrooGeeeee' at me. Not wanting to get too drunk too early I had cleverly decided that I'd subsidise my alcohol intake with methamphetamines, and in copious amounts.

Contravening every single condition of entry to the festival, I snuck my camcorder in, and I had the bright idea of filming the main stage and people walking around – getting them to shout 'Channel V' into the camera. I thought this would make me a hero at work, getting the true feeling of the festival while the rest of the team were hard at work backstage getting the big-name artist interviews.

It was all going swimmingly until around eight or nine in the evening when my consumption of alcohol, methamphetamine and random hits on every joint that a stranger had passed me reached critical mass and my body just shut down. I passed out. I don't even want to think about how much speed I'd taken or how much booze I'd drunk, but to get to a point where you've taken so much of both that your body sees no option but to go unconscious – that's probably too much.

The next day, still drunk from the night before, I called Ben Richardson my executive producer with the exciting news about the brilliant footage I'd captured. Instead of treating me like the hero I was sure I was, Ben was very upset. I'd even go so far as to say he was angry. Ben explained to me that just because I worked at Channel [v] didn't mean I could walk around the festival with a camera filming whatever I wanted. Every camera needed a camera pass and a chaperone. By taking a camera to the festival and so publicly waving it about, and especially by pointing it at the main stage, I had potentially put the entire network's relationship with the Big Day Out in jeopardy and I'd be lucky if I still had a job when I got back to Sydney. This was not how my ego had told me the conversation would go. Instead of being the hero of the day with the man-on-the-ground footage, I had potentially destroyed a multi-million-dollar partnership that had run for years.

To say I went into a panic attack was an understatement. I was having a hungover speed come-down, an unstoppable mudslide of shame and regret pushing me into the ground, and I still had to pack my bag and get to Coolangatta airport to make the next flight home. I hid the tape and never watched it again, gingerly turning up to work that week with my tail between my legs – surprised that I not only still had a job but also that Ben still wanted me to cover the back end of the tour as it stopped in Adelaide and Perth.

You'd think that after my experience on the Gold Coast I'd have pulled my head in. But no sooner had we walked into the Adelaide venue to start interviewing people about what they thought of the show than I decided that it just wasn't right to be at a festival and not have a drink. I said I needed to go to the bathroom, did a loop past the beer tent and necked two cans of Coopers – the kind in the specially printed can just for the day. With a few beers under the belt I felt that now it was OK to get on with the job at hand. Unfortunately, this didn't stop at two beers.

Next thing I know I was with the guitar player from Killing Heidi. He was a lot younger than me and I convinced him it would be a great idea to steal a golf cart and go for a hoon through the crowd. Specifically assigned to runners and those who need to get artists from dressing room to stage (which at a festival can be kilometres apart) golf carts at a festival aren't there for fun, so they definitely noticed that one was missing.

Security finally caught up with us as I was driving the golf cart out into the actual festival area, through the water-misting tent that people could walk through to cool down. A nice security man just stopped me and said, 'Mate, we need this back' and got behind the wheel and drove off. When you think about what I was doing – a working crew member, representing a major broadcast partner of the festival drunkenly driving a vehicle into a pedestrian area with seven ways from Sunday that it could have gone horribly wrong – it seems incredible. But there was a part of my personality (later in sobriety I'd call this state of mind 'the naughty boy') that was trying very, very hard to ruin everything.

The strange thing was – I was absolutely powerless to stop myself from taking these kinds of risks. The compulsion was like the irresistible desire to scratch a mosquito bite – you know it might break the skin and get infected but you just can't stop yourself. I might think, 'That's probably not a great idea', but wouldn't be able to process that into a decision that would stop the action. Unfortunately for me and many others I hurt along the way, the naughty boy was just getting started.

Back in Sydney, things between me and Paula had gone from bad to worse. I didn't know how to go about building a healthy relationship with her; all I knew how to do was outwork people. That's what had worked for me in Brisbane and in Adelaide. So I did more prep for interviews than ever before, I got there before everyone else and I left after they were gone. I just fucking put my shoulder to the cart and pushed. This didn't go unrecognised by my bosses, and soon Barry surprised me with a pay rise, not even a year after I had started. He and I were having regular conversations by now, his wisdom and drive inspiring me to try as hard as I could to rise above and outwork whatever was going on. I'm sure I was still a sulking man-child – but I was a hard-working sulking man-child.

Barry told me to just keep working and 'kill them with kindness'. I don't know how well I did with the second part but soon enough Paula decided she didn't want to work at Channel [v] any more. It was as if an enormous weight had lifted off the team and making TV about pop music became fun again.

The few months that followed Paula's departure were blissful, yet it was clear we needed more on camera talent at [v] as the few of us there just couldn't cover everything. We set up a reporter search and scoured the country for new presenters, and the two we finally settled on are now household names: Yumi Stynes and James Mathison.

By the time James and Yumi arrived I was definitely very possessive and territorial over what I had at Channel [v]. I was with one hand welcoming to these two new and talented people and with the other being domineering and dismissive. Like a child who was forced to share his toys, I was conditionally accepting of their presence, the condition being that I would continue to be a petulant idiot.

As you will remember, 2000 was a big year for Sydney. The Olympic Games were coming to town in September and due to restrictions by the IOC and their broadcast partners no one who hadn't paid to use the words 'the Olympics' could do so. So we referred to them as 'the Games' and created a nightly live TV show to celebrate them. It was like New Year's Eve every night of the week, with the streets of Kings Cross heaving with corporate-sponsored parties, catering to the collective presence of the world's elite sporting population in one place.

My visionary executive producer Ben Richardson created a nightly live show called *Rings of Fire*, with Johnny Cash's classic song as the intro music. He asked me to host this show, alongside one of Australia's most high-profile sports-mad musicians, Kram the drummer from Spiderbait. It was Kram's first time hosting live TV and so Ben asked me to guide him through it. We'd start out having a production meeting at the bar next door to the studio about 6pm with a few schooners. I had never been drunk on air, but on that show I drank heavily before, during and afterwards. I knew something was amiss when I saw highlight reels go to air and have no recollection of making the shows that were being shown in them.

A little concerned by this, I talked to one of my superiors and sheepishly apologised for drinking like that during a live TV show but was told, 'Don't worry, you were fine. It's all a part of the vibe of the city while the Olympics is on.' I took this to mean, 'Have at you, young man, fill your boots.'

Cymone and I had moved to Bondi Beach by this point, and I began to notice that on days when I went bodysurfing things felt better. There was something about being in the ocean, being humbled by the power of the waves and overwhelmed by an energy more vast than I could comprehend that made my head feel less noisy. My former bandmate Damian Barbeler was now living in Sydney with his wife Katherine Kemp, and as he was now making a living as a composer his schedule was flexible enough for us to spend a bit of time exploring the coastline and Sydney's beaches.

The conversations that he and I would have as we drove up and down the coast, combined with the physicality of tackling massive surf always left me feeling wonderful, and were a welcome respite to the stresses of work.

the world turned upside down

It was 2001. As Foxtel grew, my career profile began to rise more and more. Daryl Missen introduced me to RMK, one of Australia's biggest voiceover artists' agencies. I was able to get on the books there, leading to a lucrative side hustle that worked well for a few years. I'd read commercials for everything from cheesy radio ads urging listeners to get along to the Berry Street Tavern for a 'berry good meal', all the way to my crowning glory as a VO artist – providing the voice for Coco the monkey in the Coco Pops commercials. I got a lot more work off the back of that one.

At Channel [v], things were moving along well and the momentum was building. Occasionally we'd get sent on junkets, which is when a record company would line up a whole bunch of their artists to be in the same space at roughly the same time, and by sending across a film crew from an outlet like us they could get lots of coverage for one set of plane fares and accommodation.

Most of the time Channel [v]'s flagship interviewer Jabba went on these junkets. He had been there since the days of Red TV, and many of the artists knew and respected him. Yet in mid-2001 I was told that James and Yumi would cover the afternoon request show while I headed to the USA that September for interviews with my EP Ben Richardson and a crew which included our audio guy andy Munro (AKA Shadow)[1] and our talented cameraman Michael Jackson[2] (AKA Jacko).

We landed in LA in the first week of September 2001, staying in West Hollywood just off Sunset – I was instantly and overwhelmingly excited about being there. The first night we arrived Ben and Jacko decided we'd walk up Sunset Boulevard and get some dinner. After a few beers we set off up the street and I instantly had no filter, a little too loudly letting comments fly about what people were wearing, and more than once Ben had to pull me aside and say, 'You may want to watch what you say about strangers – don't forget we're in America and people carry guns here.' I just kept going, excitement pushing me on to riskier and riskier behaviour. Later at dinner (where I was drinking beers like I'd never tasted beer before) during a bathroom break I noticed some small crumbs of white powder on a ledge above the sink.

I'd already started to take cocaine back in Sydney; it always seemed to be around and when it was offered I did my best impression of a human Dyson. I loved the drug because it sobered me up and made me want to talk incessantly about my favourite subject – me. That first night in LA, I didn't even blink as I licked my finger and wiped up all those random crumbs with one swipe, and then proceeded to rub them onto my gums. Yup, it was coke all right. And the fact that I was doing a random stranger's leftover toilet drugs in a restaurant while overseas on a work trip didn't bother me at all.

---

1   Just a note: if your job is as an audio recordist and you often need to swing a boom pole on interviews, try to avoid getting this nickname. It was a bit unfair and he was given the nickname before I arrived but, like most nicknames, it stuck.

2   Yes, our cameraman was called Michael Jackson. A very talented operator with an incredible eye, he's a raconteur with a story for every occasion. It's fair to say I wouldn't be here today without Jacko, but more about that in a moment.

The following day we interviewed Ozzy Osbourne on the eve of the release of his new album. His massive MTV reality series had begun filming but wasn't released yet, so he wasn't quite the household name he'd soon become. The next stop was to cover a gig by up and coming LA band System of a Down, whose second album had just been released. They were playing a free show in a parking lot in Hollywood; we would get some footage of the gig and then interview them afterwards.

Hollywood is not a nice place. There's the romantic idea of it, where nobodies become stars overnight and fame and fortune are delivered on a platter, but that isn't an actual physical place. In the words of one of my heroes, Greg Proops: 'Hollywood is an idea collectively held in the heads of a million assholes.' The actual suburb of Hollywood is a rundown and nasty semi-industrial part of the city, thick with sleeping homeless and the dangerous edge of drug dealing.

Even though I'd been in the music industry less than ten years, I knew pretty soon that this wasn't a well-thought-out event. System of a Down were an LA metal band, and LA metal attracts a heavy kind of fan. The crowd was mostly Latino, and gang tattoos were everywhere. The organisers had expected 1500 people, but more than 5000 showed up. Where there should have been massive barriers to stop people from rushing the stage, the only ones there were protecting the stage and then only went as wide as the stage did. I counted five security guards where there should have been fifty.

We were ushered into a 'press' area that was a prime viewing position but separated from the heaving throng of increasingly restless fans only by the flimsy 'bike rack' barriers. The time for the show to start came and went and we could feel the air grow thicker and thicker with tension. In the back of our brains, way down right above the spinal column in the most primitive part of what separates us from animals, there's a receptor to pack mentality, and it was firing louder than I'd ever known before. Something was about to happen, and it wasn't going to be good.

One by one the other international TV crews left. As the crowd started to get more agitated and began to throw things at the stage in protest for the fact that the show hadn't started yet, I saw one or two security guards quietly remove their badges and slip away into the sea of black jeans and t-shirts. We were in the walled-in back corner of a disused parking lot and the crowd was now so massive that we no longer had an exit.

It was my first time in such an edgy situation, but not Jacko's. As a news cameraman he had seen his fair share of violence unfold in front of his lens. Instinctively, he hit 'record' because he knew that whatever tension was building was about to burst.

And burst it did when the stage manager decided to lower the band's banner from behind the drum kit. The crowd saw this as a sign that the gig wasn't going to happen, and that trigger was all they needed. Like a bomb going off, a riot broke out. Hundreds of people started to rush the stage. Those useless barriers were swiftly dismantled and passed back over the heads of the crowd. We tried to take cover with the remaining stage crew huddled behind the massive stacks of PA boxes. Jacko swung his camera around to film men who had pulled their t-shirts over their faces, rushed onto the stage and started to steal bits and pieces of equipment; others were rocking those towering speakers back and forth until they toppled right into the crowd. When we watched the footage back later, it was an absolute miracle that no one was killed, as those falling speaker boxes missed the fans scrambling to get out of the way by mere centimetres.

The stage now in tatters, the crowd looked elsewhere to take out their frustrations. Unfortunately, Jacko was in their sights and a man lunged for his camera, grabbing it off his shoulder. When Jacko caught the camera strap and pulled it back, the would-be thief spun around and king hit him, sending the big cameraman straight into the tarmac. Ben leapt over a heaving sea of bodies to dive on Jacko and protect him from the flailing blows of his assailants while both of them held onto the camera and the precious footage.

I'd never been in a fight and I had no idea what I was supposed to do. As I stood there contemplating my uselessness, the one security guard who had stayed behind came to the rescue. A well-built African-American man, he had unscrewed the steel pole of a straight microphone stand and now he jumped down from the stage towards the melee, bringing that weapon down on the backs and forearms of the rioters swarming on top of Jacko and Ben. I don't think his methods were covered by his security company's code of conduct, but this was now a survival situation and he wielded that pole with furious anger – the sound of steel crushing bone is still in my head as I write this – and eventually broke the throng of people apart enough to get Ben and Jacko out from under their attackers.

By now we were backed all the way into a corner, flanked on one side by buildings and behind us a ten-metre-high cyclone fence surrounding a school playground. Between us and Hollywood Boulevard were 5000 angry fans, and the only way out was through that fence. As Ben picked a badly wounded Jacko up off the ground I noticed that a part of the fence between two uprights wasn't set into the concrete. I pulled hard on the base of that cyclone fence and managed to bend it enough to create a small elliptical gap underneath it. If we lay on our bellies we could shimmy underneath to safety.

We escaped into the schoolyard, but we weren't out of danger yet. Some of Ben and Jacko's attackers had followed us and were feigning helpfulness, trying to get us to go this way or that to safety, but we were sure they were just trying to get us alone. We made our way across the quadrangle and found an exit gate, but it was too high for our injured cameraman to climb. I dragged a playground lunch table across the concrete, which enabled us to get over the gate and drop down to the other side. Jacko had been quite badly beaten. One of his arms wasn't really working, his head was swollen and he was bleeding.

Once we were on the ground again, I noticed that we had ended up right in the middle of a makeshift marshalling area for the LAPD riot squad. There were hundreds of cops, all in full riot gear with helmets and shields ready, getting psyched to break up the crowd. They had clearly been assembling here for a while and were waiting for the right moment to move. In hindsight that moment was probably an hour before Jacko had the shit beaten out of him, but it was too late to think of that now.

How we were going to get out of this was still a mystery; we were on foot and the street was still streaming with angry music fans looking for vengeance on anything that got in their way. At that moment a gap appeared in the ranks of mounted police and riot cops, and into that gap cruised one lone and vacant yellow cab.[3] I leapt in front of it and we all piled in, thankful for our escape from the dangerous riot. Afterwards, the true nature of what had happened really started to sink in. In a heaving and angry crowd where there were no bag checks or body searches, we had come very close to not making it out of there.

That night Ben took Jacko off to hospital where he was X-rayed and assessed for his head injuries. He was pretty messed up, but with a bit of help he would be able to continue working for the rest of the trip. It was 2 September 2001 and we were all looking forward to getting out of there for the excitement of New York City, where in just over a week we would wrap up our work trip and then head home.

After a few more days of interviews in LA, we flew to JFK for the next part of our work trip. Nothing compares to the first time you see Manhattan. As we drove in from JFK, the twin towers of the World Trade Center loomed over the southern part of the island, separated from the skyscrapers of midtown by a few miles.

One or two artist interviews fell through so we ended up with a couple of unexpected days off, which I spent walking around and looking up at things, as most NYC tourists do the first time that they go there. The record company lined us up with a few shows to see. We finally got to see System of a Down play a show at the Irving Plaza, and the following night, the incredible Tenacious D live in midtown.

---

3   In a time before Uber, LA was renowned for having about ten taxis to service the whole city. Everyone had a car, and everyone drove when they drank, so for some reason there were zero cabs when you needed them. That the one vacant taxi in all of LA happened to come driving down that street on that day is nothing short of a miracle. In fact I'm sure I heard a chorus of angels herald its arrival.

The next day we took a flight to Washington to do another interview, with r'n'b artist Maxwell. He apparently wasn't feeling too well so we waited one day, then two. On the third day, sick of waiting around, we decided to see some sights including a trip to the White House on 10 September, where we saw Australian PM John Howard leaving after his meeting with George W. Bush.

Later in the afternoon we got a call from the record company saying that the interview with Maxwell would not go ahead. This made our next day quite a tough one. We were scheduled to fly to New York first thing in the morning, travel straight to a venue for an interview with the band Incubus, then pack down and go to JFK for a flight back to LA and connect to the direct flight back to Australia. We all decided that it would be nicer to not have to do that, so instead of flying the next morning we all took the train from Washington to Grand Central Station that evening, allowing us one night in NYC and a good night's sleep before our big final day in the USA.

Around 8:45am on the morning of 11 September I woke up to what I thought was the sound of a large truck going over a road plate at the roadworks below where we were staying at the Roger Smith Hotel on 51st and Lexington Avenue. I yawned, got up to pee and turned on the TV. On the screen, I saw a gaping, smoking hole in the side of the north tower of the World Trade Center. As I flicked around, I saw that every channel was showing a version of the same shot.

I woke up Ben Richardson and said, 'I don't know if we're going to interview Incubus today.' I slipped a tape into the VHS machine and hit 'record'. About one minute later Ben, I and millions of people around the world watched as United Airlines flight 175 ploughed into the south tower of the World

Trade Center at 950 kilometres an hour. It was 9am, and the first tendrils of a fear greater than any I had ever known started to work their way into my brain.

Ben had a bit of experience in dealing with dodgy situations. He'd been through a number of coups and bloody revolts in the South Pacific and knew how to keep his cool in times of crisis. The first thing he did was turn on the radio. Searching for an alternative and independent source to verify the news from the mainstream channels was instinctive and vital, and we heard things no one talks about to this day. We heard that every bridge and tunnel was closed, that there were reports of vans filled with liquid explosives in the tunnels, and that Manhattan island was being cut off.

I didn't know what to do, but I did know that we might end up having to walk out of there – where to, I didn't know. I grabbed my passport out of the safe and told Ben I was heading down to the bodega on the corner to grab some breakfast. I stuffed my passport into my underpants and headed out onto the street. It was a warm morning and people were walking with a sense of shock and growing urgency. In the short time it took me to walk from the hotel to the store on the corner I saw that things were starting to break down around the edges. People were jostling each other just a little too much, pushing past each other and not saying 'excuse me' as they normally would; a man had his phone stolen straight out of his hand during a phone call by someone sprinting by and no one even blinked.

I walked into the convenience store, bought a few pre-made sandwiches and some bottles of water and then withdrew as much cash out of my account as the ATM would give me. There was a limit on the transactions, so I must have made five withdrawals in a row until my account balance reached zero. I figured that whatever was going to happen in the next few hours, some cash would probably come in handy.

Heading back to our hotel, I stopped in the lobby to get a coffee from the buffet, which had a flat-screen TV up in the corner of the room. The tiny restaurant was packed, standing room only, with people all with their heads craned at the locked-off shot of the twin towers burning. As I stood in the crowd of silently stunned New Yorkers, together we watched the south tower of the World Trade Center pop, buckle and then collapse in a cloud of toxic dust and fire. What I heard next still haunts me. A man said, 'Well, there it is. The world will never be the same again.'

The lift wasn't working so I climbed the five flights of stairs back up to our room, to find Ben trying to get a mobile phone to work. Since most of the telecommunications for the island of Manhattan were routed through an exchange under the World Trade Center, this was impossible. We decided our best bet was to walk down to the hotel where our crew were staying and talk about what we should do for the day. On the street, fire department trucks zoomed by, some with dents in their bonnets from massive chunks of falling concrete.

Out on the street again, the same shocked faces were everywhere. Ben and I moved past hundreds of people, most of them just standing in the middle of the street staring south towards a massive billowing cloud of smoke and dust. When we got to the W Hotel where our crew were staying, the lobby was packed. No flights were going anywhere, no one could check in or out. In the elevator, Ben and I held the door for a short, stocky guy not much older than me with a cropped haircut, carrying a small overnight bag and with a gait betraying ingrained military training. He wore a polo shirt tucked into his jeans, and on one side of his belt was a nine-millimetre automatic pistol and a badge of some kind. On the other side of his belt was the most sophisticated communications device I'd ever seen.[4] When he got out we wished him good luck and he gave us a nod. Shit was going down in a massive way and we were right in the middle of it.

In Jacko's room the TV was on too. Every single channel showed Islamic terrorist training camp videos on loop, occasionally cutting away to show pictures of George W. Bush being escorted to a nuclear bunker. The TV told us we'd just gone to DefCon 3.[5] When I saw this, I freaked out. All I wanted to do was escape. I was prepared to walk out of there if I had to and get to Canada, which I knew was only a few hours away. But there was no way off the island and everyone was trapped. I thought that whoever was doing this had planned to isolate the island and then detonate another bomb. We'd heard rumours as we passed through the lobby about nerve gas and dirty bombs, people nervously whispering to each other as they waited in line to use a payphone that wasn't working.

Convinced that the last thing I'd say was, 'Did you see that flash?' I went into meltdown. My anxiety and panic just dropped reality out from under me and I fell into an abyss of fear I'd never experienced before. Ben and Jacko, both seasoned operators, tried to tell me that though everything was scary we were fifty blocks from Ground Zero, we were

---

4   This thing had no brand name and was clearly some kind of super-high-tech government agency communications device that no one else had access to.

5   DefCon is code for Defence Condition. DefCon 1 is that nuclear war is imminent. DefCon 2 is 'cocked pistol'. DefCon 3 is 'Increase in force readiness above that required for normal readiness, Air Force ready to mobilise in fifteen minutes.' It was fucking scary.

safe and that was what mattered, but their reassurance didn't even touch the sides. I slipped further and further into fear and panic, shaking and stammering. They told me to lie down and breathe, and my body just shut down. I was in such an incredible panic that my body decided the best thing to do in order to keep me safe was to pass out. I slept for hours.

When I woke, Ben and Jacko were standing over me with a salad sandwich and a six-pack of Corona. The world might have been ending around us, but the fridges were still working. I guzzled that first Corona like it was the last beer I'd ever drink, because I thought it would be. After two more beers I started to feel a little better. They got me to my feet and talked me down from the edge. With the beers on board, I was able to process their reasoning and in their presence I felt safe again. If I hadn't been around Ben and Jacko that day, I don't know where I would have ended up.

On the night of 11 September, rumours were flying all over the place and we didn't know what to believe. That's when Ben taught me something very important: 'The first casualty of war is the truth.' With no phones working and no way of communicating to the outside world, no one at home knew whether we were OK, and we didn't know what was going to happen next. We decided that if we were going to go out, we'd go out well. So we got a table at the super-fancy restaurant downstairs, ordered some expensive bottles of red wine and ate a great three-course meal. Afterwards at the bar, Jacko and I went to work on the top-shelf spirits. If we were going to get killed in a sarin gas attack the next day, it would be a shame to leave that Belvedere vodka in the bottle, wouldn't it?

Sometime in the afternoon of 12 September I managed to get word back to Cymone that I was OK, but she'd already lived the last thirty-six hours not knowing whether I was or not. She had begun to consider for the first time what life might be like without me, and that moment would have enormous consequences for us in the future – but right then I was just so relieved to hear her voice.

Along with hundreds of thousands of others, we weren't able to leave Manhattan for about a week. We spent our time walking around the city, staring at the endless displays of missing person flyers covering every vacant wall and lamp post. In those first few days, people were pretending to make calls from beneath the rubble, giving false hope that there were survivors down there. Why would anyone do such a thing? Parts of the city would shut down occasionally, with bomb threats being phoned in everywhere.

It was a strange time, not least because the weather was glorious. It was the end of summer and with everything that was going on, not many businesses were open. When we walked across Central Park, the open greens were packed with hundreds of people just sitting in the sunshine. As we made our way from the west side to the east side, we heard the sound of a passenger jet. It was the first plane besides the circling F-15s on the first day that anyone had seen. I'll never forget that almost every person in the park stopped what they were doing and all craned their necks to the sky, watching this lone airliner cross above us while the park fell silent but for the echo of the jet engines bouncing around the concrete canyons of Manhattan.

After a few days JFK opened again for an hour or so at a time before another bomb threat shut it down. I was getting itchy feet and was trying hard to lobby for us to get as far away from New York as we could. I'd seen that Dulles airport in

Washington DC was moving OK so I figured we would rent a van and try JFK – if that didn't work we could drive to DC and try our luck there. Luckily enough, we reached JFK right in a window of opportunity and managed to get a flight headed towards LA. Once we were airborne the captain was obviously rattled, and his normal 'arrival time and weather' speech ended up being a ten-minute monologue about liberty and freedom and how if anyone tried anything on the plane, we as proud freedom-loving Americans would know what to do. It was like being flown west by George C. Scott as General Buck Turgidson in *Dr Strangelove*.[6]

Halfway across the USA, Los Angeles airport radioed back to say they were full and there was nowhere to park the plane, so we had to stop in Denver. That night at an airport motel bar, along with hundreds of other stranded travellers, I went to town, drinking to dull the fear caused by the rumours of war and suitcase nukes and dirty bombs that filled the air. The bar had screens everywhere which probably used to show sports all night, but here we were trying to have a beer, surrounded by the constantly looping snuff film of planes crashing into buildings, each network seemingly taking turns to replay that footage over and over and over again, only cutting away from that to show endless loops of Islamist training camps.

We ended up back in LA for a few days while we waited for a flight, and when we finally did get back to Sydney all of Channel [v] had turned up to welcome us home. About fifty people, with signs and balloons and everything – they were all there. Cymone wept when she saw me again, and I was so happy to be back in her arms. However, when I got back to

---

6   I'm probably going to have to start a movie playlist if you want to understand most of this book, aren't I?

Bondi and walked down to the beach for a swim, I couldn't grasp what had happened. The world was forever changed, and was closer to ending than it had ever been before, and people were just lying around on their towels as if they didn't care.

Cymone and I were only with each other for a few days, as she was off on the road for an on-camera job with Nickelodeon, so I was home alone with the cats. I'd found I couldn't watch the news any more; even seeing a person in a suit with some words at the bottom of the screen sent the same shocks of fear through my body that I'd felt back at the W Hotel. So I just didn't turn the TV on. I couldn't walk past a newsagency in case I saw a front page that screamed a headline about jihad or something equally frightening. When I got in taxis I had to ask them to turn off the radio because just the sound of a news bulletin starting sent rivers of terror across my brain.

twelve
aftermath

At work I was pretty weird. I just sat there with the thousand-yard stare. I'd be able to put on a brave face when it was time to go to air at 4pm, but I couldn't muster a smile or a positive thought beforehand. I'd just sit there and stare at the wall. Eventually my boss Jacquie walked past, did a double-take and asked whether I was OK, to which I had to answer, 'No'. Fortunately, she took my answer seriously and organised a psychologist named Phil Gorrell to come in and debrief us, not only about nearly getting killed in the riot but also having a front-row seat to 9/11. He was a total pro who had done a lot of work with emergency services in debriefing firefighters and police after trauma, so I was grateful that he came. Afterwards he slipped me his card and told me to call him if I needed anything.

A few weeks went by and nothing was changing. I'd try to wash off the doom in my head by going out for a bodysurfing session. But even under hundreds of tonnes of water, with the entire energy of the South Pacific washing over me while I waited for a break in the waves so I could surface and breathe again, I couldn't stop ruminating about what had happened and the instability that now existed in the world. I was done. If I couldn't just go for a bodysurf and enjoy the cool breeze and warm sunshine, I had to make a change. So I gave Phil a call and headed up to see him.

Phil was grey-haired and older than I was, but he moved with the nimbleness of someone who surfs every day and volunteers in his local fire brigade. After a few sessions he told me I had post-traumatic stress disorder or PTSD. I scoffed: that was bullshit. I was fine, we had been fifty blocks from Ground Zero. Sure I coughed up black stuff for about six weeks after we got back, but there was nothing wrong with me. Thousands of people had died that day, and I wasn't among them.

When I told Phil he was wrong he said nothing, just got up from his creaky old armchair, walked over to his bookcase and pulled out the *DSM-IV*, which is like the street directory for mental illness categorisation.[1] He flicked through the book until he found PTSD, handed me the weighty tome and asked me to read the symptoms out loud. As I read, it was as if someone had been taking notes on my life and then snuck into Phil's office to write them in this book, because it described exactly what was going on in my head.

It was Phil who first taught me about CBT or cognitive behavioural therapy. This is a largely self-administered form of therapy designed to identify common cognitive distortions and to challenge them with more rational beliefs. The idea is that over time you're able to challenge automatic negative or irrational thoughts and redirect them through a more rational lens. It is bloody hard, because if you've never challenged what

---

1   *Diagnostic and Statistical Manual of Mental Disorders*, 4th Edition, also known as *DSM-IV-TR*, is a manual published by the American Psychiatric Association that includes all currently recognised mental health disorders. It's used by mental health professionals to describe the features of a given mental disorder and to indicate how the disorder can be distinguished from other, similar problems. Don't be impressed, I got that definition from Wikipedia.

you believe something to be it's really confronting. However, the pain I was going through was so great that I'd have done just about anything to figure it out.

Using CBT every day, I started to feel better and slowly the new thoughts started to take hold. It was still tough trying to understand that the beliefs I had about something weren't exactly how it was and it took a while for me to separate myself from those beliefs enough to challenge them – but I started to get OK at it. I'd still need to write my 'thought diaries' every time I felt a pang of fear, but soon I didn't even need to carry around my notebook to write them on, I could do it in my head.

CBT wasn't my only coping strategy of course; there was always beer. This was a great strategy to have because that summer we went on the road with Channel [v] on a massive bus tour and drinking was all a part of the journey. We were essentially putting on a mini festival every day in whichever country town we'd turn up to, and it was absolutely brilliant. Absolutely live, skin-of-your-teeth television in front of hundreds if not thousands of screaming fans. When we were done, there were cold beers to be had, and I didn't hold back.

However, off the road things became a bit strange. I started to get quite odd about people I didn't know. Cymone had started going to an acting school and, as actors do, she had started to socialise with a new group of fun and interesting people. She of course wanted to introduce me to them and so one night we headed off to a party at a terrace house somewhere in Newtown, a suburb in Sydney's inner west. As we made our way in through the packed hallway, I felt as if the walls were closing in on me. House parties always have maximum population density in the kitchen, and it was traumatic to get out of that and towards the backyard where most people were. I vaguely recognised faces from films I'd seen and TV I'd caught along the way. I shook a few hands when people recognised me from Channel [v] but I didn't know anyone's names.

In the corner of the packed living room, someone had set up an old CRT TV with an Atari 2600 game system that had the cartridge for the game *Combat* in it. I made a beeline straight to it, sat down and started to play. While Cymone wanted me to meet her exciting and fun new acting friends, I wanted to hide in the corner. I sat there for what must have been hours, driving the little tanks around and playing the 8-bit machine while all around me the best and brightest in the Australian acting industry had a great time. I don't really remember anyone's faces – I just remember shoes. Mainly because I stared at the floor the whole time I moved in and out of the party.[2]

This behaviour obviously had a pretty big effect on Cymone, and we began drifting further and further apart. Of course I didn't realise that I was emotionally disengaging from her and from others in general, but she obviously felt it. I didn't know it was happening, and it was a complete surprise to me when she told me one day that she was moving out. Of course she felt like this; I'd been a distant, shouty but then silent weirdo whom she hadn't been able to engage with for a year. Nobody wants to be with that. In late September 2002, seven years after getting together, we were now apart.

I'd love to say that I rose above the heartache and carried on with my head held high, but I didn't. I basically sat on the couch, drank beer and didn't eat anything for about four

2   Ten years later, I interviewed Joel Edgerton for a film, and he said something like, 'Good to see you again, I've not seen you since that party back in Newtown.' I had to apologise that I didn't remember meeting him.

weeks. Sure, I'd show up to work and put on a brave face when it came to talking about pop music, but then I'd go home and writhe around in my misery.

After about the fourth week of dragging myself out of bed to sit around and mope again, I knew something had to change. Harking back to when I tricked myself into walking around the block, I said to myself, 'I'll just go and have a look at the beach.' At the time our apartment was about 120 metres behind the North Bondi Surf Lifesaving Club. I walked to the promenade and then just kept walking onto the sand. I walked in the soft sand until I got to the south end of the beach, and then kicked up into a shuffle/jog back to the ramp I'd walked down. It was probably about 800 metres in total but when I got home I felt a little bit better. The next day the misery returned the moment I opened my eyes, but I just got out the front door and walked down to the sand again. This time I ran down to the south end and then back again for a total of 1600 metres. Soon enough I was managing four, then six, then eight laps in the soft sand. I just knew that no matter how much agony would come and take a shit in my brain when I woke up, as long as I got out the door I'd be OK.

That summer really drummed into me the importance of exercise in managing my mental health. While I can no longer run due to old-man arthritis hips, I can gratefully still ride my bicycle, and daily exercise is a cornerstone of how I manage my headspace every day.

At this time I transitioned to a fully plant-based diet. It was a change that occurred over a number of years, and had started when I'd moved in with Cymone – she was lactose-intolerant, so we just didn't really have cheese in the house.

I noticed my skin clearing up, things tasted clearer, my nose unclogged, and colours even seemed brighter.

On that holiday in Byron Bay, we'd visited a vegetarian restaurant called The Piggery[3] which had a cinema attached to it. For the first time in my life I ate a magnificent green curry made with tofu instead of chicken. It was so delicious and nutritious, and as I digested the warm chilli-laced meal, we moved to the cinema in the back of the restaurant to watch the film that was included with our dinner bill. A powerful documentary called *Baraka* was playing. Shot with cutting-edge time-lapse technology, featuring long slow sweeping zooms that documented 'a day in the life of the world,' the film was clearly made with a strong environmental message.

One unforgettable scene juxtaposed the factory farming of chickens with the modern life of humans in a big city. The film showed tiny yellow chicks sliding down chutes in their thousands, dropping further into giant hoppers overflowing with the newborn animals and then into another machine where they were sorted from viable to non-viable, and then placed in cages where they'd live out their lives. Watching this powerful footage as I felt how good the meal made me feel, I thought, 'I'd rather not eat anything that lived like that.' So I stopped eating chicken.

At the same time I found out how much land, water and energy it takes to make one kilogram of plant protein versus one kilogram of animal protein. When I learned that around 15,000 litres of water is required to produce *just one kilogram* of beef protein compared to around 1250 litres to produce the same quantity of plant protein I couldn't forget it. That's a lot of

---

3   In perfect Byron Bay style, they'd converted an old slaughterhouse into a vegetarian place in order to reverse the karma on the area.

water that could be used to grow other food that people could eat, or at the very least drink. When I learned that soybeans produce five to ten times more protein per acre than dairy land, and up to fifteen times more protein per acre than land set aside for meat production, I couldn't justify that dietary choice. That's a lot of water that thirsty people could drink, not to mention the land required or even the food that's fed to the livestock that people could otherwise eat.

I'd always been concerned about the environment, but had never made the connection between my diet and what effect it was having on the planet.

Later in life I'd learn about the health benefits of eating little or no meat, and the deal was sealed even further.[4] I began to feel a lot better now that I was eating more vegetables, and not long after I stopped eating chicken I stopped eating red meat. The uptick in how I felt in my body was remarkable, mostly a feeling of lightness and vitality I'd never experienced before. The cleaner I ate, the better I felt.

After we moved to Sydney I stopped eating fish, which meant by now the only animal products I was eating were eggs and honey. When I was now the only person living in the house, I went fully plant-based and I've never looked back.

Now I was by myself, my two school friends Bubble and Luke Heggie moved in to help with the rent.[5] Evenings in that apartment were spent playing Scrabble. With four university degrees between the two of them, they are incredibly smart

---

4 While I definitely care about animal welfare, I care more about humans to be honest. The whole meat-based food industry seems to me like a colossal waste of water, energy and land – when there's a healthier, cheaper option literally growing right under our noses. An option that not only has less impact on the planet, but also our health system as the public cost of food-related illness skyrockets.

5 Bubble has a name: Dave. Bubble was just his nickname from when we were kids, and it stuck. Dave was a high-end lawyer and had the brain the size of the planet.

guys. We all got completely obsessed with the Stefan Fatsis book *Word Freak* and spent our days memorising lists of obscure two- and three-letter words so that we could crush the opposition in the evenings. We had a scoreboard, we had a league table, and we had records for highest ever word put down. Between the word-nerding and the banter, it was a great way to spend our evenings.[6] Embracing everything that Bondi had to offer, I started to take beginner yoga classes and I even began to surf.

I was a long way from being mentally healthy but that summer, between the yoga and the surfing and the socialisation with Bubble and Luke, I'd begun to form a new and more comfortable definition of myself.

6　I still have a deep love of Scrabble, and not long ago I rode my small folding bicycle down to Maroubra Beach to play a game with Luke Heggie. We now both wear glasses to play, but it's still my favourite game.

thirteen
party time

Life at Channel [v] was firing on all cylinders. Every summer before the Big Day Out we would all pile aboard a custom-built tour bus and take our request show to the most remote parts of Australia. It was great to turn up to an empty field near a small town eight hours' drive from anywhere, lower the staging truck into position and point the satellite dish at the sky, and then by 4pm see that field filled with thousands of young people who had come from all around the area to be a part of the fun. We toured with a gigantic skateboard half-pipe, a team of international professional skaters and at least one live band, and for two hours every afternoon we'd show up, turn up and rock out.

We were the biggest party to come to town in years, and it seemed everyone was there to be a part of it. It was during these tours that two things really started to kick off in earnest for me. My hearing started to get quite damaged, and drinking during the day remained a great idea. On the days where we were driving the long distances between shows (Australia is a *big* country once you get out of the cities) a case of VB sequestered from catering the night before was waiting in the fridge and I'd pretty much roll out of my bunk in the morning and crack a can. I didn't see the problem; we were on the road and this is what people on the road did. When we got off stage at 6pm, and the performance adrenaline that was coursing through my veins began to morph into anxiety, a few Coopers Pale Ales would be just the thing to settle that down so I could carry on a normal conversation without talking at 500 kilometres an hour.

With full credit to Barry Chapman, Jacquie Riddell, Ben Richardson and our director Bernie Zelvis, the shows we did were absolutely seat-of-your-pants live television, shot guerrilla-style in the middle of the bush. It was a full team effort and the whole team made shows to be proud of, day after day. Most presenters have a live TV experience about once a year, when they step in for a live crossback to the news desk for a special charity event. We not only had thousands of hours of live studio experience up our sleeves, we were building up hundreds of hours of outside broadcast (OB) expertise – a different situation altogether. It was raw, it was exciting, it was as real as real can be, and no one was coming close to making the kind of TV we were. We were running live SMS polls that sampled from across the country as we threw to a film clip requested by a kid on the phone 2000 kilometres away, from below a five-metre-high big screen in the middle of the desert to the adulation of hundreds of screaming fans. When we got back from the tours we couldn't wait to get out on the road again, to see how much further we could push what was possible with a staging truck, a generator and a satellite dish.

It was off the back of one of those tours that I returned to a stack of phone messages from a woman named Suzanne Mitchell. The voicemails said that she was from Fremantle Media and she wanted to talk about a project.

As the stranger danger was getting pretty serious for me, I did the only thing I knew – I ignored the phone calls.

Eventually she managed to call when I was at my desk and invited me to their Crows Nest office for a meeting.

Curious, I agreed and headed to their offices across the Sydney Harbour Bridge. We were meeting in the landmark Grundy Television building, the home of *Neighbours* and *Wheel of Fortune*, and I was to meet with Greg Beness. Greg was an old-school Channel 9 producer, best known for his work on the mammoth Australian Bicentennial broadcasts and for making the huge live shows for *Star Search*. He told me later that I walked in with nothing but arrogance and ego. Apparently I sat down, put my feet on his desk and asked him what he wanted to talk about. Well, we'd just come off the back of a hugely successful summer tour and I had AAA laminated backstage passes to the biggest festivals in the world. What could this company that made sausage-factory soap operas and boring afternoon game shows possibly have that I wanted?

Greg started talking about doing a singing competition show, and I was immediately turned off. The last singing contest show Australia had seen was the third series of *Popstars*, which looked as if it had been filmed with consumer-level camcorders in someone's backyard. As far as I was concerned, a singing competition show wasn't going to work. That's when he popped a VHS tape into a machine and hit 'play'. On screen came Ant and Dec, the legendary two-handed hosting duo from the UK, introducing *Pop Idol*. At Channel [v] we were well aware of the success of the format both in the UK and the USA where they'd just gone back-to-back with season two.

'The thing is, Andrew – is that this show will be *live*. Are you OK with live television?' I am 100 per cent sure that I scoffed at him. Since I'd started at Channel [v], the free-to-air television industry had looked down on what we did. We were their poor cousin, in their eyes playing in our little walled garden of the set top box. Was I OK with live television? Well, seeing it was now four years since I'd started at Channel [v], where I was a part of hosting three hours of live television every day for most of the year, I'd racked up close to 3000 hours of flight time – yeah, you could be pretty damned sure I was OK with live television.

I told Greg, 'If you're going to do this, you're going to need to do it right. It's going to need to be big. Really big. Are you going to do that?' His eyes lit up and he agreed that yes, it would be big.[1]

I was contracted exclusively to Channel [v] and I'd actually breached the conditions of my employment by taking the meeting. In the end I signed a non-disclosure agreement, which you sign when you're having a meeting about something that hasn't been greenlit yet. It means you can be told everything you need to know about a project to decide whether or not to go ahead with it, but if you tell anyone about it you'll have the pants sued off you.

I didn't quite grasp the gravity of this situation until a few weeks later when my Channel [v] colleague James Mathison took me aside at work one day and asked, 'Have you been up to Crows Nest in the last few weeks?'

'Yes, I have.'

'Have you signed an NDA in Crows Nest?'

'Yes, I have.'

'If we've both signed an NDA about the same thing, does that mean we can talk about it with each other?'

---

1 I'd come to learn a few very important things about making a great show from Greg – the first of which was: why have just one chopper shot when you can have two, and the second: everything is better when there's fireworks.

'Let's get a coffee.'

It turned out that Suzanne had approached James as well and they were angling to have us host the show together. If a production company is importing a successful overseas format into Australia, they and the network try as hard as they can to replicate every possible aspect of the winning formula from the market where it went well, and we were going to be the new Ant and Dec.[2] James and I agreed the show was an exciting opportunity. We shot a demo reel, and mercifully Jacquie Riddell saw the benefit of two of her hosts being involved in what was surely going to be a massive success.[3]

I didn't have a manager at that stage, and as I was an employee of Channel [v], it was up to Jacquie to negotiate the terms of release for me to work on *Australian Idol*, part of which allowed James and me to make a behind-the-scenes show for Channel [v] about our time on *Idol*.[4] Once the deal was done the announcement was made and we were off on the audition tour. It was May 2003, and I had no idea about how much my world was going to change.

---

2   That's why on the first season of *American Idol* Ryan Seacrest had a co-host, Brian Dunkleman. If you watch the opening pieces to camera of the first seasons of *Pop Idol* and *American Idol*, you'll see that the Americans basically repeated word for word the script that Ant and Dec used. Of course, Ant and Dec had been working together since they were fifteen on the TV show *Byker Grove*, so their natural rapport and humour were near-impossible to replicate.

3   Jacquie told me that her philosophy about the workplace was that when I went to my next job, people would say, 'How are you able to do what you do? Where did you *come* from?' That's how she approached our training and how she crafted opportunities for us within the organisation. Those were exactly the words people used when I went to free-to-air television.

4   I won't say how much money I did the first season for – but I will say this. In 2005 when I finally signed up to a management company, my tax bill alone was nearly double what I'd accepted as payment for the first season of *Idol*. Barry had always demanded that I 'know my worth' but I was still a few years away from even having a clue as to what that was.

Our producer – let's call him Colin – had no clue what to do with us. An intense man in his mid-forties, he was a very successful producer in his own right. He'd come from working on big-rating shows like *60 Minutes* all through the 1990s and had a very strict idea of how things were to be done. Colin wore winkle-picker leather shoes and high-waisted acid-wash jeans into which he'd tuck his faded Mambo t-shirt. He looked as if he hadn't been clothes shopping since 1987.

It was Colin who first told me I had a meeting at Fremantle to talk about my hair. It was 2003, and after walking through life with hair down to my waist for the last ten years, I was now rocking a full head of short, intense blond hair that needed a full head of foils every six weeks to maintain. I wore my hair in a messy style (which was the fashion at the time) and never shaved with a blade – I only ever used clippers to take me down to stubble (also, quite the fashion at the time). Colin was exasperated that I would desecrate the privilege of going on camera looking like that, and dragged both me and James – a guy who also favoured a clipper over a razor – in front of our network executive producer Stephen Tate to give us a dressing down. 'Mate, you need to bloody shave – and at least run a comb through your hair, you look like a bloody bird's nest.'

Harking back to the 'gotcha' call ten years before, I was not having a bar of this, and stood my ground. We were the coolest kids in the class – our fingers were on the pulse of the music industry, and along with the stellar pedigree of our judges we added to the legitimacy of a show that was aiming to produce a true superstar. Part of what we brought to the show was our youthful appearance. I told Colin that no thank you very much, I would not be running a comb through my hair, and the stubble was going to stay. I'm pretty sure Colin stood up, tucked his surf shirt extra tight into his acid-wash high jeans and stormed off. I got to keep my hair and stubble.

On 27 July 2003 *Australian Idol* debuted on TV, starting with the pre-recorded audition shows. Within a few short weeks we went into the now-vanished Global TV studios at North Ryde and began the live shows that took us from a Top 40 to a Top 12. On a late September night in 2003 with around 600 screaming fans packed into the legendary studio space, the intro theme blared, my floor manager Kyle Crossling gave us the cue and James and I ran out for the first of the massive Top 12 shows.

I knew we were on to something when I got back to the tiny dressing room I shared with James, turned on my ancient Motorola GSM phone and saw that it was exploding with text messages.

If being on Channel [v] had led people to stare at me when I did my groceries, being on *Australian Idol* began a whole new world of recognition. Within a week as I drove down the freeway people would speed up next to me, one hand on the wheel and the other hanging their primitive 3G camera phones out of their window, trying to take a photo of me as we hurtled down the road. Complete strangers would run up to me in the street and scream in my face 'AndrooGEEEE!', sometimes even grabbing me by the shoulders to do so. For any normal human, it was pretty scary. For someone who was afraid of strangers, it was utterly terrifying.

By the second week of the big Top 12 shows our ratings were through the roof. When you're hot everyone wants to be around you. On Sunday night after we got off air there would be a packed green room full of sponsors, record execs and people from the network. We would all be toasting another great show and would drink until the bar fridge ran out. Then we'd all pile into cabs and head into Kings Cross to continue the party. Once we got there, lines for nightclubs vanished, private booths appeared out of nowhere, drink tabs were thrust upon us and I warmly accepted invitations into the 'back office'.[5]

I'd usually find myself at home somewhere around three or four in the morning, and at seven my phone would start to ring with radio interviews to promote the elimination show that night. Every five minutes from seven until nine I'd take a call from another station, telephonically travelling from coast to coast as the nation woke up and wanted to talk about what had happened on the show the night before. Now, I can't say that those interviews were my *best* radio, in fact they were probably woeful and angry. Because I was probably still drunk and high I would get cantankerous when all people wanted to talk about was my blond hair, and I would berate regional radio announcers for not doing their research when they didn't know what the letter in my last name stood for. I was being a selfish, arrogant fuckwit, and I was doing it live on radio right around the country every Monday.

Most days I'd get to work at Channel [v] and have to sweep my desk clean of the event invitations, so if I wanted to I could go out every single night of the week and never pay for a drink. I was drinking as if all manufacturing of beer would cease tomorrow and would often show up for work at Channel [v] completely wrecked from the night before. There was a coffee shop next to our studio on Bent Street at Fox Studios, and most

---

5   I mean the small room in a no-longer-there nightclub away from prying eyes, where cocaine could be inhaled in privacy and the ensuing blabbering and facial gurning could be maintained without too many onlookers.

days the show would be brought to you by two double shot soy lattes and 400 milligrams of ibuprofen.

While it's no news to you by now that alcohol and I were in an ever-decreasing death spiral, as I was now earning more money than I knew what to do with I'd regularly go clothes shopping and blow $1000 on clothes I'd end up never wearing. It was the early 2000s and with Tsubi jeans and Bondi Fashion exploding there was no shortage of $300 t-shirts for me to waste my money on. When that didn't make me feel better, I'd go out on the hunt.

As you know, Cymone had been my first real girlfriend and only the fourth person I'd ever slept with. After seven years with her ended I suddenly found myself single and on one of the highest-rating TV shows in the history of Australian broadcasting. To say I participated in risky sexual behaviour would be an insult to people who take risks. My self-worth and self-respect were utterly absent, and I waded into the waters of one-night-stands with zero care for myself or for the emotional wellbeing of any woman I was with.

When one woman told me I was being followed by a private investigator hired by her husband, instead of feeling remorse that I was willingly participating in the destruction of a marriage, I shrugged it off as funny. When once in my life just the *thought* of catching an STD had been enough to send me to the clinic, now I was booking myself into anonymous late-night bulk-bill doctor's offices on an almost monthly basis to pee in a jar and get another course of antibiotics to kill off whatever bacteria were festering in my urethra.

There was a time towards the end of 2003 where I'd slept with more different women in a week than there were days. Sometime towards the end of that week, I caught up with my dear friend Grant for a much-needed drink. I shared with him what had been going on and he gave me a stern warning. 'Be careful of your Qi, man. Your life force is draining out of you. Every time you come, you let go of a part of who you are.'

He was right. I was hollow inside, shaking and frightened. But I didn't understand what he was telling me. I was only doing what all the rock-star biographies told me I should be doing. I was living the dream, right? I was David Lee Roth and Robbie Williams all at once; this was supposed to be what all men aspired to achieve, wasn't it? But if this was what happiness looked like, it sure didn't feel that way. I was empty, lonely, and unable to stop. Unfortunately it would take a while for me to finally change my behaviour, and like any good addict I would go on to hurt a lot of people before I did.

1 – Mum on her graduation day with her mother, Aldona, and her father, Jonas, 1966. Three doctors in one photograph. To say my Lithuanian family was stoic would be an injustice to stoicism.

2 – My dad, Michael ('Miša') Günsberg (below), visiting his childhood friend Igor Konak (above) who was studying in Oxford, 1968. Dad had only just escaped from Czechoslovakia when this picture was taken.

3 – Mum and Dad on holidays in Europe, June 1970. We only found these photos after Mum had passed away, and it was so wonderful to see her and Dad so happy together. Before kids, before Australia, before all the fighting. It made my heart sing to know that these two once had a real happiness and love for each other, and it brought me incredible peace to see them like this.

4 – Me, Dad and the legendary Mitsubishi L300 Express, somewhere between Brisbane and Adelaide in the summer of 1984–85. Mum took this photograph on her Pentax 35mm.

1 – Living the guitar hero fantasy in my Brisbane bedroom, circa 1987, pulling shapes on my first electric guitar. I don't think Eddie Van Halen would have worn Kmart summer PJs however.

2 – Long hair, long shorts, and apparently all of the flannel in Brisbane. Feeble's Junky promo shoot circa 1994. Left to right: Sam Hemphill, Andrew Morris, me, Ant Gough, Andrew Dunn.

3 – My band, Feeble's Junky, playing at the Queensland University of Technology O-Week 1995. Left to right: me, Sam Hemphill, Andrew Dunn. I'd just enrolled and ran from a lecture to set up for this gig. After the set, I loaded the van and headed back into a tutorial. Of the three things I did at uni that day, this was the only one that I truly loved. I quit QUT four weeks later. (From inside slip cover of Feeble's Junky EP)

4 – Five strings, barefoot and funky with Feeble's Junky. Left to right: Andrew Dunn, Ant Gough, Sam Hemphill, me.

1 - My DJ career was intense but short-lived - here I am playing tracks for a friend's glam-metal-themed 40th at World Bar, King's Cross, 2005. You can't see that I'm wearing tights here, but I was fully committed, including the Derek Smalls enhancement.

2 - On the roof at Elizabeth Allnutt's apartment building, Military Rd, North Bondi 2004. Elizabeth was my photography mentor, and would often call me up to do shoots together for fun. The glint in my eye betrays the kind of lifestyle I was chasing at the time. Loose would be a small word to describe it. (Elizabeth Allnutt)

3 - Blurry times at a house party in Bondi somewhere with Elizabeth. Between her and Yumi Stynes, they taught me nearly everything I know about taking a great picture.

4 - Sunshine Village, Banff, Canada, circa 2004. My instructor Cameron and I had just hiked to the top of a peak to snowboard down some fresh powder. Later that week I broke my hand.

1 – Backstage at the Big Day Out January 2005 with the Channel [v] team. Left to right: Danny Clayton, Maya Jupiter, Me, Yumi Stynes, James Mathison.

2 – Clowning around at Homebake at the Domain, circa 2004. Every year at Channel [v] we went live backstage with the interviews the music fans wanted to see. Fair to say I was soaking up the festival vibes in this one. Left to right: James Mathison, Grinspoon drummer Kris Hopes, my producer Jade Skelly, frontman Phil Jamieson, me. I played alongside Kris and Phil back in the day, so it was always a kick to interview them from the other side.

1 – Take 40 Australia had just won the 2006 ACRA for Best Long-form Show, for our U2 special. I saw my childhood TV hero Jono Coleman at the Sydney Convention Centre and asked him to show off the trophy to my fish-eye camera.

2 – Recording Take 40 Australia's Backstage special at the 2007 ARIAs. It was always a treat to chat with Ben Gillies, Chris Joannou and Daniel Johns from Silverchair. By this point I'd come to accept that they were the better band for Sony to have signed – my old band probably couldn't have written *Diorama*.

3 – In U2's home studio with Larry Mullen Jr and Bono. I flew to Europe and back in 72 hours with only carry-on and was on the ground in Dublin for less than 18 hours to make this interview; back just in time to get on air with Channel [v] that weekend. This interview won us an ACRA award.

1 – Me, James Mathison and about 10,000 *Australian Idol* fans on the Sydney Opera House steps. Unless you host the Olympics, you never, ever get to make television like this. *(Stuart Bryce © 2005 FremantleMedia Australia Pty Ltd)*

2 – Backstage at the ARIAs with the original Australian Idol, Guy Sebastian. He's still so successful because he's not only talented beyond words, but he works harder than anyone else and will not compromise on the quality of his product.

3 – Rehearsing 'the walk' from the forecourt of the Opera House onto the stage of the Concert Hall. We needed to get this travel from one location to the next second-perfect, because the fireworks and orchestral cue wouldn't wait for anyone. The late Kyle Crossling, our brilliant floor manager in the foreground, taught me more about hosting live television than anyone I'd worked with.

1 - Afternoon dress rehearsal at Stage 5, Fox Studios meant we needed to make sure the wardrobe didn't clash with anything on camera. I'm wearing thongs because the promo that we just shot was only from the waist up. I used to enjoy wearing toenail polish - it helped me focus on stage. With all the pressure of live TV, I was the only one who knew my toenails were painted, which was enough to bring a smile to my face as Kyle would count me in. (© 2008 FremantleMedia Australia Pty Ltd)

2 - In the makeup room with James Mathison, backstage of season five of *Australian Idol*. Judging by the weapon of a 35mm camera I'm holding, my photography adventure was certainly in full swing at this point.

3 - Circa 2008, going by the hair. I love playing with the big toys in television. There's a fine dance that happens between director, camera operator and presenter that needs to be perfectly choreographed to make sure that you get that big 'wow' shot just at the right time. Rehearsing these moves always paid off when we went live. (© 2008 FremantleMedia Australia Pty Ltd)

1 – High above Sunset Boulevard, Beverley Hills, 2006. Taking some time out from a dinner party to shoot a frame in my mate Andi's bathroom.

2 – Shooting interviews for the Superbad film junket, 2006, on Universal Studios, Soundstage 22. I knew that Michael Cera (left) was a camera nerd so I brought a swing-lens panoramic camera with me. Jonah Hill took this shot. If you look very closely, you'll see him – he didn't wind it on when he clicked the shutter and it was a double exposure.

3 – *The Hot Hits Live from LA* makes its debut. I wore a tux because I knew it would be a special moment. This was the first time a radio show had a permanent broadcast set up from another country back into Australia, and it took incredible technical creativity to make it happen. (Day 176 of my 365-day self-portrait challenge.)

1 - Getting my makeup done for the audition episodes of *Live To Dance*. Dodger Stadium, Los Angeles, 2011.

2 and 3 - *Live To Dance*, Studio 46, CBS Television City, 2011. Primetime, US Network television, live across America on CBS. It was at the time technically the best work I'd ever done. *(Photograph 2 courtesy of CBS Photo Archive, Getty Images)*

1 – My younger brother Martin and I have taken a few cross-country road trips together, this one was from Melbourne to Adelaide and back again, 2012. Martin is also an avid photographer, and we'd stop whenever we found what looked like a great photo. He shot this cracker of a frame of me holding my beloved Hasselblad Xpan amongst a sea of flowers.

2 – Dodger Stadium, LA Marathon start area, March 2012. Running with Daniel McPherson was one of the true joys of living in LA. He and I did a few trots together and I'd often pick his brain for tips on endurance racing (the man is a weapon when it comes to triathlon). I loved marathons because I enjoyed pushing through barriers of endurance to see what was on the other side, and then later in life when things would seem hard, I had the experience of 'just keep going' to draw from. If you ever get a chance to go for a run with Dan, do it.

3 – Monday Tiles with Luke Heggie at Bronte, 2018. We both need to wear glasses to play now. He gave me a pantsing this game, but I got him back in game two with 'Azaleas' on a double word score.

1 – Dad and I took a special trip down to Melbourne for the Australian premiere of the musical *Spamalot!* in 2007. Here we are at the Prince of Wales Hotel, St Kilda. Dad gave me a gift by introducing me to Monty Python. I adored staying up late with him chuckling to the absurd TV we'd watch together.

2 – Shooting stills on Willie Ebersol's film *American Thief*, downtown Los Angeles, 2013. I liked to take the Polaroid with me because people always got a kick out of having a print to take home with them that day. The t-shirt, 'I'm a Photographer … NOT a terrorist!', was apt in the USA at the time.

3 – Brisbane, 2014. Dad found his father's old Kodak roll camera and wanted to give it to me. I asked him to show me how my grandfather used to hold it, and he kindly demonstrated. This camera takes incredible photos.

4 – Ein Hod, 2009. Everywhere you go in Israel you're surrounded by history. A young building is over 250 years old. It certainly gave me perspective over the passage of time and what different cultural claims to land mean in my own country of Australia. *(Noa Tishby)*

Deep in the darkness, March 2014, London. I took this photo because I wanted to remember what my face looked like when I was completely lost in the psychosis of paranoid delusions, and the perfectly kind and simple solution to the relentless ruminating agony in my head was to end my life there and then. You can see in my face that I am in very real physical and emotional pain. After I shot this I went for a run through Kensington Gardens, where I had visions that I was running along the bottom of the new sea floor, the trees around me all dead and skeletal like you see in underwater photos of dams that have been made of flooded valleys.

My mentor told me that 'the problem with crazy people is that they don't know they're crazy'. Sure, I knew, but that didn't make the pain any easier to bear. It took a very long time before I stopped having days like this.

1 – On set of *The Bachelor Australia*, season one, 2013. I've always been a fan of documenting my work (as you can tell), and this was the first dressing room door sign with my new name.

2 – In the make-up room of *The Bachelor* season two with keeper and designer of 'the hair', Carla Mico. We had our first day in television together in 1999 when she was on work experience and I was on Channel [v], and we still get to work together now. She's an incredible human and even introduced me to my wife, Audrey.

3 – Live tweeting *The Bachelor* while at the poker table in 2015. For over ten years, roughly the same group of ten guys has gathered around a table for a $20 poker game. Sure, there's a league and points awarded, but none of us are really there for the cards. Left to right: Steve Martinez, me, Barrington Calia, Ruben Meerman, Benjamin Scott. *(Josh Cilento)*

4 – Counting the roses for Sophie Monk's season of *The Bachelorette*. It was a real pleasure to help someone I'd known since the start of her career find a person to fall in love with, and I was truly sad when it didn't work out. The weight gain caused by the OCD meds is pretty evident in this photo. *(Courtesy of Warner Bros. International Television Production Australia Pty Limited, © Warner Bros. International Television Production Australia Pty Limited)*

1 – My 365 Exhibition, Mart Gallery Surry Hills 2010. In a time before Instagram and live-blogging, I took a self-portrait every day for a year, documenting a most remarkable year in my life. It was unintended but I ended up documenting the end of *Australian Idol*, the beginning of *Hot Hits*, me leaving Australia for the USA (you can see me showing off my green card in the pic over my left shoulder), but also the last six months of my drinking and the first six months of my sobriety. This exhibition legitimised me as a photographer and I couldn't be more grateful to Mel Nahas and the team from Canon who made it happen. *(Lisa Maree Williams, Getty Images)*

2 – Survival Day march, Brisbane, 2017. I'm an immigrant to Australia, and I feel it's important to recognise the history of how our country came to be what it is today. Part of that recognition having an open and honest look at the effect that colonisation has on our Indigenous people – effects, community attitudes and policies that are still felt to this day. I'm always proud to march next to Nathan Appo, a man doing great work within the community with 'Deadly Choices'. On the left there is my sister-in-law, Sally Queitzsch, and Nathan is carrying his niece Kirriana Appo in his arms. *(David Williams, Gilimbaa)*

1 – I took this Polaroid of my now wife, Audrey Griffen, the first time she cooked us dinner. She showed up to the Bondi apartment Channel Ten was renting for me during season two of *The Bachelor*, with all the ingredients to make a curry from scratch – even flour and a rolling pin to make roti. She also brought a little pill box containing Fijian spices, which soon filled my apartment with the glorious aromas of the delicious meal to come. I'm sure Audrey also brought a secret extra spice, one that made me fall in love with her as we talked and joked and awkwardly looked at each other over her magnificent meal.

2 – Nothing but nothing is better than going to Disneyland with a ten-year-old. This trip in 2015 with Audrey and her daughter, Georgia, was the best time ever.

1 – Barefoot under a canopy of ancient melaleuca trees in the Hunter Valley, January 2017, taking our first steps together as husband and wife. Together with so many wonderful friends and family, Audrey and I danced and ate and danced again, all of us celebrating late into the hot summer's night. *(Justin Aaron)*

2 – On holiday in Quebec, Canada, with the two greatest women I know. Audrey and Georgia, all smiles at -25°C, January 2018.

fourteen
crash

The first season of *Australian Idol* came to a rapturous conclusion in November 2003. We broadcast live from the most famous performance space in the world, the Sydney Opera House. Thousands of people were there and we were live across the country to what would at the time turn out to be the largest television audience ever assembled for a non-sporting or non-news related telecast. We started the show out on the front steps of the iconic building, surrounded by fans, all there to see our two finalists, Guy Sebastian and Shannon Noll. Unless you're a TV presenter who works on the Olympic Games an opportunity to hold down a show like that never comes along. Yet here we were, live on the steps of the Opera House with no autocue, surrounded by heaving masses of humans and doing the best work of my life.

The first half of the show built to the arrival of our final two. As we stood on the front steps in front of the cheering crowd, the first shell of a massive fireworks display exploded above our heads and it was time to go.

As we all raced underneath the giant white sails of this glorious building, our floor manager Kyle stopped us in our tracks. We only had ninety-seven seconds to dash inside, get out of one suit and into another and then walk out on the main stage of the concert hall in time to the end of a musical and pyrotechnics cue that would wait for no one. Even though we were running, Kyle suddenly stopped and made us look up. He said to Guy and Shannon, 'See that? That's for you. Don't forget this moment.' We all stood there for just a few precious seconds soaking in this extraordinary moment in our lives. We were snapped out of it when Kyle shouted, 'OK, now *go!*' and we carried on with our race into the building and through the backstage area, jackets flying off and pants being stepped into as we ran. Through impeccable timing and incredible teamwork, when the big key-change hit, Guy and Shannon walked out onto that stage of the concert hall and 3000 people rose to their feet in boundless adulation.

At the end of the show, Australia had crowned Guy Sebastian their winner and it felt as if all the confetti cannons in the southern hemisphere went off at once. After what seemed like forever, Kyle gave me the 'we're clear' signal and the show was over.

I should have been satisfied and happy with what I'd been a part of creating, of being a part of a cornerstone of Australian popular culture, but instead I was left with an immense emptiness and the feeling that none of what we'd just done had mattered at all. I felt neither proud nor satisfied. I felt no emotion whatsoever. I just thought, 'Well, what the fuck am I supposed to do now?'

I headed back to the dressing room. James and I had gone from a shared broom closet with a mirror at Global Television to the conductor's suite at the Sydney Opera House. Essentially an entire apartment with a 180-degree view of the Sydney Harbour Bridge, this room had a five-piece lounge setting, its own immaculate bathroom, a full bar and a Steinway grand piano about three metres long. I imagined that this magnificent instrument had probably helped warm up the tonsils of Pavarotti, accompanied Yehudi Menuhin as he got ready for the big room, and warmed up Dame Joan Sutherland for her triumphant final show. As I stood alone in the room, all the splendour and history of this glorious instrument were not lost on me as I used its immaculately applied black lacquer lid to chop up some lines of cocaine.

Unfortunately not the coke nor the many beers I drank over the coming days did anything to fill the gaping chasm inside me. Rather than feeling satisfied with a job well done, I felt as if nothing I had done mattered. Something like one in four people in Australia had watched that finale. Rather than feeling that I'd been a part of something great I felt as if they had given me the job as a favour and that I was utterly worthless.

I began to descend into a strangely oscillating headspace. I'd begun to wear a trucker hat when I left the house so I didn't have to return every stare that came my way, but I'd still be checking to see whether people were looking at me. Even though I was so afraid of the attention, I would still check to see that people had noticed me.

In the midst of all of this I got a call from a flamboyantly camp publicist I knew. He was in very high spirits, and seemed to be in the middle of a big noisy lunch. He told me he wanted me to meet a friend of his. Before I could ask who, he put me on the phone with a woman who had an American accent. She told me that her name was Noa and that she was from Israel. A few days later she and I met down on Bondi Beach near my house. As we lay there on the sand chatting about her life in LA and what I'd just done here in Australia, I had another moment not unlike the one I'd had about the Beastie

Boys a few years before. I could see my career as a crosshair target just bobbing there where the sky met the ocean. As I thought about Los Angeles and what's possible there, I decided to create a show that I could do out of Los Angeles so I could spend time with this woman. As that idea came into my head, I clearly saw those crosshairs now sitting about one-third of the way up into the sky. Even though Noa left back for LA a few days later and we had known each other for so little time, I knew meeting her would change my life forever.

The rest of that summer passed in a blur of blond hair, beer and Big Days Out and my drunken rampage across the country continued unabated. At the Melbourne show of the Big Day Out I experienced a hypomanic state for the first time that I knew what to call it. The Flaming Lips were on that tour, and their show included twenty to thirty people dancing on stage in furry animal costumes. I first danced with the band in Sydney dressed as a giant chicken and it was amazing.[1] By the time the tour moved to Melbourne I had the whole routine dialled in. Finishing broadcast work with Channel [v] just beforehand, I raced over and found Corey the animal wrangler backstage and reserved my costume early. I slipped away for one or two beers before go time and when I got backstage Metallica were letting off angry fireworks across the showgrounds. I dressed as a giant koala and excitedly waited to go out in front of the thousands of fans and dance once again.

The excitement within me built and built and soon I couldn't keep still. As we waited for the band to start, I

---

1 I'd stood in the crowd the night before and watched the show, with 10,000 weeping people as we all sang the closing lines to the Chemical Brothers' 'The Golden Path', all of us collectively singing an apology to lovers from the past. They're a really great band.

couldn't stop dancing even though the pre-show tape wasn't really playing anything worth dancing to and the house lights were still blaring. I looked around and saw that most of the crowd were just standing around waiting for the band, except the odd person who was also dancing hard to music no one else could hear. When the band started playing and we hit the stage I felt as if lightning was coursing through my veins. As the music swelled I felt as if I was experiencing the collective positive energy of the audience channelled through my body. It was like the final scene of *Raiders of the Lost Ark* but in reverse – I was the Ark of the Covenant and the good-feeling lightning was shooting from every person in the audience right into my chest. It was my most intense and incredible high, and I was experiencing it dressed as a giant koala. Later I discovered that this is a pretty good definition of a manic state.

When the band started the show on that tour, hundreds of giant balloons were thrown out into the audience, an explosion of colour and tactile connection between the band and the crowd. Some of the balloons would be thrown back towards the stage, and I would dive to catch them so they wouldn't crash into the drum kit or keyboard stand, helping (well, at least I thought I was) the crew clear the stage of the inflatable obstacles. One of these balloons managed to bounce over our heads and fly towards the backdrop behind the drummer. As I ran to retrieve it, I saw the side of the stage was standing-room only with people who had all come to witness the astonishing spectacle of the Flaming Lips show. Jumping to grab the balloon, I landed at the feet of renowned Australian author and broadcaster John Safran. I knew John and we'd played scrabble together a few times, so when I saw him I instantly exploded with joy at seeing his face. Instead of being happy to see me though, he looked shocked and concerned.

'Are you OK?' he shouted over the strains of Wayne Coyne asking 'If we realised'. I let go of the balloon, held his shoulders and screamed, 'I'm fucking amazing, man!', eyes rolling back in my head.

'You look as if you're about to burst right out of your skin,' he replied.

I didn't think anything of it, let go of him, and ran back to join the other dancers. What could he have been worried about? I felt better than I'd ever felt in my entire life. I was covered in apparently permanent goosebumps from the crown of my head to the cuticles on my toenails. This feeling was better than every line of speed and coke I'd ever snorted combined, all wrapped up in a silvery shot of tequila and delivered with the explosion of a thousand orgasms as I hurtled upside down on a rollercoaster through the finale of a New Year's Eve fireworks spectacular. I felt that if I'd wanted to, I could have breathed fire.

As anyone who's tried drugs knows, there's a point when you don't want to be high any more, and you start to put other drugs into your body to try to come back down to earth a bit. After a while I couldn't stand the ride any longer and wanted to get off. But as anyone who's experimented with drugs also knows, the problem with getting *really* high is that there is an equally powerful low. Unfortunately for me, as this particular mental high hadn't been brought on by any drug, the low was deep, devastating, and lasted a long time.

The lows felt like the world itself was ending and that a chasm to hell was about to open up and swallow me whole. You'd probably think that feeling as awful as this after a night out might cause me to go about my next night out differently, but you'd be thinking that with *your* brain. I have the brain of an addict – so my rationalisation was simply, 'I guess I'll have to do it *differently* next time. Brilliant! I know, instead of finishing with the tequila, I'll start with the tequila. That was clearly the problem. Let me send some texts out and see who wants to party …' I was trapped in a near-daily cycle of unstoppable binge and devastating regret, and I couldn't break out of it.

I spent my thirtieth birthday in Banff, Canada, on a snowboarding trip. Noa and I had stayed in contact and she had come up from LA to meet me and hang out for a while. After a few days she headed back to LA as it was pilot season, an important time for an actress to be available for auditions. I stayed on to make the most of the mountains and the wonderful snow.

In the most clichéd way possible, on the last run of the last day I slipped and landed hard, breaking the third metacarpal in my left hand. Luckily I was in Canada where the health care system is fantastic, and the next day I managed to get an appointment with an orthopaedic surgeon down in Calgary who had made his career putting rodeo champions back together. I was scheduled to have surgery in the morning and fly back to Sydney that night. So after he'd finished drilling some new scaffolding into my hand bones to keep them together, I asked the doctor for some painkillers for the flight home. The good doctor hit me with the heavy artillery. He didn't even blink when he gave me a massive bottle of Percocet, a potent mix of oxycodone and paracetamol, one and a half times stronger than straight morphine. It was good for the plane home, and it was good in the days that followed.

Less than a week after I got back from Canada the 2004 TV Week Logies were awarded.[2] We managed to find a suit that would fit over the splint I was wearing while my hand healed, and in preparation for the big night I washed down a few Percocet with some frosty Crown Lagers so my hand wouldn't hurt during the ceremony. And that's about *all* I remember.

Later that year I was named the Cleo Bachelor of the Year. The next morning I was a guest on the Nova 100 radio show in Melbourne and legendary Australian comedian and all-around super sober guy Dave Hughes was hammering me that I didn't remember him. I don't recall exactly the conversation because it was a) breakfast radio and b) I was away from home and definitely either still drunk or hungover from the night before, but I do recall that he was quite rightly pissed off that I didn't recall meeting him. When I challenged him as to where exactly it was where we met, he just replied, 'Mate, I gave you a bloody Logie!' I was so blitzed on synthetic morphine and booze that I don't even remember accepting Australian Idol's award for the Most Popular Reality TV Show for 2003.

Unfortunately this was not an isolated incident. Aside from the experience at Channel [v] with the Olympics show we did, I never drank on air – or at least not when I was working on *Australian Idol*. On *Idol* show days I'd wake up somewhere around noon and go for a run in the soft sand down on the beach to get my head straight and sweat out the sin of the night before, and leave by 1:30pm to make it to work in time for rehearsal. A few coffees and a meal break later we were ready to go on air, so I'd down half a can of Red Bull and hit the

2   They're essentially our Emmys, or BAFTAs, or whatever other night you have when all the TV people cram into a fancy ballroom with everyone they ever have or ever will work with and spend the entire evening either trying to line up a new job, a new lover, or both.

stage. If we went off air at 9:00pm I'd have a beer in my hand by 9:02pm and the night's drinking would begin. Considering my stranger danger was now reaching fairly intense levels, I'd usually grab one or two bottles of red from the green room cupboard and sneak them home where I could drink alone and undisturbed.

While I know that Anthony Callea had a great voice and that Casey Donovan is an incredible talent I can honestly say that I don't remember the second season of *Australian Idol*. 2004 was a year of me pushing the envelope as far as I could with sex, drugs and rock 'n roll. *VICE* magazine had recently begun to be distributed in Australia, and I was actively trying to emulate the tales of debauchery that filled its pages.

The cycle was intense. I was afraid of strangers, so I drank. When I drank I became an arsehole, and then strangers reacted to that, so I drank more to dull the need to make everyone like me. Wanting to fill the gap of human connection and the need to be liked or wanted, I'd try to convince a woman I'd just met or someone I had been texting to stay the night with me, and of course the sex that sometimes followed didn't fill the gaping hole in my self-worth at all. The next day I would feel so hungover and remorseful that I couldn't deal with talking to anyone. I'd pull a trucker hat so low over my face that I would walk in public negotiating my route by watching where people's feet were going. My local cafe knew what I had for breakfast every day, and they'd kindly deliver my order to the table without my even having to speak too much at all. Drinking was no longer just a thing I did when out at functions or down at the pub with friends. It was something I had begun to do alone, in my house – where I could get as smashed as I liked and no one had to know.

It was in 2004 that my drinking took its first confirmed kill in my career.

Voiceovers had proved to be wonderfully lucrative.[3] I showed up one Tuesday morning after a massive night of beer and wine alone on my couch for a VO session for a client I'd been working with for years. The gig was worth upwards of $15,000 a year to me – not bad for fifteen minutes' work once every four weeks. My every exhalation reeked of alcohol and my liver's inability to process it, and I slurred my way through the script. The engineer pushed me to do take after take, I kept slurring and messing up the script, and as the engineer kept pushing me I started to get mad. In the end I arrogantly stated, 'Look, you booked me for an hour, it's been an hour – you've got the take, and I'll bet it's the first one I did too.' With that they let me go, and I huffily drove back to Bondi to get ready for my day at Channel [v].

While I'd been fired from jobs before (that phone call from Dave when I was removed from Resin Dogs), most things kind of faded away and it wasn't until much later that I realised they were gone. When I realised I hadn't been booked on a VO job for a while I decided to take the initiative and call the agency. When they told me the truth I was arrogant enough to say something like, 'Look, I'm just *too famous* now to do regular VO work. When people book me, they're getting an endorsement for what's just a regular fee. From now on I'll only take endorsement jobs, no more reading commercials for suburban RSLs.' It's fair to say that no big endorsements came my way, and I was never hired to do another voiceover through that agency.

---

3   Cymone started doing VOs at the same time I did, but she has risen to great heights in the industry. For a while she was the highest-paid female voice artist in Australia, and she still ranks right up there. While you may not know her name, I'll guarantee you've heard her voice.

In the middle of all of this I kept thinking what life might be like with Noa. She came out to Sydney that winter and I'd managed to fly to LA for a weekend to see her in between *Idol* shooting days. I learned a lot from that trip: a) Life's too short *not* to jump on a plane and fly to Los Angeles for a weekend to see the woman you've got a crush on, and b) If you work with a friendly photographer you can set up paparazzi-style photographs to sell to an Australian magazine, and then get a kickback to cover the cost of said trip.[4]

When Noa came to Sydney for a few weeks over the summer, a massive New Year's Day party was happening at the Bondi Icebergs just below my place. When everyone started to arrive at my apartment to go down there, I was still very dusty from the night before. However, it was nothing that a few bumps of Escobar's finest wouldn't help me shrug off, I thought, and went down to the club. The thing about making decisions when you're drunk and high is that you're completely divorced from your ability to recall what happened last time you were drunk and high. It suddenly seemed like a really great idea to take a hit of ecstasy. I'd had the drug before and I wanted that feeling again, so when a stranger offered it to me on the dance floor, I didn't even hesitate to wash that little pink pill down with a swig straight from a bottle of Veuve Clicquot. To quote Steven Tyler from Aerosmith: 'The problem about telling kids not to do drugs is that things like ecstasy feel fucking fantastic. Who wouldn't want to feel like that?'

Steven was right. As Sneaky Sound System blared Justice Vs Simian's 'We Are Your Friends', the feeling I had experienced on stage with the Flaming Lips returned, this time wrapped

___

4 These are the things that we did in a time before Instagram #sponsored hashtags.

up in what felt like cuddles and orgasms. I got higher and higher, the music got better and better and I was covered in goosebumps, wrapped up in a blanket of love for everyone and everything. I never, ever wanted this feeling to end.

However, as I've mentioned before, the problem with getting *really* high is that afterwards you get *really* low. And while I'll never forget how wonderful that drug made me feel, nothing was ever the same after that. That pink pill was the one that truly popped my brain. Of course I'd read that one pill or one hit might be enough to change your brain forever, but I ignored all those warnings, they were for serious drug users. I was at the Bondi Icebergs, surrounded by Australia's sexiest people at Australia's sexiest party in my sexy black shirt while people danced on the tables above me and surfers were carving it up at the break below. This pill would be *fine*.

In the following weeks and months, anxiety and panic went from being experiences once or twice a week, and usually after drinking heavily, to acute incidents I'd feel many times a day – and I didn't even need to be hungover. By the time we were turning around for season three of *Australian Idol*, I was a jumpy, frightened mess.

When we pulled into a city we would set up shop at a hotel and stay there for up to two weeks while we shot the audition episodes. We weren't the lowest-profile team when we came into town, and I'd yet to learn to book rooms under an assumed name, so when I started getting phone calls to my hotel room from girls who sounded like they were still in high school I freaked completely out. They were probably just having fun at a sleepover somewhere and daring each other to call the hotel, but in my head I'd already been busted for associating with underage kids and my career was in ruins. I took the phone off the hook, and wrote angrily on the 'Do not disturb' sign, 'This means do not disturb. I don't need towels, I don't need housekeeping, please send all deliveries to the front desk' and taped it to my door.

Just being outside was terrifying, and I couldn't stop my brain from catastrophising every tiny mistake I'd made. My head started to flash back to everything I had ever done wrong, and then draw a line to the worst possible scenario that could happen because of that. I'd furiously write out my cognitive behaviour therapy columns for each crisis I was imagining, and the very *moment* I breathed a sigh of relief at having worked through and processed what was troubling me, a new fear would spike into my brain, my body contorting in pain, and I'd have to start the whole process again. I just couldn't stop. It was as if my brain only wanted to exist in this state of terror. This went on for days. Whenever I wasn't at work, putting on a happy face for the cameras and faux-celebrating with the victorious singers who had proven to the judges that they were worth going to the next stage of the competition, I was trapped in a hotel room, trapped inside my head, surviving solely on packets of cashews and beer from the minibar.

This behaviour continued once I got back to my house in Bondi.

Whenever I wasn't at work I was hiding in my home. I couldn't bear to go out unless I'd fortified myself with three or four beers before leaving the house.

The one saving grace was that I had absolutely wonderful friends. There was Grant, whom I'd known since Brisbane days, now working at Sony music studios in Darlinghurst. Through Grant I met Steve Martinez, who became a surfing, drinking and poker buddy. Steve introduced me to a regular poker game held every Wednesday night. Initially I was very reluctant to attend because the room was full of strangers, but the men who sat around that poker table became, and continue to be, a very important part of my life.

When I met these men we were all pretty much in the same boat. We were ten guys of similar age, some starting their first adventures into cohabitation with long-term girlfriends, some just out of long-term relationships and partying hard. At first I was intense with them, trying to exert control, but after a few weeks I relaxed and started to thoroughly enjoy not only the banter but the incredible support these men offered. The wisdom of this group of guys got me through a lot over the years, and when the shit really hit the fan they were there to dust me off and help me back out into the world.

So while every other day of the week was a day to be afraid of, Wednesdays started to be a day I'd look forward to because that night there would be the camaraderie of the card game to safely explore a new way of relating to other people, one where I didn't bark at people I didn't know.

fifteen
loss angeles

After the *Australian Idol* tour of 2005 I was shuttered up good and tight. Being on the street was increasingly frightening and every gaze from a stranger felt like a stab in the side. I started to become afraid of even speaking with people that I worked with. This led me to getting my first real manager, to whom I handed over my contract negotiations, stalled mainly because they meant that I would need to talk to people and possibly even negotiate.

I already had *Australian Idol* and Channel [v] and I'd just been offered a new job doing a TV commercial for Ford Australia. I still honestly believed I'd been given the *Australian Idol* gig because someone felt sorry for me. This is not a great bargaining position to take but I didn't know how to push for anything more, so I hired a manager and handed over the deals I had lined up, sending him in to battle for me. Sure he took 20 per cent but he was an absolute machine. He ended up getting me more money than I knew existed for a job like mine. I was on holidays with my youngest brother in Japan when he called me to tell me that between Channel [v], *Australian Idol* and the Ford deal I'd bill over $1 million in 2005.

I knew nothing about what to do with all this cash. I had grown up with parents who, like so many people without money when they were young, had no idea how to handle it when it came in regularly. Even though they were well paid doctors they had often lived from pay cheque to pay cheque.

I now had to hire someone to help me invest this money in a clever way, so I did. Being so afraid of interacting with people had left me with a habit of saying and doing *anything* to finish dealing with someone I didn't know as quickly as possible. But instead of evaluating the advice my financial adviser gave me I'd rush into his office, rapidly sign countless pieces of paper without reading any of them and get out of the room as fast as I came in.

You might think that this is a terrible way to invest the large sums of money that I was now making, and you'd be absolutely right. I just didn't want to have anything to do with the success that I was having, and it showed. If there was a dodgy agribusiness that was put to market in 2005/6, I'd be the stupid idiot who'd invest six figures in it. When it all settled down, I'd blown over $600,000 on complex tax-minimisation schemes, all but one of which went south. I wish that I could tell you this was the end of me wasting my money, but I'm sorry to say that way more was to come.

Given that just walking down to the beach for my run in the morning had begun to chill me to the bone, I came up with a brilliant way of avoiding people looking at me. I'd leave Australia. I'd recently been handed the reins to the biggest radio countdown in the country, the landmark Sunday afternoon show *Take 40 Australia*. I could now offer a publicist over 150 radio stations around the country and a national TV show with just one interview slot. With that in mind I managed to convince both Channel [v] and *Take 40 Australia* that it would be a great idea for me to be based in Los Angeles for a few months between the end of the *Australian*

Idol auditions and the beginning of the live shows. The talent wranglers went into overdrive lining up interview slots, and I booked a ticket to LAX.[1]

Landing in LA to be with Noa, whom I now called my girlfriend, was as if a huge weight had lifted from my shoulders. When I walked down the street nobody stared or whispered comments. I would run twelve kilometres up to the top of Runyon Canyon and back every day, just loving to be away from everything that scared me so much about being in Australia.

The interview schedule became super-busy and I started work. I was given access to artists of higher and higher calibre, including Madonna, U2, Oasis and Jamiroquai, and soon I was being flown back and forth from LA to Europe just to get thirty minutes on camera with some of the biggest bands in the world. When I wasn't away, I was relishing the time spent with Noa. She was driven, fascinating and excited to show me around the city she called home. I was a vegan now, and had always struggled in Sydney to eat out or to go grocery shopping. In LA, we ate at a different vegan restaurant for breakfast, lunch and dinner, and at the supermarket where we shopped there was an entire aisle of different kinds of tofu. *An entire aisle.*

---

1   It was around this time in my life that I became deathly allergic to economy class. I felt as if I'd break out in a rash if I had to sit at the back of the plane. Up in the front, your seat reclined flat, they'd bring you as much alcohol as you could drink and because it was business class there was a handy little privacy screen that you could pull up so you didn't even need to make eye contact with the person next to you. You were even allowed into the business class lounge before your journey, where you could start pouring three-finger gin and tonics at ten in the morning if you wanted. Qantas would sell you this incredible experience for only $10,000 return. It took me years to get over myself and only in sobriety did I discover that sitting in economy isn't actually that bad. I weep when I think about how much money I wasted so I could sit alone and binge drink at 40,000 feet.

In LA, we lived less than two kilometres from where they filmed *American Idol* and thanks to reciprocal connections with the production company that made *Australian Idol* I got to go to the legendary Studios at CBS television city to watch the highest-rated show in America go live. It was like seeing my future. This is what I wanted. I felt as if this is where I belonged. I *had* to figure out a way to stay.

When it came to building my career in Australia though, I was so utterly focused on moving to the USA, and so consumed by fear, that I dismissed one incredible opportunity after another. Shortly after I returned to Australia from that LA trip I got a call from Network Ten's production and development manager Tim Clucas. He had read that I used to be quite fat, and that my personal story involved getting my health together and losing a ton of weight. He told me that he felt this would bring an incredible angle to the new weight-loss reality show the network was going to make in a few months, *The Biggest Loser*. I was channelling nothing but ego when I told him that I wasn't focusing on new opportunities in Australia at the moment, I was living in America whenever I wasn't on air at Channel [v] or *Australian Idol* and the commitment to make this kind of show would scuttle my plans to hunt for work in the States.

While that was true in my head at the time, I didn't tell him that an enormous wave of shame covered me as soon as he told me that he knew I used to be fat. The idea of playing off that and making it public, the flashback photos that would come out in the press, the whole concept of so solidly identifying with my former body size was utterly mortifying.

He asked me one more time and I gave him a polite but firm no, having thrown the first match that would burn the bridge of Australian television behind me.

The Biggest Loser went on to run for eleven years. I could have had two gigantic shows on air every year, propelling my career into the stratosphere. I said no to what could have been over a decade of solid income, endorsements, a new body, you name it – I threw the whole thing away because I was eating my own bullshit and calling it cake, and was afraid and ashamed about my body.

Being back in Australia was like being in a maze of mirrors. In my head whenever I walked down the street I felt hundreds of eyes on me, judging me. I would sometimes go three days without leaving the house for anything but work; it just felt safer to stay behind my front door. A front door that I now needed to check was locked between five to eight times when I lay down to sleep at night. I would finally wind everything up, get into bed and turn the light off, and then wonder whether the front door was locked (it should have been, I hadn't opened it in two days). I'd turn the light on and walk down the hallway to check that it was, and then climb back into bed, turning the light off when my head hit the pillow. I'd lie there for about thirty seconds before I had to turn the light back on and repeat the process. I'd repeat this behaviour again and again until I was finally tired enough to fall asleep before the next rumination started. I'd do the same thing with the oven, the front window, and sometimes I'd drive halfway up Bondi Road and have to turn back around to make sure I'd turned the stove off. Sitting around the house all day used to be a mind-numbing thing, but now there was broadband internet I had endless stimulation. Unfortunately for me, that stimulation came in the form of internet poker and porn.

On the outside my life was pretty incredible: I had a girlfriend in another country, I travelled the world and interviewed the biggest stars on the planet. *Take 40 Australia* was the number one countdown show in the country. Alongside James I hosted a massive TV show and was plugged into the epicentre of the music scene with Channel [v]. The reality was that when I wasn't on camera I was boarded up in my house addictively chasing massive losses by playing internet poker, drinking alone and incessantly masturbating.[2]

My management would occasionally call and ask me whether I was interested in hosting this event or attending that function. I'd say 'no' to pretty much all of them because the last thing I wanted to be around was people. But one gig came through, a voiceover for a film trailer. They'd requested me specifically and the money was great, so I agreed and headed over to the backlot of Fox Studios, making sure my face was hidden by a trucker cap and a hoodie.

Grunting my arrival to the receptionist, I took a seat in the waiting room. In those days there were no real smartphones and when you sat in a waiting room, you did what the room was built for. You just sat there and waited. I didn't even text anyone or play snake on my Nokia, I just sat there in silence across from the receptionist, who typed away quietly. The audio engineer came to get me, and I headed to the safety of the sound booth where I could finally pull the hood back from my head now I was safe and locked behind a double-walled soundproof door. I knocked the script out in less than ten minutes and everyone in the control room was happy. I thanked them all by name and made a beeline for the front door, and I was moving fast.

My path from the audio suite to the front door across the waiting room took me past the receptionist and I did all I could

---

2   Now I see that I was clearly an alcoholic struggling with a gambling addiction *and* a porn addiction. In my head, though, I was just 'hanging out at home'.

to avoid eye contact or a reason to interact with her. 'Oi!' she said. 'Oi! Andrew!' I turned and saw she was holding out a folded piece of paper. She was a woman in her early forties with kind eyes and a knowing smile.

'Look.' She pointed at my upturned hood, mirrored sunglasses and excessively lowered trucker hat and made a circle with her index finger. 'I've worked in the music industry my whole career, I've seen this before and it's no way to go through life.' She handed me the piece of paper. 'Here, go and see this doctor. He'll help you. I've seen him help many people who do your job. He's very busy but if you tell the receptionist I sent you, they will be able to squeeze you in.'

I was completely shocked and ashamed that my secret was out. I thought I was the only one who knew how afraid I was of the world. I scurried out of there and headed to my car. When I got home I stuck that piece of paper on the wall above my monitor. By this time my apartment looked like a bad episode of *Hoarders*, with stuff piled to the ceiling, goat tracks cleared between the junk all over the floor, and my walls covered by random bits and pieces I'd stick on there with BluTack. As I hid in my bedroom, hour upon hour spent mindlessly clicking on internet poker games and scrolling through endless porn of ever-increasing intensity, that piece of paper stared back at me. I would stare at that piece of paper for over a year.

About now Channel [v] moved from Darling Harbour to North Ryde forty-five minutes away. The hipster, inner-city employees of Channel [v] who walked to work in their double denim delights fled the company in droves. New employees came into the company and soon the office was full of people I didn't know. It was no longer a hub of excitement, creativity and great music – it was now a place full of strangers that I flat-out feared. Channel [v] became so frightening that I just stopped showing up.

I don't know why they kept paying me, because I was simply never there. The words of Craig Bruce, who had advised me to leave if my heart didn't race with excitement, started to echo in my head. My heart was racing all right, but with pure panic. Rather than face my employers and tell them why I wasn't showing up, I did what I had come to find was a great way of dealing with problems. I left the country.

Flying via Bangkok I headed to Israel to get to know Noa's homeland and see whether I could connect with my Jewish roots. I don't know what they put in the air in Israel, but the moment I landed I felt at home. I'm Jewish on my father's side; the feeling of belonging was probably because I was suddenly surrounded by a culture that was one of my father's obsessions. Everything about the country seemed familiar to me, and within hours of arriving I was able to drive around Tel Aviv without a map.[3]

It was a wonderful time, mainly because I didn't have to speak English to *anyone*. I could walk down the street in Tel Aviv and with my small amount of Hebrew I could order a coffee in peace or read my book on the street and no one cared. Noa, who had come over from LA, took me on the grand tour – from Jerusalem in the west to the Dead Sea in the south and up to the sea of Galilee in the north. She didn't hold back and over those three weeks I got a crash course in the intense

---

3   Years later when I started to study Kabbalah I told a rabbi about this happening in Jerusalem too, and she said, 'Oh that's easy, it's because you'd been there before,' referring to reincarnation. I still don't know if I believe in reincarnation, but I can tell you that it was pretty strange to suddenly be intimately familiar with parts of a city I'd never set foot in. It's not like it's based on a grid or anything; the place has been there for *thousands* of years, and is arranged like a rabbit warren.

political situation, met some wonderful people (including the man who would inspire me to change my name), drank some fantastic espresso and ate the most remarkable food.

When I finally returned to Australia, the moment finally came when I decided to leave Channel [v]. I was hosting a live show in Melbourne's massive Federation Square. Thousands of kids were there to see the incredibly popular emo band Dashboard Confessional. I watched the same thousands of kids sing every single word to every single song, most of them with tears streaming down their faces they were so moved by the lyrics. I, on the other hand, felt absolutely nothing. The music meant nothing at all to me.

When I started at Channel [v] I was twenty-five and frothing with excitement about every single band I heard. I was now thirty-two and largely detached from the music filling festival lineups and music charts. Craig Bruce had been right. If I didn't get excited every time the mic went on, I should get out of the chair and let someone else have a turn. I shared this reason with my boss and told him it was time for me to go. What I didn't share with him was the *real* reason I was leaving – that I was too scared to show up to work because the office was full of strangers and I was utterly mortified to be out of my apartment. I hadn't quit anything since university, and this felt like a decision based solely in irrational fear.

Now that I no longer worked at Channel [v], I had essentially created a five-day weekend for myself. I worked on *Australian Idol* on Sunday and Monday nights, and recorded *Take 40 Australia* on Monday morning. Fortunately, and due to Steve's presence in my life, I'd begun to venture further out my front door and had taken to surfing enthusiastically. I tried to get out in the water most days; having someone you've promised to meet at the south entrance to the beach at 6am was a pretty great motivator to get out of a warm and cosy bed. No matter how hungover I was, every time I got out in the water I felt better. We began to explore the coastline of Sydney and beyond, and pored over weather maps and tide times searching for the right conditions that a 32-year-old beginner could handle.

Another *Australian Idol* audition tour came and went, and I was lost in a maze of beer and locked hotel room doors. Part of me knew that using alcohol was probably not the best way to manage my anxiety, so I had begun to run in the mornings no matter what city we were in. Unless I was really dusty, I'd put in an hour or so every morning, which would usually get me about eight to ten kilometres under the belt. If I didn't run, it was hard to get through the day.

The moment that tour was over, however, I'd escape to LA to start the hunt for work there. Noa lined me up with Adam Sher, an agent friend of hers who worked at the William Morris Agency, one of the biggest in the USA. It couldn't have been a more perfect fit, as Adam already represented the man whose career I wanted to emulate – Ryan Seacrest.

Adam lined me up with general meetings all over the city and I got to work. A 'general' is a meeting with a production company or network where you basically get to know each other over a tiny bottle of Arrowhead water. You pitch yourself and the kinds of projects you'd be interested in, and at the end you all shake hands and talk about how you'd love to find a project to work on together, then you get your parking validation stamped by an intern and you race off to the next meeting. Because Adam was such a heavy hitter I got to meet the biggest decision makers in the industry: ABC, CBS, NBC,

Fox, the CW, Fremantle, Endomol, 3 Arts – you name it, I went and drank a small bottle of water on their sofa. To get around the anxiety that crippled me so much back in Australia I replaced the worthlessness I normally felt with unbridled narcissism. I let my ego take over, and I'd walk into those meetings and dominate the room with personality. It was an unhealthy projection of who I was, but it seemed to impress the Americans. I should say here that the Aussie accent wasn't too much of a problem – all I had to do was say the letter 'r' and flatten my vowels out. Soon I was getting invitations to come in and get on tape for this or that project and it seemed that everything was going exactly to plan.

Once I went all the way to a meeting with heads of the massive US network ABC for a singing contest reality show called *The One*. A mix of *Idol* and *Big Brother*, it was one of many potential giant-killers the other networks were firing at Fox in an effort to get some of that enormous *Idol* audience. It was down to me and a talented guy called George Stroumboulopoulos. He was the Canadian version of me. We were the same age and had the same radio and music TV pedigree but very different accents. After a few follow-up meetings with the heads of the network, Adam and I crossed our fingers. Alas, the gig didn't come my way. Less than a year after I'd decided that I was going to move to America I'd come breathlessly close to a network gig. Both Adam and I were disappointed, but chalked it up as a massive win.

I went back to Sydney for the live shows of *Australian Idol* with fire in my belly. I might have missed it this time, but I absolutely was going to get a network gig in America. It wasn't a question of if, but when. Now I knew what was possible for me in the USA my ego just roared to life.

My days were on repeat: massive live show, massive night drinking, massive regret and shame the next day. If you're getting bored with constantly reading about massive nights of drinking and drugs that ended with shame and remorse the morning after, I apologise. However, this is what the life of an addict looks like. When normal people have these shameful and regretful moments, they generally try not to repeat their experience. As an alcoholic, however, I'd just keep repeating the same behaviour hoping for a different result. I was still drinking and using, hoping that I would find the magic that would finally make me feel like I belonged.

Through the drinking and using, the shame and humiliation I brought upon not only myself but those I loved was something I am still working to repair. I drove my family away from me, my work colleagues away from me, and I was increasingly driving Noa away from me, drunkenly watching her wince in pain as the guy she loved shamed and embarrassed her in public and private time after time. As our relationship was a part of the fantasy world I was creating for myself – one that had all of the ingredients that on paper would lead to happiness – I couldn't let her get away. I also had to get to LA to make sure she didn't leave me. I loved and was unhealthily obsessed with her, all I wanted to do was to be around her and to live in LA with her. I was sharing this desire backstage one day with former *Australian Idol* judge Mark Holden and he just held me by one shoulder, looked me in the eye and said, 'Seal the deal, G!' Marriage had been on my mind for a while, but like many men I had been afraid of pulling the trigger. During one of my morning runs, I reflected on my desires and what Mark had told me and the answer was clear as day. I'd ask Noa to marry me.

She said yes.

help wanted

Being in LA brought freedom of movement and the idea that I could reinvent myself to a whole new group of people. I felt far less afraid of strangers, or so I thought. But soon Noa started to see the fear in me and I'm sure it freaked her out. Once we were lost looking for a restaurant while driving through West Hollywood so she pulled over, rolled the passenger window down and told me to ask a waiting valet parking attendant where the place was. The car came to a stop, my window went down and I froze. I couldn't say a thing. The poor man stood there staring at this wide-eyed blond guy petrified in the front seat, and Noa had to lean across me to ask the question.

I could tell that she was concerned about me acting like that and for me that was the final straw. When I got back to Sydney I pulled the piece of paper off my wall that the kind receptionist had given me and finally made a time to see that doctor.

In early 2007 I met Dr Ian Chung. His office was plastered with photos of him with superstars; all the pictures had autographs on them and comments such as, 'You saved my life'. My favourite photo was of him walking across the tarmac from a small aeroplane carrying a medical bag as he followed Mick Jagger, who was waving to photographers.

I told Dr Chung what was going on and he explained to me that I had something called social phobia: fear of meeting people. He taught me a relaxation technique to use when panicky thoughts started to cascade, adding that meds would help. He insisted that I couldn't just take the meds and expect this social phobia to get better. They would form a part of a treatment protocol that involved hard work on my part in reshaping how I thought about things. I said I'd rather have a few beers than numb my brain with drugs and he understandably got angry.

After we arranged another appointment he gave me a DVD to explain what social phobia and social anxiety were. When I got home I hit 'play', and it was as if the production crew had simply stuck a camera through my window and filmed my life. I had been thinking I was a special snowflake and that no one knew what it was like to be me, but it turned out I was exhibiting bog-standard symptoms.

Ian and I worked together to try and turn things around, but the fear kept getting worse. By now I was refusing every single invitation to any event or even social functions, except for poker night in a dark room full of familiar faces. But when I ran off to LA I couldn't ask Noa to halt her vibrant social and work lives in order for me to hide in our apartment. I started to freeze up and lurk in corners at dinners with her friends, and more than once I had to ask for a few moments to calm myself before walking into a work function that she had to attend (in LA *everything* is a meeting). The daily running was helping to lift me out of it for a few hours, but the gloom would descend on me again by the end of the day. No matter how much I drank to try and numb the fear, it was getting worse and I didn't seem able to stop it. I was a long way from the happy blond guy with the big smile she'd met on the beach in the middle of a carefree summer.

Back in Sydney one afternoon I just couldn't handle the noise in my head. I cancelled everything and hit the soft sand for a jog. However, this time it didn't make me feel better. As I ran past the North Bondi surf club, watching the ancient, portly men in their budgie smugglers wander out for their daily swim, I felt as if someone was standing on my chest. I was running pretty hard so a tightness in my chest was to be expected, but this actually felt like a weight was being pushed upon me, as if I was lying on my back and being squashed from above. The sensation defied physics: how could I feel heavy pressure on my chest when I was upright and jogging? A few minutes later I felt I was being held by the throat, as if invisible fingers were crushing my neck to stop me from breathing.[1]

The two phantom sensations were brand new and completely terrifying. I ran all the way up the hill to my house where I called Dr Chung and begged the receptionist for an appointment. She must have heard the urgency in my voice and said I could come in at the end of the day. When I got there, I begged him for meds to make this feeling stop. He had to tell me that the drugs wouldn't kick in straight away. We were going to start with Lexapro, a garden-variety SSRI,[2] increasing the dosage by minute increments, so I wouldn't feel any different for a few weeks.

---

1   Not a tightness inside my larynx where if you tense really hard you'll sound like Brian Johnson from AC/DC, but an actual physical pressure pushing around my throat. It was very strange.

2   Selective serotonin reuptake inhibitor. Increases the levels of serotonin in the brain. I don't have any proof, but I'm pretty sure that the ecstasy pill I took a few years before popped my brain and all the serotonin leaked out.

He was right, and it took a while before anything changed. But I stuck with it and after about a month on a low dosage of Lexapro I began to feel better and I had a profound realisation. Why had I not accepted the offer of meds back in 1999? *Why* had I wasted nearly a decade of my life drowning in fear and panic?

The meds made peak emotions far easier to deal with. But I was still drinking, and contrary to doctor's orders I wasn't doing the necessary extra work to reshape the workings of my brain. I just took the drugs and expected everything to get better. Dr Chung explained that I was a sports car, and the sports car has five wheels if you include the steering wheel. The wheels represented diet and exercise, sleep, living with a purpose, cognitive behavioural therapy and the meds. You couldn't drive the sports car unless all the wheels were working – it would be lunacy. I seemed determined to prove him wrong and drunkenly sped down the road in my three-wheeled Lamborghini.

Back in LA that spring of 2008, *Idol* was turning around for a sixth season, *Take 40 Australia* was crushing the ratings, I was getting married later that year and I felt unstoppable.

In a fit of astonishing hubris I fired my 20 per cent manager and told the network to send me the *Idol* contract for negotiating directly. I printed it out and over a few beers took a red pen and marked it up with language I'd learned from my fiery Year 11 accounting teacher. I knew absolutely nothing about negotiating or delicate diplomacy and I was scrawling angrily on this contract – in red pen – as if I was the greatest presenter in the world and they were lucky to have me. When it came to the dollar figure, I had heard the phrase 'open high and then meet them in the middle', so I took the amount they'd offered and straight up doubled it. If Kyle Sandilands was getting a million dollars a year, I should get at least close to that. I faxed the contract back and waited for them to call to say, 'Thank you for coming back to work for us, we'd love to acquiesce to your demands.'

The phone did ring. Network executive producer Stephen Tate called me to say, 'What are you doing? David Mott saw the figure and the blood just drained from his face.'[3]

I replied, 'Yeah, man, it's negotiation – I go high, you counter and we meet in the middle.' I hung up feeling that I'd sent a clear message about my position. The thing was, so did they. Two weeks went by without a phone call, a fax or an email. Finally, after a text from an inside source I read the words that no person in business ever wants to see: 'They're exploring other options.' I'd grabbed the most wonderful, incredible thing ever to happen in my career, taken a massive ego-shit on the floor and rubbed narcissism poop in its face, and now I was surprised that they had walked away. The next text from the insider nailed the coffin shut. 'They've hired Ricki Lee to replace you.'[4] My *Australian Idol* career was effectively over.

I'd made some foolish investment decisions, I had two mortgages in investment properties and I was committed to outlay a huge amount of money in management fees and mortgage repayments. While *Take 40 Australia* was a great gig, there was no way it was going to pay the bills.

With the time differences between Sydney and LA, these few weeks meant that evenings were a very tense time as that's

---

3   David Mott was the then programmer at Network Ten. He'd commissioned *Idol*, and approved my employment. He was right under the CEO and the gatekeeper of my career.

4   Ricki Lee had been a fan favourite contestant from the first season of *Australian Idol*. She's lovely, with a wonderful career in her own right.

when the Australian phone calls would get made. Noa had said 'yes' to marrying a guy who was on the up, and here I was crashing and burning before her eyes. We didn't watch TV during those nights as we tried to process what was happening. But I noticed that I wasn't as terrified about exploding everything as I thought I'd be. In the middle of all the financial future fear, it appeared that the meds seemed to be working.

I started to pick up the pieces. When I fired my manager back in Sydney I'd had initial meetings with another manager, an industry legend by the name of Mark Morrissey. After the silence from Network Ten I called him in a panic and begged him to please save my career and take the percentage of whatever he managed to get.

Mark truly is a master of his craft. Using every nuance of his experience he managed to walk the furious Network Ten executives back from their decision that I was now finished. Like Trinity at the end of *The Matrix* after we'd seen Neo die, he was able to bring my career back from a complete flatline.[5] If you've never negotiated anything before, the idea is that each party comes into the negotiation with 'leverage'. You have something that they want, they have something you want – and you work out a value for that something together, whomever having the most 'leverage' usually coming out on top.

Yet not even Archimedes and his very, very long lever could move their position.

Miraculously, Mark did.

There's a phrase I'd learn later in recovery, 'Find humility before humility finds you.' The money they finally offered smashed me in the face with humility and then made me a

---

5   Spoiler alert: If you've not seen *The Matrix* by now, I might have just spoiled the ending for you. That's OK, because the bit after that in the film is still awesome.

house and bed of humility so that I'd have to wake up every day and be surrounded by nothing but the wreckage that's caused when I let my ego run things.

Without Mark Morrissey my career would have ended there and then.

I humbly went back to *Australian Idol*, which was now a three-host version of the show, and the cycle repeated again. In the break between the auditions and the live shows I headed to Israel with eighty-six friends and family to travel around the country for a few days before marrying Noa in the ancient Israeli city of Caesarea on the shores of the Mediterranean.

In that part of the world, everyone you've ever known or worked with comes to your wedding. By midnight on the day of the wedding there were more than a thousand people there, all invited guests. I was so overwhelmed and terrified by the scale of the day that I emotionally detached from the situation and switched into being an observer. Like the driver of a Japanese mecha-robot I sat behind my eyes and watched as the ceremony took place. I was so detached that I didn't emotionally connect with saying the vows. I completely missed the part where you feel that emotional shift within you as your husband or wife commits themselves to you in front of everyone that you care about. It's as if I wasn't even there.

While I was supposed to be in the happiest time of my life, things were just getting worse. Now the stakes were raised, Noa and I fought more and more. I now understand that arguing with me during that time in my life was like trying to hold a snake by the neck to stop it from biting you, only for it to morph into a thousand spiders that would sting you all over your body only to then re-form as a snake, peacefully coiled on the floor legitimately wondering why you were so mad.

When James Mathison decided to leave the show at the end of 2008, I went it alone on *Australian Idol* in 2009. I dearly missed having James to work with. I learned something new from him every single day, and without his vibrant energy and humour, trying to carry the show alone was hard work. I wasn't naturally funny in the way James is, and I had nowhere near the timing that he so effortlessly displayed. It took me a few weeks to get used to taking up more space on camera and I essentially had to relearn how to do my job. It was a difficult challenge and one I relished tackling, but it was tough to do that training on live television.

Looking back now, there were warning signs that *Idol* was coming to an end. At the Logie Awards we had won Best Reality Program three years in a row. When they're reading out the nominees, the camera cuts to you for the victory celebration or the 'oh, good for them' clap you're forced to do if you don't win. We went from having a camera standing by for our 'loser shot' to no camera at all. Our grand final for 2009 was no longer inside the Sydney Opera House; we were now just on the front steps. We had no helicopters and no fireworks. As I signed off in the final moments of that show as the confetti rained down, I shouted, 'See you in 2010!' but I knew in my heart that it wasn't going to happen.

A few weeks later back in LA I called my network executive Stephen Tate and asked him if they were going to do another season, to which he said something to the effect of, 'I can't tell you yes or no, but I know that I'm not going to be executive producer any more and I've not heard anything about another season.'

In the end I had to read about the show being axed in the newspaper.

That wasn't the only kick in the groin I got that year. *Take 40 Australia* was the biggest radio countdown show in the country, and it was produced by a media company called MCM. The same company produced a similar countdown called *The Hot Hits*, hosted by Kyle Sandilands and Jackie O. I was just a voice on the Southern Cross Austereo network on a Sunday afternoon delivering the number one countdown in the country. Kyle and Jackie were anchoring the 2Day FM breakfast radio show in Sydney and were crushing the ratings there. A decision was made way above my head to put the flagship personalities of the network on the flagship countdown in the country. In hindsight, it made perfect sense.

In the same meeting that the MCM execs were told that *Take 40 Australia* was being given to Kyle and Jackie, they were told that *The Hot Hits* was getting the axe. Thinking quickly, Tony McGinn and Simon Joyce, the head honchos at MCM, pitched a show we had been talking about for years between ourselves – a show made from LA but for Australia: *The Hot Hits Live from LA*. It was an extraordinary moment of quick thinking, without which I would have been completely fucked.

I would now have a radio show that allowed me to live in LA but broadcast back to Australia – the exact show I'd thought about that day in 2003.

a long way down

Starting a new radio show from scratch takes a lot of work, particularly with the technical challenges of going live across multiple stations in another country every single week. Other people had done shows back to Australia from overseas – in Oscar week, Grammys week, or for the occasional Royal Wedding – but no one had ever had a permanent setup to broadcast on a weekly basis.

MCM built an incredible team around the show, with some of the most skilled radio operators I'd ever worked with making up the LA side of things. The pressure was immense: *The Hot Hits* was a brand that MCM had been running for fifteen years and we were under enormous stress trying to make four hours of network radio every week. Because of the time difference we would broadcast out of the landmark CBS Radio building on Wilshire Boulevard at 9pm on a Saturday night, Sunday afternoon in Australia.

We tried *really* hard in those first few weeks, but we just couldn't get it together. The network wasn't happy, the team's leadership was malfunctioning and I was panicking. Overnight, the show's format changed from a four-hour magazine-style show to another countdown. I was back to weekly airchecks with Brian Ford, my old program director from B105 who was now a heavy-hitting radio consultant.[1] I'm sorry to say that I didn't approach them with the humility I'd had as a mid–dawn announcer. I was inwardly furious that someone would dare tell me how to do my job (even though I was clearly not doing it very well at all), and I'd grudgingly accept the direction I was given. My ego and arrogance were beginning to blowtorch the whole thing.

The conflicts within the LA leadership of the team were also very difficult to deal with, and I responded in the only way that I knew. I began to drink even more.

Noa and I had just bought a house in LA to renovate, and we'd got the loan based on income from *Australian Idol* and *Take 40 Australia*. Both were gone now and I was under the pump. My drinking began earlier and earlier in the day. I went from sunset drinks to afternoon drinks to a drink with lunch on a Wednesday by myself for no reason except that it was now noon. I tried to offset the anxiety and fear with exercise, which did work temporarily, but it was starting to be no match for my problem.

Each year pilot season would bring planeloads of well-known Australian actors to town, hoping to land the roles that would propel them to stardom.[2] One was Australian acting

---

1   This is essentially a performance review of the show. Like when a football coach goes through the game tape and points out flaws in the play.

2   Pilot season – or as I liked to call it, pirate season – is an eight-week vortex of hell if you're an actor. It's the time of year when the big networks take all the scripts that have been commissioned out of their development roster and commit to making one show and one show only to see how it works. If the show *does* work they'll hopefully commission a season of episodes. The stress on the actors is incredible because over the course of three ten-minute auditions (one initial, one callback, and one for the network) and one or two meetings you could essentially change your entire life. But even if you get booked for the show, it's not a sure thing. I know an actress who was cast as a recurring character on a pilot and when the show got picked up for series they *recast* her character. Every single person you see on an American TV show has been through this horrible, psychologically punishing process. It takes enormous fortitude to survive, and I hope I never ever have to do it.

legend Daniel MacPherson. We had met once or twice but we were both represented by Mark Morrissey, so we arranged to go for a hike up Runyon Canyon. Dan carries the glorious sunshine and ocean breezes of his Noosa home wherever he goes, and just being around him makes you feel you're basking in the warmth of a perfect summer's day.

I'd taken to mixing up my running to the peak of Runyon Canyon with hiking to the top carrying a weighted backpack. The day he and I hiked to the top of the mountain I had an extra thirty kilograms on me. As we descended from the peak my foot slipped on the gravel path and I came crashing down like a hurdler in mid leap. As I landed I felt a 'pop' in my right knee and when I stood back up that leg was most unstable. That night my knee was in so much pain that I couldn't sleep, despite necking huge amounts of ibuprofen, so it was off to get an MRI the next day.

I won't go into what it's like being exposed to the US healthcare system, except to say that I'll do everything that I can to maintain universal healthcare in Australia because I've seen the alternative. A nice doctor dressed in theatre scrubs told me that I'd torn the medial collateral ligament in my right knee. It would take about twelve weeks of physio to heal, but I'd get back to running after a while. He told me to take 400 milligrams of ibuprofen for the pain and come and see him in two months. When I told him I'd taken 600 milligrams the night before which hadn't helped, he didn't even hesitate when he said, 'Oh, OK – I'll give you some Vicodin.' This is the drug of choice for celebrities with prescription painkiller addictions, and I now had an orange bottle with one hundred pills in my bathroom cabinet.

I've had a few injuries in my life that have caused pain, I've broken bones and torn a few ligaments, but nothing has compared to the pain of this injury. Walking, sitting, standing, even lying down, I was in agony. And that's where Vicodin came in. When you take it, you still feel the pain but *you just don't care.* Unlike Percocet (a synthetic opioid that blocks the pain receptors by putting a heavy wet blanket on your whole body that shuts the world down around you) on Vicodin I could go about my daily activities with no problem. I also discovered that when I washed the Vicodin down with a few beers the effect was even better.

However, the Vicodin only took care of the pain in my knee. It didn't help with the pain of being under immense pressure from work as the very last tenuous thread of my once-almighty broadcasting career hung off a show that was struggling to get through our non-ratings test period to survive a full commission.

My drinking was bad, especially when Noa wasn't home. A successful actor and producer in her own right, she was often away on work trips to New York or Israel, and when she wasn't home I'd blow the doors off.

I had always scheduled flights the day before an interstate morning meeting or any work in another city rather than taking the early flight out. This was solely to hit the bar at the airport lounge, drink on the plane and get annihilated alone in a hotel room. I'd done that for more than fifteen years but now I was starting to schedule all meetings early in the morning so that my workday would be done sooner and I could start drinking earlier. Eventually I began to cancel the afternoon meetings, saying, 'Something had come up back in Australia that I have to deal with.' As soon as I was off the phone I'd walk into a bottle shop to buy a six-pack and some whisky. The moment I was back in my garage and the car was back in 'P' I'd crack the first beer before even turning the engine off.

I was ashamed of what I was doing but absolutely unable to stop.

I hated that I'd start to get itchy for a drink earlier and earlier in the day, hated that I was walking to the fridge, hated that I was reaching for a can of beer on a weekday morning, hated myself as I cracked the ring-pull, hated that I was lifting the can to my lips ... but as soon as that first sip of beer washed into my mouth, all of that self-hate vanished. For about three seconds. The moment after I'd swallowed the beer, I'd fall into a pit of shame for drinking at this time of day. And the best way to get rid of those feelings? More drinking.

People who have never had a problem with drinking may be wondering why I simply didn't have that drink. I'll try and explain it. Imagine you're sitting on the beach with the love of your life, your toes in the warm sand, holding hands and enjoying a wonderful sunset together. Right then you notice that the biggest, nastiest mosquito that's ever flown has just finished slurping your blood; the bug flies off *just* before you slap your arm.

About ten seconds later the most intense itch you've ever experienced starts from the site of the bite and the itch builds and builds so you can't think about anything but scratching it.

Everything wonderful about that moment vanishes right then and there. All you can think about is scratching that itch. You are no longer present to the sunset, the touch of your lover, the fragrance of the flowers in the air nor the warmth of the sand on your toes. Your mind is completely consumed with scratching that itch and you cannot rejoin reality until you have done that.

Every single thing around me stopped mattering, and nothing could continue until I had had a beer.

It became quite difficult to hide from Noa that I was drinking like this, and she was understandably concerned to see the man she married clawing at the fridge door as if I was Lyndsey grabbing for Virgil Brigman's scuba mask as she was drowning in *The Abyss*.[3] Like any good alcoholic, I assured her that I didn't have a problem and I could stop whenever I wanted to. What she didn't know was that I'd tried to stop many times before, but it just wouldn't stick. During that final season of *Australian Idol* I'd tried to not drink the whole time we were doing the live shows, but I only lasted about six weeks. I'd try driving to an event so I had to stay sober enough to drive home, but by the end of the second beer I had already decided to leave my car parked wherever it was and had ordered a double Jägermeister shot and two more beers. Every time I promised myself I wouldn't get plastered I failed. It was as if I was stuck on a convoluted Rube Goldberg machine, and once it was set in motion there was only one possible outcome.

I'd start by opening the first beer, but no matter what I tried, no matter how many different ways I tried to behave, it was inevitable that by the time the night was over, something would be broken, someone would be angry and I couldn't remember a thing that happened.

Alcoholics describe rock bottom as getting to the lowest low that you'd ever experienced, so low that you look up

---

3 You might have bought this book for an insight into what that guy on the telly who changed his name is on about when he talks about mental illness – but you didn't count on getting a bunch of recommendations for obscure James Cameron films, did you?

and realise that the only reason you're face down in shit is because you put yourself there. You have to get there before you can make a lasting change in your behaviour. I dragged along the bottom for some time like an anchor dragging over a precious coral reef, trying to find purchase but causing untold destruction that would take decades to repair. But I wasn't quite at rock bottom. Not quite.

In May 2009 I'd begun to document my life, taking a self-portrait every day for a year as part of an online photo challenge called '365'. I'd always loved photography and was looking for a project that would really push me. I was just taking a photo every day – but what I ended up documenting was the end of *Australian Idol*, me getting my green card, leaving Sydney and moving to LA and, most notably, the last six months of drinking.

I excused my puffy face in a few photos, saying I was tired. Actually I was plastered, and sometimes I took the photographs with my eyes closed in an effort to try to disguise their lost look.

The final days of my drinking involved utter humiliation of myself, Noa and many of her colleagues. She was in New York City for a work trip and I had tagged along, mainly because I loved to be in New York City. Since the PTSD after 2001 it had taken some time to be OK with going back, but happily I was able to reframe my NYC experience after a few visits. I was able to enjoy it for the diverse metropolis that it is, eating in every vegan cafe, running through Central Park and watching people come and go like the tide. While Noa was busy taking meetings, the chilly days dragged on. I walked around New York City looking for places to shoot my 365 photograph for the day, stopping into a bar for a beer here and there. But I didn't have a drinking problem, I was just exploring the city.

Because there were many people involved, many of whom I care about very much even though they're no longer in my life, I won't go into the gruesome play-by-play details of the final night I ever drank. But I'll give you the highlights.

It started with me drinking double martinis with a mate who is a partner at one of the big three investment banks in downtown Manhattan. Here's a tip – don't try going toe-to-toe with a man who is used to making deals that could gain or lose hundreds of millions of dollars before his second cup of coffee on a Tuesday. I've met a few NY bankers and they're all quite similar. All over six feet tall, all strikingly handsome and physically powerful, and they can all drink like they have a spare liver back in their penthouse.[4] From there we met Noa and some very important people she had been working with that day. We sat down to dinner and before the bread hit the table the third martini had kicked in and I was already shitfaced.

Of course, I just kept drinking and by the time we paid the bill, I had utterly humiliated her, yelled at and frightened strangers, vomited on myself in the bathroom and been nothing short of an absolute pig. One moment I was stumbling out of the restaurant, and suddenly we were back in the apartment arguing; I don't remember more than that. Next thing I recall I was on my knees in the apartment mopping up my own piss with my socks. I'd passed out on the sofa and had got up and peed against the wall thinking it was the toilet, but I don't remember doing that.

---

4   Given the eye-watering wealth and access to advanced health-care that normal people couldn't even dream about, the spare liver scenario is probably already real.

I was just suddenly conscious with wet knees, using my socks to try and sop up the lake of urine that was rapidly leaking out over the hardwood floor.

I'd love to tell you that this evening was an isolated incident – but it wasn't. It was the thing that had started to happen every single time that I drank. It wasn't the one big night that ended it all – it was no smaller or bigger than any of the other evenings I'd been drinking through over the past months and years.

This was just one more night – one of a series going back to when I started drinking as a teenager – that ended in pain for someone who loved or cared about me, and nothing but shame, humiliation and regret for me.

But now I realised that I *just couldn't* do it one more time.

It was inevitable that this was exactly how every night ended when I started drinking like I did. There seemed to be nothing I could do to change it. I was trapped in a pattern of behaviour that was on an ever decreasing spiral and ever increasing velocity.

Alcohol wasn't my problem, it was my solution. Unfortunately for me, the amount that I needed to drink to feel safe, accepted or even normal was now impossible to maintain.

All I did do was cause chaos and destruction wherever I went, wreaking havoc on those who loved me, and those I worked for.

That morning in New York City, the words of the great Chinese philosopher Lao Tzu flashed into my mind: 'If you do not change direction, you may end up where you are heading.'

That was it.

I had to stop.

Noa took the early flight out of NY the next day and called me from the airport. 'When you get back to LA we're going to need to talk about your drinking,' she told me.

I said, 'I'm sorry. I know I can't do that ever again.' She had no reason to believe me this time, but I was committed to change. *All* I wanted to do was drink – but I wanted *not* to go through that kind of night again just 0.1 per cent more. All that happened on 13 March 2010 and I've not picked up a drink since.[5] How did I do that?

Well.

That's where the work really started.

---

5 It's important to emphasise that for around 50 per cent of recovering alcoholics, a relapse is a part of that recovery. I haven't relapsed yet, but the odds are 50/50 that I will. I *have* accidentally taken a sip of a drink passed to me in a club that was supposed to be soda water but turned out to be a vodka soda, and again on a camping trip after a run when I mistook a jug of morning-after melted margarita mix for a jug of fruity water. Both accidents sent me into a panic that I'd start a relapse but thankfully I waited until the effect of the tiny amount of alcohol passed, called my mentor and talked it over. I'm so sensitive that I can't even drink kombucha, as the taste of the fermentation is enough to set off the triggers. It's a pity because apparently that stuff is really good for you, even though it looks super-gross when you make it.

eighteen
it works if you work it

In order to stop drinking, I knew that I needed help. I'd tried by myself to stop a few times, and that clearly hadn't worked out well at all. I already knew about 12-Step fellowships, having once attended a meeting to get support for dealing with someone I knew, so I was aware that they were around and were easy to get to.

A few months before all of this I'd met a handsome and talented photographer from New York – let's call him Glen.[1] Glen was built like an Adonis and utterly gorgeous, as if a picture-perfect Tom of Finland cartoon had come to life and started walking around in the real world. He was gifted in the way that only true artists are, he was having an enormous amount of fun, he was the life of the party and he was sober. I'd only known sobriety to look like depressed people sitting on folding chairs in a dark church basement sharing stories of how much they had fucked up their lives. I didn't know sobriety could look so good or so successful. If I could get just the tiniest bit of what Glen had, it would be better than what I had now. I called him and asked for help.

He said he was going to a meeting that afternoon and he'd be happy to take me along. Glen is gay, so the first few fellowship

---

1   It's not his real name, but in an anonymous program you don't out other people in the program.

meetings I went to were all gay meetings in West Hollywood.[2] What I heard was people with completely different upbringings and experiences describing their relationship to sex, drugs and alcohol as if they had been living exactly the same life as I had. I learned again that maybe I wasn't such a special snowflake after all. Maybe I was just a standard base-model addict who did and said and believed exactly the same things as every other addict.

I can never thank Glen enough for taking me to those first meetings when I was still shaking and wondering whether I'd ever be able to clean up the enormous mess my behaviour had made. You've seen the movies, so you'll know that there's steps that you're encouraged to take to achieve physical and emotional sobriety.

But I was an arrogant, ego-driven alcoholic, so clearly those steps weren't for me. I thought all I had to do was not drink and everything would be fine and I would no longer need to go to those meetings. This was a very poor decision on my part.[3]

What happened was that alcohol, the drug I'd been using to manage my rapidly deteriorating mental health, was no longer safe for me to take. So I essentially came off my meds without any real substitute for the depressant that I'd been using every day to manage my moods. Instead of my life getting better, it got *inconceivably* worse.[4] I thought I was being very smart by

---

2 West Hollywood is probably the gayest postcode on the planet outside of San Francisco.

3 This is called the 'pink cloud': it's a term used to refer to the feeling of elation and happiness usually felt by someone in early sobriety. All right – you're sober now! People in the meetings cheer when you tell them you've got 21 days clean. Everything is fine and you don't have to do any more work – you have figured everything out … It's a very volatile part of sobriety where relapses can occur.

4 If you didn't read that in the voice of Vizzini from *The Princess Bride*, please go back and do it for me. If you don't know who Vizzini is, I will be more than OK if you put this book down for two hours and spend the time watching one of the most perfectly written films ever made. I'll still be here when you return. Or don't. As you wish.

thinking I could not drink on my own, but I was just doing what so many alcoholics have done for decades: I was 'white knuckling', holding on for dear life, hoping that things would get easier, desperately avoiding the rigorous introspective work required in order to actually get sober. Because let me assure you – there's a big difference between 'not drinking' and 'being sober'.

In the first few days of not drinking, the sunsets were the worst. Sunset was usually when I'd crack the first non-guilty beer or wine of the night. I'd try to go for a run or do something else when the urges hit, and they would pass soon enough. But instead of admitting to myself that I had a problem with alcohol (the big and scary first step) I wrote down in my notebook, 'I'll just not drink until I can have a healthy relationship with alcohol.' It was the same trick I'd used to get myself out the door for a walk around the block nearly twenty years before, and the same way that I would trick myself into attacking a massive pile of dishes or laundry that needed to be put away. I'd just say, 'Oh, I'll only wash one dish,' and then I'd be standing there with the soapy sponge in my hand and one clean dish in the other, and it would be nothing to pick up the next one and the one after that. However, it took only a few weeks for me to realise that if I wanted that healthy relationship with alcohol, I could indeed have it – but only if I would never, ever drink again.

When you stop drinking a few six-packs a day, two things happen immediately: you lose a ton of weight and you realise you've got more pocket money than you thought. My face soon no longer resembled a balloon with eyes, and I wasn't going to the ATM three times a week to pull out another $100 for booze money.[5] The radio show carried on, and thankfully when a change was made with the management, the show finally started to fire up.

The ratings were in and we got the full commission for the year – we were going to be OK. It took an enormous amount of work for a show that was only four hours once a week, but when you market the show as the 'latest from the entertainment capital of the world' you need to spend a lot of time doing the interviews that give the audience the access you promised them.

I'd often find myself flying in and out of NYC in the middle of the week to participate in film junkets. They were just like the record junkets I'd done for Channel [v] back in 2001. For the actors spruiking a movie, it must be utter horror to be asked the same questions every five minutes, all day long, for a week straight. For me, it was waiting in a long and silent hallway, shoulder to shoulder with various members of the Hollywood foreign press complaining about how terrible the film was or that they'd drunk through their minibar and couldn't get the film company to pay for a restock. Then I'd get shuffled in to spend four minutes trying to pry anything more than a three-word answer out of a tired and defensive actor who had been trapped in that small room trying not to answer personal questions for the last five days. It was a long way from getting phone calls like, 'Madonna is in LA doing interviews and she wants to know why you're not on the interview list. Can you get over there straight away?' Humility was still coming to find me wherever I turned, and it would be a long time before I'd go and find it willingly.

---

5    $100 a few times a week seems like a lot, but in a desperate attempt to avoid admitting that I was an alcoholic I'd started buying expensive bottles of red wine – because if I was buying fancy bottles I was a connoisseur, not a carouser.

It was on one of those cross-country plane trips that I met a woman who changed the way I was seen as a photographer. After we hit 10,000 feet and the seatbelt sign went off with that non-familiar 'ding', the woman I was sitting next to (in the very, *very* back of the plane, still much to my distress) opened up a laptop that had a Canon asset control sticker next to the trackpad. In the hope of having some interesting conversation on the six-hour journey back from New York City I pulled down my camera bag from the overhead locker and not-so-subtly opened up the front of the backpack to get out my Kindle, exposing my Canon 5DII DSLR body and arsenal of lenses that I carried with me every day before I zipped the bag back up and returned it to the overhead stowage.

After a few minutes, she said, 'I see you're a Canon shooter,' and we were off. We got to talking about my photography and the '365 Days' project I was working on. She got very excited about the prospect of Canon Australia sponsoring an exhibition in Sydney when the project was over. Once again serendipity stepped in and leapfrogged my career. Turns out that this woman was one of the heads of marketing for Canon USA, and right there and then using the in-flight wifi (which was still a novelty) she emailed the head of marketing at Canon Australia to introduce me and float the idea of a sponsored photographic show. In September of 2010 the fantastic Canon team did just that. They paid for the expensive printing process, helped me get national TV publicity and offered incredible support throughout the month-long show.

As I stood in the packed Surry Hills gallery on opening night, I whispered to a few close friends who had come to support me that they were standing in the middle of my last six months of drinking and my first six months of sobriety.

Seeing all the photographs blown up and hung on the wall was a stark reminder that incremental change, made every day, can have a massive effect on your life.

After the exhibition, I returned to LA from Sydney on a Monday one month later. The week I got back to the USA was the most intense week of work of my life, and it shows why basing yourself in the heart of the business you're in can be a valuable strategy.

That Thursday I got a call from Adam Gelvan at WME. He told me to get to a meeting the next day with the production company Shine to talk about a new show on CBS. Negotiations had broken down with the host they had lined up for the show, and there was a chance I could be their guy. At eleven the next morning, and I met with the team behind a new dancing competition show called *Live To Dance*, Paula Abdul's first new network outing since leaving *American Idol* the year before. As they were rolling tape in New York City for the first audition show in six days' time, they were very serious and we got down to brass tacks quickly. By close of business that day they had sent a deal over to my lawyer and I was faxing back the signed contract at ten on a Friday night. The show was all but locked away, I just needed one more tick of approval – from the show's executive producer and star, Paula Abdul.

That Sunday afternoon I went to meet her at the legendary Polo Lounge at the Beverly Hills Hotel. She was sitting right at the rear of the outdoor garden, secreted away on one side of a booth with her back to the room, her pet chihuahua Bessie Moo chilling by her side in a Louis Vuitton dog carrier.

The first thing that strikes you about Paula is that she is absolutely tiny. She makes Kylie Minogue look like Brienne of

Tarth.[6] She also carries about her an air of artistic eccentricity that befits someone of her immense talent. Paula was utterly sweet and charming, very excited about the show she was making. It was clear as we talked that her technical knowledge of stage production is unsurpassed – she really is one of the greatest choreographers of our time. We drank herbal tea and spoke for around an hour, and then I headed home to pack as I was on a flight to NY the next morning regardless, to cover a film junket for *The Hot Hits Live From LA*. As I was packing my bag I texted James, the show's executive producer, and asked how many pairs of boxer shorts I should put into my bag. I was cheekily asking whether I was going for three days (my original schedule) or whether I would be there for another week making this show. James told me to pack for a week, and the next morning I headed to LAX for the 6am flight.

Somewhere over Kansas I hooked into the on-board wifi and my Blackberry inbox exploded. It was official, I was the host of CBS's new show *Live To Dance*. As the news had been published on the big trade news websites already, industry people I'd worked with in the USA from day one, even people I'd only ever taken one meeting with, were emailing to congratulate me. When I got off the plane my voicemail was overflowing with similar messages and I excitedly called Noa, my family and friends.

I called my agent back in LA to find out how the job had come to me so quickly. At other times when I had been up

---

6   Brienne of Tarth is a very tall female character from the TV show *Game of Thrones*, played with extraordinary feminine power by the very talented Gwendoline Christie. If you've never seen *Game of Thrones*, start with the early seasons – I don't mind if you tap out once everyone starts being able to magically teleport across the vast continent of Westeros in what seems to be hours, when at the start of the show they needed two episodes just to get to the neighbour's castle to borrow a cup of sugar.

for a big network show I had needed to meet with the head honchos at the network to get the final tick of approval. But for this gig I never met anyone from CBS. It turned out that back in the summer of 2006 when I was having 'general meetings' with everyone in the LA industry, I'd met an extremely talented woman named Jen Bresnan who worked at a cable network called The CW. We had a great conversation and left hoping that one day we would get a chance to work on a project together. Right after we'd met, Jen Bresnan was named senior vice-president of Alternative Programming at CBS, looking after all the shows that weren't news, sport or drama. Jen had seen my name on the list and given her approval based on a meeting we'd had four years beforehand.[7] The lesson is that every meeting, no matter how small or seemingly unimportant, could be the one that changes everything.

Once the film junket was done I moved from the humble press hotel to an opulent suite in Tribeca where the Shine crew were staying. A gift basket so full of vegan snacks that it would have needed two people to carry was waiting in my room and there was a limitless tab on the room service. The next two days were spent scooting around NY with a stylist putting together an outfit and meeting the production team I'd be working with. That Friday we decamped to Liberty Park, New Jersey, with an astonishing view of the Hudson River and the Statue of Liberty, and prepared to roll tape on the first 'audition' show of the season.

---

7   I've found that if you leave people with a positive emotion, when they remember your name they'll feel that positive emotion again. It's like having a cheerleader in the room even though you're hundreds or even thousands of kilometres away.

nineteen
always learning

If the difference between cable and network TV in Australia is the difference between economy class and first class on the A380, the difference between network TV in Australia and network TV in the USA is the difference between flying the A380 and the Learjet.[1]

When I showed up to the set, I wasn't sharing a broom closet with another co-host, as I did on *Australian Idol* – I had my own bus. An entire bus converted into a motor home with transformer-like sides that would expand out to create more space in the middle. There was a full kitchen, shower, makeup stand and satellite TV. I had my own makeup artist, hair stylist, stylist, personal assistant and tailor. *A tailor.* She was set up with a sewing machine and an overlocker and everything to make any necessary clothing adjustments, no matter how small.

The level of attention to my needs was over the top to say the least. It was: 'OK, Mr Günsberg, we're ready for you on set now, your golf cart is waiting, can I get you a water? Would you like cold or room temperature – no don't open it yourself, please let me do that, I'm just being told we won't need you for

---

1   When you see Dwayne 'The Rock' Johnson snap out an Instagram standing alone on the tarmac in front of a small jet plane with the caption 'heading off for 72hrs, 86 interviews and 12 countries to talk about my *Fast and Furious* 15 #blessed #fast15', he's standing in front of a Learjet.

two more minutes, would you like to go back to your trailer? No, please don't stand – *I need a seat for the talent and I need it now* – here, please have a seat, oh, no, it's no trouble, are you done with that water? Seems they're ready for you now, would it be OK if we make our way to set? I have asked the crew to stop work so you can walk without having to step over anything while we walk … is there anything particular you'd like for dinner? I know you're vegan and enjoy Thai food, here's four menus from the nearby vegan Thai restaurants, pick what you want, I'll have it ready when you're done, oh, no, please, it's no trouble, here just through this door, *talent on set, we have talent on set*, OK your crew is already rolling, here's your producer, let me take that water if you're done? Should you need me I'll be right over here to get you back to your trailer after you're finished.'

Living a sober life and taking the humble road was something I was trying to do more and more. But I have to tell you that when your ego is being stroked like that and you're made to feel so important, it's bloody hard to keep your feet on the ground. Fortunately I knew that this was the biggest chance I'd ever get in my whole career, so I had to have a clear goal. All I wanted was to be utterly professional. I wanted every single person from the network execs, story producers, directors, camera operators, sound operators, all the way down through the union grips and stage hands, right to the drivers who shuttled us 200 metres from trailer to set in a golf cart – I wanted to show every single one of those people that I was the most professional guy they had ever worked with. If I did that, I'd do my job the best I had ever done it. It was a good way to frame going into the gig because on that show I feel that I did the best work of my life.

I just had to deal with one large problem first. The execs felt that my look for the New York shows was a bit off, and they needed my styling to have a bit more 'pow'. Back in LA they sent me to a house just above the Comedy Store on Sunset Strip to meet legendary Hollywood stylist Jessica Paster. Racks and racks of clothes filled every single room; there was no furniture in the home at all. When I asked Jessica whether she lived there she replied, 'Oh, I used to, sweetie, but I ran out of room so I moved across the street. There's more clothes there.'

She asked me to try on outfit after outfit, so I needed to take my shirt off not only in front of her but also in front of the endless scurrying interns and assistants whose job it was to fulfil her every request: 'Get me a brown belt with a closed buckle. It's in the belt room, third from the end on the fourth rack of belts.' An assistant would also run in and shoot a Polaroid photograph of every look and then run out again.[2] My body shame was still intense, but fortunately Jessica noticed this. She pulled a changing screen off the wall so I could hide behind it. Wearing the clothes she put me in, I'd looked better than I had in my entire life. When someone is a master at their craft it really shows.

That is, until she asked me to put on *the cardigan.* It was winter in LA and despite what you see on TV it gets absolutely freezing at night – the place is in a desert, after all. Jessica's mirror was elaborately adorned, glorious and floor-to-ceiling. At that time I weighed eighty-six kilograms with almost no muscle on my upper body. Wearing that too-tight cardigan I looked like a plastic sack full of pumpkins. While Jessica

---

2   If only we had known that Polaroid film would be discontinued later that year, we wouldn't have wasted so much of it …

rummaged around in a rack behind me preparing the next ensemble, I mumbled to her in embarrassment, 'Um … Jessica, I'm sorry but I think I'm a bit too lumpy to wear this.'

She took one glance at me, and with a flamboyant wave of her hand that sent the tinkling sound of bangles through the air, she said the words that would change everything. 'Oh, don't worry, sweetie, we'll get you a girdle.' As I stood there in shame having my photo taken by one of her assistants I made a resolution. I'd fought for years to get that job, I'd worked my entire life to be able to do it, I'd left my family, friends and career back in Australia for it, I would be the first Australian ever to host live network prime-time TV in the USA. There was *absolutely no fucking way* I was going to do that job wearing a girdle.

As I drove back home I called a trainer I knew. Natasha Fett, a powerful woman who was direct in her very German way, was not only a trainer but a vegan chef. We met the following day in a coffee shop down in Santa Monica and I told her what I needed. We were shooting the audition shows that week but in twelve weeks we would go live across the country. I wanted to make sure I made the most of this gig looking and feeling the best I'd ever felt in my life. She didn't flinch when she heard my timeline. 'Twelve weeks? I can do it. We start tomorrow.'

For the next twelve weeks Natasha cooked for me and coached me through training sessions on the Santa Monica stairs that left me invigorated. Natasha is an absolute machine, a powerhouse. She did every rep of every single exercise with me and I was only one of four or five clients she had that day. Once when we didn't have the power bands to help me with a set of chin-ups so she simply used one hand to push me from my feet, to get all eighty-six kilograms of me high enough to edge my chin over the bar. *With one hand.*

With the SSRI meds now able to do their job because I was no longer flushing them out of my kidneys with rivers of beer, I was able to be a lot more calm about eating, too. My relationship to food was beginning to change because I now knew that no matter what, wonderful and nutritious food was waiting for me when I got home. Previously if I had felt hungry while I was heading home to eat dinner I'd panic and pull over to a service station so I could grab two nut bars and a sports drink which I'd mindlessly wolf down, even though I was less than thirty minutes from home and food. I'd do this in the morning before lunch, too. I associated hunger so closely with fear that I'd do anything possible to avoid it. However, with Natasha in my life I was absolutely committed to hitting the screen looking and feeling my absolute best. You only get one chance to meet America for the first time, and I wanted everyone to be blown away.

Besides the workouts with Natasha I'd begun to go on long bicycle rides through the hills of Griffith Park near home. I hadn't yet graduated to the road bike but I was relishing the freedom that comes with getting where you're going on pedal power alone.

Soon enough the weight started to absolutely fall off my body. Natasha's nutrition plan was timed to perfection and twelve weeks after we first started working together, as promised, I now weighed seventy-two kilos. I'd dropped fourteen kilograms in twelve weeks.

Live To Dance made its debut on 4 January 2010. We opened with strong ratings and an audience of more than ten million people. The first two shows were the auditions we'd taped back in October, and on 12 January we broadcast live. We were broadcasting from CBS Television City on the corner of Fairfax and Beverly, the very same studio complex as *American Idol*. My parking space was the second one from the front door, next to none other than *American Idol* executive producer Nigel Lythgoe.[3]

Continuing a practice I'd begun back in the later *Australian Idol* days, I meditated for twenty minutes before going on as a way to focus myself. Doing live prime-time TV out of LA means you go live at 4pm when east coast time is 7pm. As my floor manager Harvey counted me down from near the vast LED screen, I took the relaxing breaths that Dr Chung had taught me, and when Harvey patted me on the back to send me on, I strode out with the confidence that only relentless preparation and rehearsal can give you.

As I walked I understood the significance of this moment. I was now the first Australian to ever host live, prime-time network television in the USA. I felt so good that I flipped the mic with one hand and caught it again as I eyeballed the camera – a risky trick I'd learned earlier in my career – but one that showed the hundreds of screaming fans in the audience and the millions watching at home that I was in control.

I've talked before about the feeling of peace that I get when I'm working, and in those moments where I was addressing the camera straight down the barrel, it was the closest I've ever been to complete serenity. Of course, there was intense pressure leading up to it. My entire career had been sharpened for this exact moment, my entire future career depended on the job I

---

3   In LA things like where you park and what order you appear on the call sheet are all status symbols that get fought over during contract negotiations. It's a pissing contest. Tugg Speedman's agent in *Tropic Thunder* isn't a parody – that's a reflection of actuality.

did at that moment, but as I spoke (being sure to lean on the letter 'r' so people in Kansas would know what I was saying) in my head was absolute silence, and I felt complete bliss.

During those six weeks I feel that I did the best live work of my career. While the show didn't rate as well as the network had hoped, I was thrilled with the job I'd done, and the feedback from colleagues within the LA TV industry was extremely positive.

I now weighed seventy kilos for the first time since I'd been a chubby teen. I was looking great and feeling greater, and the next thing to do was to just sit back and wait for the offers of new shows to flood in. The phone would be ringing off the hook any moment.

Nope. Nothing. Absolutely zip. Even though I'd hired a manager to help me make the most of the heat around my US TV debut, that was it. When it was clear we weren't coming back for a second season, I was absolutely heartbroken. To be painted with the brush of a cancelled show is to walk around LA with the stink of failure all over you.

I kept going out and meeting for jobs, but I'd begun to lose hosting gigs to people who were already pre-famous. To host live national prime-time TV takes a specific set of perfected skills. At the time, there were only a handful of people in LA who could do the job I was doing. However, the hosting gigs had begun to go to people who were already known to the public. I began to get passed over for WWE wrestlers, ex-cast members of *Glee* and even an ex-Olympic gymnast. Unfortunately for me, the networks just kept hiring people who were already household names, despite their lack of live hosting skills, and my prospects for more work in the USA vanished.

The market was shifting under my feet. I had to think of something else to do.

In 2010 I had become involved with a group of entrepreneurs called Summit Series based in LA. Initially introduced to the group through Noa, it was in hanging out with them that I had met people who were doing exciting, world-changing things every day. I started to investigate marrying my experience and knowledge in broadcasting with the exciting developments taking place in start-up tech.

To put it simply, I had come up with an idea for a platform that was like Shazam for TV and radio shows. It would listen for an inaudible ultrasonic sound broadcast over the TV signal and then unlock content on an app, offering rewards for watching or listening longer. This technology has of course since been deployed very successfully by many different companies in the form of 'watch along' apps that unlock content as the show rolls on, but in 2011 the technological possibilities were only just becoming available.

Through contacts I'd made at Summit I began to fly to San Francisco every week to pitch my idea around the venture capital companies up and down Sandhill Road, ground zero for venture capital in Silicon Valley. I managed to raise some decent angel funds, enough to get the project started, but when I got back to LA and it was time to hire people to begin work on the project, it was clear that now, at the end of 2011, my marriage was falling to pieces all around me.

For months Noa and I had been growing further and further apart. I was under a lot of financial stress; after I lost *Live To Dance* the funds we were relying on to complete the renovation on our Studio City home were just not there. On three separate occasions that year while I was paying not only the mortgage on the property but also colossal bills for completion of the pool or replacement of the roof, my bank account hit absolute zero. I was bone dry. We were now down to overdrawn credit cards to help us get by, but as we kept separate bank accounts I didn't want Noa to know. I begged my business manager to help me keep her from finding out that we were in such dire trouble, convinced that if she found out our marriage would be over.

As anyone who's gone through financial stress knows, pain and fear shoot out of you like Neo exploding out of Agent Smith at the end of *The Matrix*.[4] No matter how small the issue between you, the underlying fear of financial insecurity manifests in every word and action. On top of that, I was doing absolutely no work to find out the reasons that had been behind my drinking. I became awful to be around, with nothing but fear and jealousy underlying my every interaction with Noa, who understandably wanted to be around me less and less. I was clinging to a piece of broken furniture after the wreck of the *Titanic*, but instead of using it to help me float I was swinging it around, driving away not only my wife but every offer of work.

I was under so much stress that I was beginning to twitch and spasm uncontrollably. One day while getting dressed, I stood in front of the full-length mirror in the closet once I'd put all my clothes on, and staring back at me was a man with rounded shoulders, sunken eyes that seemed to be winking at two different people across the room at once and hands that were scratching imaginary itches all over my body. I was a wreck.

---

4   That's two *Matrix* references. You'll really have to see it now.

We began to fight almost all day, almost as if we were addicted to arguing, but the arguments repeated a script that was as predictable as it was sad, a script that was only altered by how much meaner I became.

Knowing I was on a clock that was ticking down, I decided to finally get serious about becoming sober emotionally as well as physically. Through someone I had met at a meeting I was introduced to a wonderful human being named David, the man who would become my mentor and guide me through those dark days and the months and years that followed. He set me to task on doing the real work of getting sober, but just as before, when I was asked to dig in the dirt to figure out where in my life I had hurt people, I balked and went back to circling in white-knuckled fear. Noa and I tried to find a therapist who would help us, but after the first meeting with her it was clearly evident that the intervention had come way too late. In December 2011 Noa asked me for a divorce.

I had believed that only Noa and I knew that there were problems between us, but I was clearly wrong. Six months before, a friend of mine, the LA-based Aussie entrepreneur Nick Bishop, had given me a key to his house in nearby Coldwater Canyon. He said, 'Just in case you ever need it, we have a spare room, we won't ask a thing, and I won't tell anyone you're there if they ask.' I was in such denial that I thought, 'Why in the hell would Nick give me a key to his house? Why does he think I'll need a place to stay? Sure, Noa and I have fights sometimes but we've got the perfect power-couple relationship. Everything is fine.'

After that appointment with the therapist I went back to our house in Studio City, got the key from my desk where I had put it six months before, and headed to Nick's. Luckily for me Nick had been the CEO of a massive LA advertising agency. He had not only mentored hundreds of employees through difficult times over the course of his career but he had been divorced himself, so he knew exactly what I was going through. Within hours of my hearing Noa say, 'I want a divorce', Nick sat me down at his dining-room table with an open exercise book, and got me to write down my thoughts about how to handle what my life would now be, and how not to make things any worse than they were.

That same day I called my mentor. When I told him what was happening, the first thing he told me to do was write down ten things to be grateful for. 'I don't think you heard me, mate. My wife wants a divorce! What the fuck do I have to be grateful for?' I said.

'Sounds like you might need to write down a list of twenty things. Did you swing two legs over the side of the bed this morning to stand up and get on with your day? There's plenty of guys down at the Veterans' Hospital who couldn't do that. That's one thing to be grateful for, and I'm sure you can come up with nineteen more,' he told me.

The other thing I did that day was to go to a fellowship meeting. Between Nick, my mentor and the meeting, after one of the worst days of my life, while I went to bed in emotional pain I was also full of gratitude that I had so many people willing and ready to help me.

It was also lucky that I was training for the 2012 LA marathon with Gidi Grinstein, an Israeli friend. Gidi runs a non-partisan policy institute that tries to provide solutions for the astonishingly complex political issues facing Israel. During the peace accords in the early 1990s he was the youngest person at the table. He is an inspiring man and he loves to run marathons. Because he had a young family, the only time Gidi could train for long runs was late on Sunday evenings, and the day after I found out my marriage was over I went for a sixteen-kilometre run with him. Each week on those runs, he counselled and guided me mentally through that horrible time.

Whatever else was happening in those early agonising days after my marriage ended, I would always do two things. I'd go for a long run and I'd go to a meeting. The run, with the release of all those endorphins, emptied my body of many of the physical manifestations of painful emotion, and the meeting helped me share the burden of what was happening in my head. Without both these things I'd have been in a lot of trouble.

I was doing pretty well until Noa needed to head back to Israel for a work trip right before Christmas (there is no Christmas break in Israel for obvious reasons). I had to move back into our home to look after the dog. Everything went to shit. My mind started to whirl in fear and agony. I was unable to sleep and at one point found myself walking around the house yelling at the walls. In the past when I had been overwhelmed with such emotion I would do everything I could to escape: I drank, I used, I shopped, I gambled, I masturbated. While there was definitely alcohol in the house, it was all I could do to not pick up. But now I knew that the only way out of these flames of fear was to walk through them.

This is where the power of the 12-Step fellowship came to the rescue. It was 23 December 2011. It was two days before Christmas and I was alone with the dog in the cold and empty house, going absolutely nuts. I'd learned in the program to call people before you do anything. I was initially very scared of strangers in meetings asking me for my phone number, but after a while I had realised how powerful communication could be. I'd put the numbers of everyone I'd met at a meeting in my phone with a keyword so I knew who they were. It was six in the morning LA time, way too early to start hitting up people on the west coast, so I started calling people I had met at meetings in New York: 'Hi, we met once at a meeting and you gave me your number. I really need to talk, is now an OK time?'

I'd typically tell them what was happening, and that I didn't know what to do next, but I did know enough to make a call instead of pick up a drink. They'd always respond with empathy and advice, making me feel that they had really listened. Then I'd ask if they were OK, and for a moment we shared the commonality of our struggle. I'd usually talk for about fifteen minutes until I settled down. By the end of the call, the knowledge that at least two of us were in this thing called life together made me feel OK enough to get off the phone.

But it wouldn't take long before my head would start to whirr again, and with a shaking hand I reached for my phone once more and called the next person on my list. I did this all day long. When it got late enough in the morning I started to call people from LA. When it got too late in LA I started to call Australia as the people there started to wake up.

When I first stopped drinking I was given this sage advice: 'You don't have to go the rest of your life not drinking, just the rest of today. All you have to do is get your head down on to the pillow tonight without taking a drink, and you've done this perfectly.'

By the time I got in bed at 10pm on that day I had called twenty-three different people, many a number of times. I couldn't tell you what some of them looked like, as I'd met several for only a few seconds after a meeting when I'd told them I enjoyed what they had shared, or vice versa. But I can tell you that every single person I talked to that day made time for me. Every single person made me feel that they understood the pain I was in, and helped me get through the day without taking a drink or worse. Relying on the support of others in times of intense crisis was new for me, and this was a time when reaching out literally saved my life.

I had learned from the fellowship about 'my own best thinking'. Until then the best ideas I had, the *very smartest thinking I could do* had left me divorced and with a career in tatters far away from home. I needed some new ways of doing things, because clearly my ideas weren't working out too well.

I called every guy I knew who had been through a divorce. Those back in Australia I asked, 'What did you do that worked? What helped you feel better?' and those in LA I asked to meet me for lunch. Within two days I had lined up a lunch every day of the following week with a different man who had been through what I was going through right now. In the words of my unofficial landlord, Nick Bishop, 'Divorce is a popular sport.' Again, everyone made time to talk to me, not just about the emotional issues but about the financial and legal ramifications – and how after a failed marriage, each and every one of them had rebuilt his life, to be a much bigger one than before. The advice and guidance I got from those men saved me from reacting in resentment and from making financial decisions based in anger, and helped me find purpose in going through the experience.

The most profound words came from Gazza, one of my poker mates. In his glorious Scottish accent he said, 'Mate, I know it's awful now, but you've got to picture your life at the moment like an old-school set of scales. Right now you're lowest of the low, you cannot get lower. But each day if you stay positive and do the right things you'll put a little weight on the other side of the scales, slowly, slowly, day by day, and then one day you'll be back to where you can feel happiness again. The day after that you'll be back in a place where you can feel happy, and from there it's a quick ride back to the top. Just make sure you remember to make each day a little better than yesterday – that's all you have to do.' My best ideas had fucked up my marriage, torpedoed my career and lost me my house. Once I started following other people's ideas, things started to get better.

Because I was training for the LA marathon, my daily run brought me great relief. If your brain is relatively healthy, you probably have most of the chemicals and hormones already within you to make you feel better – all you need to do is the physical action required to release them. I could be feeling like my life was over and I was another single, broke, divorced guy crashing in someone's guest room – but after two or three laps around the six-kilometre loop of the nearby UCLA campus I'd feel that my life was now full of possibility and opportunity.

It really was that simple.

There were also the fellowship meetings. At first I'd head to men-only gay meetings because Glen went to those and I was afraid to go alone. While the message was clear and helped me a lot, something was missing. I bumped around LA looking for a meeting where the people were more similar to me, and a few people suggested I check one out in a bar above a famous rock'n'roll club. A fellowship meeting *in* a bar? Well, I thought it couldn't hurt, so I went.

As I looked around that room I recognised some faces. I'd heard that LA had a strong celebrity sobriety scene, which just goes to show that addiction can come and get you no matter how rich and famous you might be. So when I looked from person to person I thought, 'Oh, I've interviewed you', or, 'I've got all of your albums', or, even, 'I've camped out to buy tickets to your show'. At that first meeting an older rock 'n' roller described walking offstage after a second encore with thousands of people screaming his name – and *still* he felt that it wasn't enough. I'd felt exactly like that. I wanted to know how he could now live his life, and how he found what made him feel what was 'enough'.

The meeting kicked off at noon every day of the week. I'd get there early to grab a seat, sometimes on the floor because that was all the space that was left. It was packed, and they were clearly *my* people. I hit that meeting every single day for months, I made some great friends and heard some inspirational stories. The most profound of which came from a tiny woman in her sixties who had come to Hollywood chasing fame in her late teens and spiralled into a vortex of pills and sex and parties that lasted decades. While I was never an underage go-go dancer in Las Vegas, the way she talked about how the world felt to her, the way she described her emotions when dealing with love and intimacy and connection to others – she was telling my story word for word. It was as if she was speaking for me, but with a lazy southern drawl and a larynx that sounded as if fifty years of cigarettes and booze had crossed over it.

Going to the meetings was one thing, but in order to deliver me from the pain of what my life had become, I needed to do the work. They're not called 'steps' for nothing, and taking those steps was vital in the healing process. If you want anything to change in your life – it requires action. Sometimes, the only way out of the flames is through them.

Like many people in the fellowship I had taken a few tentative steps – admitting I was powerless, understanding that something bigger than myself was needed to free me from the control of that power, and trusting that the universe would deliver me the life I was meant to live, if only I let go of constantly trying to control everything. However, I had stopped short of the real work, the searching and fearless moral inventory of myself that would turn up the 'why' behind the drinking and behaviour that had destroyed my marriage, my career and my relationships with others.

Every day, sometimes many times a day, I spoke with my mentor. I put my best ideas to one side and just did what he told me to do. I had to remember that my very best ideas had landed me divorced and with a career barely hanging by a thread, so instead I needed to listen to the ideas of someone who had a healthier view of what was right. Of course my ego didn't want to be told what to do in the slightest and resisted the humility being thrust upon me, but I just had to let that ego have a violent tantrum in the corner while I got about changing who I was as a person.

Every day I made time to sit down, pencil in hand and just do the work. Of course it was confronting, but I knew with all my heart that I never wanted to put myself or another person through what had just happened ever again – and imagining that possibility was more confronting than putting pencil to paper and beginning the rigorous introspection, so I just pushed on. I asked myself tough questions, and tried as hard as I could to fearlessly be accountable to myself and my mentor as to what motivated me as a person to behave the way I'd behaved. Over the course of the weeks and months that followed, I did the work to not only figure out 'why' it was that

I drank the way I did, but how that would show up in every other part of my life. As I looked back at those pages, I clearly saw all the ways I had become a person who had ended up in this situation. I became willing to let go of all those forms of behaviour, and then set about learning how to catch them whenever they showed up – and quickly admit when I was wrong and try my best to make things right where I could. I wasn't perfect, but I was making progress.

Through the course of following those steps and deliberately living them from day to day, I was given an incredible gift. I was slowly able to change who I was as a person. I was able to change how I felt about the world, and how I treated other people. I got the chance to live the rest of my life not being the guy that did the kind of things I had done. As my mentor told me, I now got 'the chance to not be that guy anymore'. And that was a better feeling than any beer could ever give me.

The daily work I did with my mentor was so important in those weeks and months – as was the work that I did for my job. *The Hot Hits Live From LA* was still doing OK, we weren't killing the ratings but we weren't getting cancelled, and that was enough. Every week I got to make radio with one of the sweetest, kindest and most professional humans I've ever met – Natalia Perez. Like me, she had got into radio through the street team and then started to make herself indispensable around the station, at LA's world-famous KIIS FM. Natalia's compassion and love of her work were like standing in the sunny spot in a cold room – she brought warmth and love and kindness to every day I worked with her. She helped guide me through that difficult year just as much as anyone. I loved to work with her, but unfortunately it wouldn't be for much longer.

hi, i'm osher

As you know, for most of my life I have never been known by my given name. I had barely escaped the lingering teenage nicknames when the professional ones arrived. There had been the 1990s FM radio nickname of 'Spidey' which stuck with me for four long years of midnight to dawn radio, and it always felt strange. Then I was 'Andrew G' all through Channel [v] and through six seasons of *Australian Idol*.

On one of my journeys to Israel I had met with a revered shaman in Tel Aviv. He told me about the power of a name, and how what we call ourselves affects our lives. He had a vocabulary of about a hundred words of English and had known me for around two minutes before he asked me my name, my mother's name, my birthday, place of birth and time of birth. Once I told him these things he hoisted many weighty tomes of star charts, calendars, and planetary atlases onto his large table and opened them. All I could make out were columns and columns of numbers and coordinates. Then in his limited English he proceeded to tell me in astonishing detail exactly what kind of person I had been on every birthday, what friends I had, how long they had been in my life, times when I fell in love, out of love, how I lived, my fears and joys, the times I had nearly died. It was incredible. I'm the son of two doctors and I was brought up to believe that if there's evidence, something is to be believed. Though I have a healthy streak of cynicism, when this total stranger described me in such amazing detail I was listening to what else he had to say.

He explained that the path I was on led to darkness and possibly grave illness, but seeing the expression on my face he assured me I could avoid this. 'Change the energy around your name, you will change your life, and change your path,' he said.

I chose the name of the coolest man I've ever met. He was an ex-commando cameraman I'd worked with in Israel, a guy with a body and a jaw straight out of a Calvin Klein ad, so cool he made Brando look like a hobo. His name was Osher. When I told him I thought that was a cool name, he replied: 'You know what it means in Hebrew? Happiness.' He then took a long drag on a cigarette, winked and strode off to effortlessly direct an incredibly complex shoot we were working on.

So that's what I went with. I didn't have to tell anyone this was now my name – I just had to know it was. That's who I was in my head. I was still calling myself 'Andrew Günsberg', and gradually I started signing emails with 'Osher'.

So a few years later, on my thirty-eighth birthday, fresh from divorce and looking for answers – when I needed a reboot so very badly – I did two very important things, and they both happened at around 10,000 feet above sea level. I was in Vail, Colorado, with my poker mate Jaxon, who had dragged me out to the mountains to try and perk me up. After thirteen years I was a bit bored with snowboarding so I went and rented some skis.

I carefully clipped them on and climbed aboard the chairlift. I don't know if it was the mountain air, or my brain remembering how to ski again for the first time since I was a teenager, but I went up the mountain that day a snowboarder named Andrew, and came down the mountain a skier named Osher. Simple as that. I felt I was shedding my old skin and my new name meant that I was a completely new incarnation of myself.

From that moment on, I introduced myself as 'Osher' to everyone I met. The change in my life was remarkable. So much of who I am now as a man didn't exist before that day. I barely recognise the way I used to operate. With a new name comes an entirely new experience of life, and finally I feel I have ownership of who I am and what people call me. I am not someone else's nickname. I am my own.

I started to use the name on *Hot Hits Live From LA*, and slowly began to integrate it into the TV interviews I was then recording for the national nightly news show *The Project*. In marketing that's known as a 'soft launch'. The real aggressive rebranding phase had yet to happen, but I had a few career moves yet to make before I got to that point, and not all of them in the 'up' direction.

I believed on one level that during my whole career the universe had been paying attention. When I put it out there that I'd like to interview the Beastie Boys on Channel [v], the universe provided. When I wanted to create a job in LA for Australia that would help me stay in America so I could explore a relationship with Noa and chase a career there, the universe provided. When we were renovating the house in LA and colossal invoices would drain my bank account dry, within twelve hours a job would appear out of the blue, and the fee was the *exact* figure that I needed to pay those invoices.[1] I don't

---

1 That happened twice, once with a huge telco campaign I was a part of and another time with an in-cinema interview show that I did. It was uncanny. I couldn't enjoy the income of course, it went straight to building a pool or fixing a roof or something like that.

know what I did, but something somewhere was looking out for me. So the next thing that the universe did really sent me sideways.

It was closing in on December 2012 and my contract for *Hot Hits Live From LA* hadn't been renewed. Radio contracts are normally rolled over by October or even earlier, to lock the talent down for the coming year. The radio company were delaying, and I thought that I'd push things along by getting a solid answer from the universe.

After the divorce settlement, which we worked out amicably in felt pen on the back of a bakery bag that I then photographed and sent to the lawyers, I had a little bit of money left over. It was just enough for a deposit on a house. So I put some money down to buy a modest studio apartment on Electric Avenue in Venice, just off Abbot Kinney Boulevard. I signed all the paperwork and had everything stamped on a Wednesday and headed to NY for a film junket the next day.

Now my chips were on the table, the universe knew what was at stake. My manager Mark Morrissey and I decided to find out what had happened about the *Hot Hits Live From LA* contract, so he gave the company a call. Their answer wasn't the one I wanted to hear. Between the radio network and MCM they had decided to 'explore a new direction', to fire me and hire a talented young Australian broadcaster, Maude Garrett.

In the past, rivers of resentment would have flooded into my brain, I would have acted out in anger and pain and probably made some calls and done some things to hurt a lot of people. I won't lie – I had that feeling for about the space of a breath. But in sobriety I had learned to perform something called 'contrary action', a form of cognitive behaviour therapy in which you try to catch yourself just as you're about to repeat the old and damaging behaviour and force yourself to do the opposite.

I'd learned to put the words 'of course' in front of every problem I felt horrible about, every bad thing I felt had been done *to* me. It helped me see my role in the situation and in a strange way flipped me out of victim mode and into a place where I felt empowered. Take the statement, 'My wife wants a divorce'. It's open to victimhood, blaming another for the problem. It's a powerless statement. But saying, 'Of course my wife wants a divorce', leaves the way open to exploring *why* it's happening, looking at one's own role in it and, better yet, seeing the possibility of change.

So when I heard the news I took a long breath and said to Mark, 'Of course they're hiring Maude Garrett. She's ten years younger and she speaks more directly to the demographic. Why would they want a sad, divorced thirty-eight-year-old man talking to their teenage audience about happy Justin Bieber songs? It makes sense. Good for her.' I meant every single word from the bottom of my heart.

I hung up the phone feeling shaken but OK. My next call was to my business manager to cancel the purchase of the apartment, my question to the universe having been answered rather robustly. I'd learned that mood follows action, so I went out for a sunset run along the Westside Highway and then hit a meeting in mid-town Manhattan. Later that evening an email pinged into my inbox. It was Michael Cordell, the executive producer of *Bondi Rescue*, a documentary series about the lifeguards on Bondi Beach that I'd narrated since the show's inception in 2005. He explained that in pitching the show for the following year the network wanted to explore a first-person format, similar to other observational reality shows. This meant that the stories would no longer be told by a narrator, but through master interviews with the lifeguards themselves. He wanted me to be the first to know.

I leaned back in the hotel room chair and contemplated what had just happened. I'd lost my last two jobs in the same day. I was now unemployed, divorced and a long way from home.

I called my mentor. 'David, I just lost my last two jobs in one day. I'm unemployed.'

'I'm excited for you, pal,' he said. 'Looks like the universe has bigger plans for you than what you were doing.'

I was furious. 'Mate, I don't think you understand – *I just lost my job*. The one that pays my bills. I'm unemployed, I'm now going to be paying rent out of my savings, I'm just another divorced loser whose life has ended up in the toilet.'

He responded, 'No, I heard you the first time, and I need you to understand that I am actually excited for you. You're not doing anything and that means that you can do *anything*. I believe the universe wouldn't have taken those two jobs away from you on the same day if it didn't have something way bigger lined up for you, pal.'

David's military-precise redirection of my self-centred misery was incredible. He stopped me from falling down into what's called a 'pity party', helped me keep my chin up and see this as a positive. I used the trick I'd used earlier: 'Of course they've gone in another direction. Every show needs to freshen up to stay relevant to the audience. I'm glad they got commissioned for another season even if it means I don't get to be a part of it. I've loved every moment I worked with that team and I'm proud of being even a small part of the success of the show.' It helped.

My business manager Jeff and I figured out how long I'd have on my current level of expenditure before the money ran out and I'd have to pull the parachute and head back to Australia. If I stuck to a budget with the money Jeff had saved up I could probably last eighteen months, as long as I flew one way and in the back of the plane when I finally raised the white flag of defeat. Had it been up to me I'd have spent that money the moment it hit my account. If it hadn't been for Jeff, who knew how to manage clients that worked in a seasonal industry, my apartment full of stuff would have been left in a pile on the street and I'd have been on QF12 back to Sydney that night.

So here I was, divorced, unemployed and paying my rent out of my savings while living in a foreign country. I did my best not to explode in panic, and I tried to keep to a routine. I ran ten kilometres every morning, hit a fellowship meeting every night and spent my days just trying to figure out what to do next. The running intensified and within a few months, I was running a half marathon on trails every Saturday just because I could.[2]

David's words echoed in my head: Because I wasn't doing anything, I could now do *anything*. My next job didn't even have to be in TV or radio if I didn't want it to be. I did my very best to remain open to any and all possibilities. At one point I thought I might do an MBA, inspired by the conscious capitalism happening in the start-up scene, and wanting to be more skilled if I decided to do something about it. I'd given myself about six weeks to think before I had to go out and get a regular job, and in the middle of that time I got a call from a

---

2   Where I ran was a trail that was used to service a former Nike missile site that
     formed part of the US's air-defence network back in the 1960s. If you're ever in LA,
     it's an absolutely brilliant run. You can't believe you're in a city of more than twenty
     million people up there.

mate called Dan Lack. He ran a small-scale conference called Meeting of the Big Minds at his ranch in Texas and suggested that I take part. It was limited to ten people, each brought there for the ability to help other members of the group, a super-concentrated networking event. There were only two media people on the conference, the others were social entrepreneurs.

I convinced Jeff that it was a good idea for me to pay the money and go, and soon enough I was on a plane to Houston. Besides buying fancy cowboy hats and shooting revolvers at beer cans on tree stumps (not a bad way to redefine a relationship with beer), I met people on that conference whose influence was life-changing. Someone told me about the THNK School of Creative Leadership in Amsterdam, which offered an eighteen-month course in creative leadership, teaching design thinking and problem-solving. This was more achievable and affordable than the full-length MBA courses I had been considering. I also met the power couple screenwriter Kiran Ramchandran and author Mei Mei Fox. They encouraged me to put all my skills into TV format development. Both of them had been where I was, and they told me the only way out of this kind of unemployment is to create the next job you are going to do. There wouldn't be a knock at the door offering me a three-year prime-time network hosting job. I had to create the show that would bring me that gig myself.

Back in LA I went down to an office supply store where I bought two huge whiteboards and all the colourful pens.[3] I started to create a show based on my recent experiences of online dating. The last time I'd been single there had been no

3   My former EP from *Australian Idol* Greg Beness once famously told me, 'If you have a whiteboard, you can make a television show.' At the time I didn't understand because I thought you needed things like a studio and cameras, but now it was all beginning to make sense.

cameras on phones, no Facebook and certainly no Tinder. Yet I had been finding myself swiping left and right on my couch every night, only to go out on a date with someone whose photographs had been taken five years and fifteen kilograms ago, or a woman in a relationship with her boyfriend (or even husband) who was clearly lining up the next relationship to jump into.

So I created an in-studio dating show that asked a contestant, man or woman, to pick the answers on a standard dating website quiz that lined up with those given by a panel of beautiful men or women. I called the show *The Real Deal.* I was creating a show I could host and have a ton of fun with, but also one that explored the difference between what we *wish* to be true in the people we find most attractive and what is actually true. As I was soon heading down to Australia for my cousin's wedding, I asked my manager in Sydney to line up some meetings where I could pitch the show around the various networks while I was there. The first meeting I took was at Network Ten. They had always been so good to me and we had a great relationship, so I pitched my heart out.

They bought the show in the room. I was now in development on a show I was not only going to host but had created. If Kiran and Mei Mei hadn't told me I could do that I wouldn't have thought I was allowed to. All I had needed was permission to behave.

I headed back to LA and began development of the show in earnest. I was working with a small team of development producers and the aim was to mould my original pitch into a living, breathing TV show. We had weekly sessions where we tried to work the format I'd pitched into something that would last for years. It was tough for me, as I was trying to stick to the simple and fun 5pm dating show I had originally conceived, yet the team were trying to throw in elements of other successful shows. When you are the creator and executive producer of a format, part of the job is to make sure the core idea of the show stays true. The process was more difficult than I had thought. Regardless, the message I was sending out to the universe was that I was prepared to go back to Australia to shoot a show about dating, a show I could shoot in less than three months.

Not four weeks into the development process, Mark Morrissey called me late one night. 'How would you like to come down to Australia to host *The Bachelor*? Stephen Tate wants you to screen test for it via satellite this week.' At the time, *The Bachelor* was undeniable in the US market. An absolute juggernaut of ratings success, it had created multiple spin-off series which included *The Bachelorette* and *Bachelor Pad* (which would later become *Bachelor in Paradise*). The show claimed multiple weddings, babies and breakups, and the stars of the shows were on every magazine cover and *Dancing With the Stars* episode.

While I had been pitching an untested format into the narrow-margined Australian market, Ten had secured an absolute certain ratings winner. It's like me pitching a custom-made burger stand to Westfield and then seeing them buying a franchise of McDonald's because it's worked so well elsewhere. It was no contest. It was six months since my broadcasting career had come to a crashing halt, and to be wanted again – certainly by Ten, the network I knew so well – was a nice feeling. 'When do they need me in the booth?' I asked.

I wore the only suit that still fitted me (the daily running had me slimmer than usual) and headed off to the studio where the satellite link was going to take place. The screen test went off without a hitch, and Mark called me the next day with good news. I'd be heading down to Australia in July 2013 for a ten-week shoot for season one of *The Bachelor Australia*. It would be my first time back on TV since *Idol*, and my first time back on TV since I'd changed my name.

I got on the plane back to Australia for the job, and I won't lie – it felt nice to turn left.[4] The 40,000ft drinking binges were behind me, but I still made sure I told the cabin manager to please make sure no one offered me alcohol. I wasn't going to drink any, but it was still nice to not have to constantly make the decision not to.[5]

---

4 Turning right means you're down the back of the plane in economy. Turning left means you're up the front in business class.

5 Same goes for minibars in hotel rooms. Whenever I check in to a hotel I ask for the alcohol to be removed, or if it's super late at night I just take it all out and hide it somewhere in the room so I don't have to look at it. Don't do this in a room which has those systems that charge you for the minibar item if you simply *move* it; you'll have some explaining to do.

twenty-one
back in the saddle

To be returning to Australia to work on a format that had seen spectacular success in other markets was incredibly exciting. Some people don't get seven episodes into their TV careers before they get cancelled. *Australian Idol* had run for seven seasons. I had already enjoyed the most terrific TV and radio career anyone could want and here I was about to get another shot at the title. I was determined to approach *The Bachelor Australia* as I'd approached *Live To Dance*: simply to be the most professional person any of the crew had ever worked with. While I'm sure there were some days when I didn't achieve that goal, I tried my absolute hardest to be the very best person they could possibly have hired for the job.

Working on *The Bachelor Australia* was very different to working on *Australian Idol*. I'd not done much pre-recorded television before, as my only experience had been live TV. When it's live you rehearse and rehearse until everything is burned into your muscle memory and when the red light goes on and you're live it's like a ski run through the moguls all the way to the bottom. Hopefully being live brings out the magic in the moments and you don't make too many mistakes. If you've rehearsed enough there's more magic than mistakes, and afterwards you all pat each other on the back and look forward to getting closer to zero mistakes next time. When it's pre-recorded, we'd shoot it and cut it all together later. It was nice to have the challenge of learning some new skills, but I was grateful to have thousands of hours of live experience because when it came to capturing the emotional reactions of our cast members (which is ultimately what we were there to do), you could only tell someone the big news once. While we weren't live I really had to get that right first time every time.

With humility and gratitude, I approached that first season of *The Bachelor Australia*. I had been given a gift of yet another massive franchise, and if we all did our job well we just might get to ride this one for a few years.

It was when I was in Sydney to shoot that first season of *Bach* that I finally decided to start my podcast.

I'd been in LA during the explosion of podcast content in the early 2010s, and seen the dramatic rise in independent digital broadcasting. Radio was still in my blood, but the kind of radio I wanted to do wasn't available to me. In fact, podcasters were making shows that you'd never hear on any kind of radio station ever. They were reimagining the format of spoken audio entertainment in ways hitherto unheard of, and I wanted to be a part of it.

I'd had a few dry runs in LA, interviewing Natasha Kufa, Dan MacPherson and the Australian actor Grant Bowler. With Grant's interview I even shot a Polaroid portrait of him as a way of capturing him on that very day in two different ways. This is the format I wanted to go with – a long form interview and a portrait shoot – but I just hadn't had the balls to pull the trigger.

When I got back to Sydney to do *The Bachelor Australia*, I wanted to start a podcast so badly I thought I would burst, but

I just couldn't make the first move. I was frozen in inaction. That's when I remembered some of the wisest words ever spoken to me. I'd once had the good fortune to have a drink with Bob Lapointe, the man who brought KFC, Pizza Hut and Sizzler to Australia. This man is one of Australia's most successful businessmen and has had astonishing success in the horse-racing industry. I asked him what one of his golden rules was and he simply crooned in his glorious Canadian accent, 'Whatever problems you think you'll encounter, problems that you think will be so big that there's no point even starting your business – those problems are never as big as the problems you actually encounter. So just start the damn thing.' So with Bob's sage advice on board I decided just to go for it.

One evening while accompanying my standup comic friend Luke Heggie from club to club in Sydney while he was working out new material, I bumped into another great Aussie standup, Scott Dooley. We got to chatting and when I felt enough confidence I just asked him straight out, 'Hey, how would you feel about coming on my podcast next week?'

'Yeah, I'd love that,' he said. 'Tuesday's good for me.'

Scott didn't know that I did not have a podcast. I also did not have microphones or a sound card and I did not know how to edit nor even publish a podcast. None of that mattered. Scott was coming around on Tuesday and I had to learn it all before then. The following morning I went out and bought a pair of microphones and a sound card and spent the day learning how to put a podcast on the internet before I headed off to count roses for the night. Dools was the first of now more than 230 people I have interviewed for my show which I publish every Monday. It's the radio show I always wanted to make, and it has brought me more opportunities than I could possibly count. The book you are reading is being published because of a chain of events and connections that led directly back to one particular podcast episode recorded during those first ten weeks of shooting *The Bachelor Australia*.

I was single and starting to take my first steps back into the world of dating. Dating on meds, however, is quite difficult. Many of the bonding receptors in my brain were dulled down so I'd often go out on dates with wonderful women but feel absolutely nothing. It wasn't fair on either of us. In Sydney I asked Dr Chung about coming off my meds for a while. I'd been doing really well and was interested to see how I'd cope with life now I was sober and working a program.[1] He agreed. It was a tricky start, like going from that nice and smooth part of the freeway straight to gravel, and at speed. The sharp edges of the world had been blunted for so long that it took me a while to adjust to the new, higher volume of life. I'm happy to report that sex off meds and completely sober was actually pretty incredible. Being able to connect with a lover without a haze of alcohol or pharmaceuticals was just wonderful.

The Bachelor Australia launched to great acclaim and the network had a hit on their hands.[2] I headed back to LA, and it was nice to land with some heat behind me. In a seasonal job like mine you just don't know if your show is going to get picked up again, so you're constantly dividing your time:

---

1 Sobriety fellowship talk for 'doing the work to stay sober'.
2 To be honest, you really never know if something's going to work or not. You do your best, everyone on the set loves it, and when you go live with it, something about it just doesn't click, or you're up against a monster hit show on another channel. You just have to try and do your own job as best you can and hope that it sticks.

50 per cent on the current project, 30 per cent on hunting down the next one and 20 per cent on building the one in five years from now.

With development on my dating show halted (fair enough too, why would Ten want two dating shows?) I began creating the next show, and the next.

Unlike when I first landed in LA where I was effectively trying to hide, in sobriety I went out of my way to nurture work relationships. When I started reaching out to people to pitch shows they said 'yes' to the meeting. That's the thing about LA. Success is a tradable currency, but so is the *potential* of success. Everyone wants to hear the idea that will go ten, twenty or even a hundred times bigger. So even though producers are super-busy making their massive network shows they are always on the lookout for the show that will run when their current one ends. In the words of my great LA manager John Ferriter, 'The only show that has never been cancelled is the news. You need to be ready for the day your incredibly successful show isn't picked back up for another season.'

Now I was back in LA, I had to do something else to keep my head busy. When you stop drinking, you've got to find something else to do with the time that you used to spend drinking. Inspired by Dan MacPherson, I'd bought my first proper road bike and added cycling to my head-cleaning exercise regimen. I was single, and worked my own schedule so I'd get two to three hours of riding done most mornings, just climbing up and down the Santa Monica mountains. It was during this time that I met the incredible vegan ultra-athlete Rich Roll who would sometimes kindly slow down to a crawl so I could run alongside him in Malibu Creek State Park, or as we climbed bicycles up the impossibly steep parts of Mulholland Drive. For me, part of staying sober was to have sober heroes. People who lived a life I wanted my life to look like. Rich is one of those people. He showed me the secret trails of those hills and I spent many hours running solo through the mountains, just me and the forest. There's not many men on this earth as fit or as wise as Rich, and having the honour of being able to talk to him about whatever was going on in my head as we ran and rode was truly a privilege.

Being off meds meant that the weight was really starting to drop off. I felt as fit as I'd ever been, and with a regimen of weekly psychologist appointments and daily meetings I was trying to keep my head fit as well. Not knowing whether *The Bachelor Australia* would continue, I finally enrolled in the THNK School of Creative Leadership in Amsterdam. I'd need to be in the Netherlands for the first part of the course in February, which coincided nicely with a TV gig I'd picked up in Israel. They wanted me to come out there and shoot a pilot for a new big-money TV game show that was hoping to challenge *Who Wants To Be A Millionaire*. While it would be a little strange heading back to Israel for the first time since the divorce, I was looking forward to seeing old friends.

Meanwhile back in Australia, things had started to turn a corner. Off the back of *The Bachelor Australia* I'd been asked to host the 2013 ARIA Awards.[3] It was a job I'd dreamed of doing for years. When you're on a roll things move quickly – a breakfast radio gig showed up at NOVA in Sydney, three weeks on air filling in for Fitzy and Wippa with the delightful Rachael Finch. I was trying as hard as I could to do my very, very best on those jobs. I'd been given a second chance at life

---

3   The ARIAS is our version of the Grammys, but with fewer twenty-minute long
      performances from baby boomer bands like The Eagles.

and I was not going to do the heart-bypass-patient-going-back-to-eating-burgers routine. It was with as much humility as I could muster that I took those jobs and worked hard to give them my best, and I'm grateful they came my way.

I spent the week of New Year's Eve of 2014 with friends in Miami and had a torrid holiday romance with an Argentinian DJ who was also there on holiday. Romances like these burn very brightly for a few days while you're together, and when everything's done you kiss and you're glad it happened rather than being sad it is over. However, once we both got home, we began to reach out to each other again – there was something more there than '*bienvenido a Miami*'. So we organised that the following week she'd fly over from Miami when her holiday ended and instead of heading back to Buenos Aires she would come to LA to hang with me for two weeks.

It's fair to say that when I was off meds that time, my ability to regulate the ups and downs of my emotions was quite limited. My only reactions were all the way up to eleven in either direction.[4] Understandably, this became too much for anyone else to bear. My affections were nothing short of smothering, and when things didn't go my way I essentially threw temper tantrums. Instead of just enjoying a relaxing few weeks exploring the early stages of a relationship with this talented woman I mashed the relationship accelerator to the floor and it felt like I was essentially driving a truck through a school zone at 100 kilometres an hour. I had yet to have a functional relationship in sobriety. I had no idea how I was supposed to behave or indeed what it felt like to fall in love when your brain

---

4   I'm referring to guitar legend Nigel Tufnell who famously had a custom-made Marshall amp that didn't just go up to 10, it went all the way to 11. It was one louder. There was a 'rockumentary' made about his band, Spinal Tap, which I thoroughly recommend you check out.

isn't pickled with booze. Only later did I figure out that I wasn't falling in love with this woman, I was falling into obsession. I also started to learn that my ability to know when people are upset was quite compromised. I struggled to recognise other people's emotions. I would have to wait until things burst before realising that I had been in the wrong and had hurt someone else – but by then it's too late, isn't it?

The two weeks was up and she headed back to South America. I was broken. I had had such high hopes for what might have been – but she understandably didn't want a part of it. When you think about how a sober Australian living in LA could possibly start a relationship with a DJ who played 'dark house' in nightclubs that *open* at 5am half a world away – it doesn't really make sense, does it?

After she left, I moped around the house for days before I decided to straighten things out, as we'd played around shooting some photos for her next flyer in my living room and the furniture was all over the place.

As I cleaned up I started to find notes and gifts all over the apartment. She had left them there on the last day while I was out for a run. The come here/go away nature of it all was very confusing. I called her and she told me she missed me and it might be nice if I came down to Buenos Aires in a few weeks so we could be together.

I hit the gas again. Within ninety minutes I'd booked a flight, booked hotels for us, booked day trips, all kinds of things – all of them on special on non-refundable travel deal websites, of course. I called her the next day with the exciting news but she was furious that I was coming down and had booked the trip without talking to her. A day later a WhatsApp text would ping on my phone: 'I miss you.'

I was very confused, and the stress was starting to mount up. Coming off meds is a big move for anyone who has shown they need them to live a mostly normal life. For me, it was a case of weighing up benefits versus side effects. Sure I wasn't waking up in crippling anxiety every morning, but nothing was exciting any more. Food tasted bland. The world and everything in it had gone grey. Even the giggle of a small child passed through my brain without even touching the sides. Is that living? Is that what it is to be human? Just a lump of meat walking around eating and shitting and doing a task for money so you can buy more things to eat and then shit out later?

I wanted *so very much* to get by without meds that I was enduring a state of mind that was rapidly becoming worse and worse, but I just gritted my teeth and tried to cope because I *didn't want to give in.* Red flags sailed past me like I was on the giant slalom of anxiety heading straight down. I was lucky to get four or five hours of fitful sleep a night. Every day I'd make my bed and have to put at least two corners of the elasticised fitted sheet back under the mattress because I'd thrashed around so much in my sleep that I was stripping the bed while I was still in it. I kept running trying to make things better but the effects of the run would last a little less than an hour and soon I'd be shouting at the walls again.

The stressors kept piling up. The come here/go away situation from the woman in Buenos Aires kept dragging on, turning my unhealthy obsession on and off like a strobe light. On top of this the network hadn't yet ordered a second series of *The Bachelor Australia* so I was technically unemployed again and paying rent out of my savings in a foreign country. I was gearing up for the big-budget pilot shoot back in Israel, a trip to visit mates in the UK and the first week of school at THNK in Amsterdam. There were swirling fears about the strangers I would meet on the first day and more fears about being back in Israel for the first time since my divorce.

That's when my father got very sick. In a behavioural pattern not atypical for doctors, he had lived a life contrary to the advice he'd spend his career giving out. He drank and smoked and ate almost nothing but stinky meats and cheeses. His lifestyle choices had put him into hospital back in Brisbane. His lungs were failing him, and when one collapsed and he required surgery, the fact that his 'healthy' lung looked more like a wet and deflated balloon meant that the surgery to help him was very high-risk. My brother called to let me know he was in ICU and I should keep a bag packed in case I needed to make a mercy dash back to Australia. So I did.

twenty-two
into the darkness

The next day I woke up as I always did – in a fit of fear around 5am. I'd stopped setting an alarm because it no longer mattered whether I did or not. The moment I reached the peak of a REM cycle I'd be awake and flooded with adrenaline. I lay in bed trying to calm myself in vain for about an hour before wandering out of the bedroom around 6am. It was 21 February 2014.

I made coffee as I did every morning, and then sat down to read the *New York Times* on my iPad as usual. I leafed through the articles and checked the weather. Over the years I'd paid close attention to scientists' warnings about climate change and government policy solutions. Next to the weather report the *New York Times* wrote 'this last month is the 145th consecutive warmest month on record', a way of reminding us all that yes, the world was warming up.

At that very moment something in my brain burst open and pure, white-hot fear came pouring out. Thoughts and fears cascaded faster and faster and I was completely unable to stop them. In that moment I was certain that Greenland, both polar icecaps and all the glaciers in the world were definitely going to melt. The cataclysmic climate projections would make most of the planet uninhabitable. Oceans would rise, every society on earth would crumble as agriculture, food storage, power and transportation came to a halt because it was too hot to grow anything, or every piece of vital infrastructure was now covered in fifteen metres of stormy seawater. I was certain that civil order would break down at any moment as everyone in LA realised what was inevitable. It felt as if all of those things were going to happen today, and that if people were smart they'd start getting ready for doomsday as soon as possible. The most terrifying thing about this was that I felt as if *I was the only person who knew or cared.*

It was a long time before I could get up from the table. I was aware that I was in the most intense panic and anxiety episode I'd ever had, and I knew that all I could do was to go for a run. My daily run was down to the Santa Monica pier and back, a quick and easy ten kilometres to get the gremlins out of my head so I could get on with my day.

However, I wasn't far down the jogging path when I knew that something was very, very wrong. I looked up at the palm trees swaying in the gentle ocean breeze high above me. Instead of seeing a picture-perfect palm tree against the blue California sky I saw the crown of the tree like a perverse water lily, now resting on what was the new sea level some fifteen metres above me. Everywhere I looked I saw waves crashing over the houses and relentlessly destroying everything. I saw the famous *Baywatch* lifeguard towers floating at strange angles as they drifted against their concrete moorings with the water level high above them. I don't know if these things were hallucinations, but they were pretty real to me. My brain started to tie every single piece of auditory and visual input back to my terrifying fear.

As I crossed a driveway, an older-model Mercedes idled as its owner chatted to her neighbour. It was all I could do not to run straight to her, reach in and turn her key to shut the engine off. Didn't she know that her emissions were sending us all careening towards a terrifying end? Wasn't she aware that her car was pumping CO_2 into the atmosphere so fast that polar bears were drowning for the first time in history because they'd run out of ice floes to swim between?

I kept running, only to see two more ladies out for a walk, both holding disposable coffee cups. I wanted to shout at them. Didn't they know that those aren't really recyclable? Did they realise how many trees had died so that they could use that piece of cardboard for less than five minutes? Did they not care that the carbon footprint required to pick, roast and transport their fancy single-origin coffee beans from across the world was utterly unsustainable?

I had once sat under a waterfall in Litchfield National Park in the Northern Territory. It was a spiritual experience to feel thousands of litres of water cascade over my body, water that had travelled hundreds of kilometres and would travel hundreds more before it lay still. The energy of that falling water transferring into my body had elated me, making me feel closer to nature than I had felt before or since. This was exactly the same, except I was trapped under that waterfall, and the energy I was absorbing was full of horror and doom.

No matter how hard I ran, the roar of the fear drowned everything out. My plan had been to run five kilometres and then turn around, but the next thing I saw had me running back home. A young father, probably in his mid-twenties, was proudly walking down the path with a sleeping newborn baby strapped to his chest in a BabyBjörn. He was smiling, enjoying the perfect late winter's day and occasionally looking down at his slumbering child as if this was the best moment he'd ever had as a father. It was all I could do not to run up to him, grab him by the shoulders and scream in his face, '*What the fuck are you doing?* Why would you bring life into a world that is going to be on fire, underwater and at war over resources all at the same time? What were you thinking?' Luckily for us both I stopped before I got to him.

I knew I had to get home, and fast. My thoughts started to physically hurt, and just like being flicked on the ear by a bully as a kid, I'd flinch as I felt each thought pierce my body. It wasn't just a thought, though. I felt actual physical pain, as if I were being injured, my brain unable to differentiate between what was real and what was imagined. In an effort to stop the pain I began to swat the air as if I was being attacked by a swarm of sandflies at sunset. I also started to grunt or inhale sharply through gritted teeth as each painful thought hit me.

Rounding the final corner home I noticed a man shuffling along the path ahead of me, shirtless and wearing pants a few sizes too big for him. A member of Venice Beach's large homeless population, he looked absolutely filthy. He had recently wet himself and a bloom of urine spread up the back of his pants and down to his knees. As I came to overtake him, I saw that he had a strange rectangle shaved into the side of his otherwise unkempt hair. As I got a close look at him, two things chilled me to my core. He was younger than I was, maybe in his late twenties, with the stink that only living with mental illness on the street can give you. And as he shuffled, he was also grunting, swatting and flinching. We were doing exactly the same thing. I don't know whether he knew something was wrong but I knew that something was malfunctioning in my brain and I needed help, fast.

The moment I got in my front door I called my mentor David. He was a professional drug and alcohol counsellor, and an expert in dealing with dual-diagnosis cases like me.[1] I don't think I drew breath for about three minutes as my torrent of words full of fear flowed down the phone line. The moment I stopped to breathe he simply said, 'You need to get some professional help, and fast. Can you call your therapist?' But my therapist couldn't see me until after the weekend so I called my doctor back in Sydney. He said I needed to find a doctor as soon as possible, but not to turn up to the emergency ward at the hospital – I might get involuntarily committed and I'd have a terrible time trying to get myself out.

The problem was that by now it was Friday afternoon and I was flying to Vail, Colorado, for a ski weekend with a friend in a few short hours. So I gave up and caught the plane. As we took off, I looked down at the oil refineries just south of LA and saw the complicated towers and tanks being smashed about like toothpicks from giant waves, the oil spilling mercilessly out into the ocean.

As my friends and I drove up to Vail from Denver airport we started to pass empty, snowy hills on the way to the mountains – and all I could think of was that soon this would be brown and barren desert with piles upon piles of houses clambering for space up the steep faces like a Brazilian favela, everyone clamouring for a safe place as far from the rising ocean waters as possible.

That night I woke in terror every hour, sitting bolt upright in bed, desperate to get out of there. But where on earth would be safe? The answer was 'nowhere', and I plummeted deeper

---

1 Dual-diagnosis means you're not only alcoholic, but you're gifted with a mood disorder as well as an addiction.

into a pit of despair. Too afraid to raise with my friends what I was going through, I gritted my teeth and carried on with the weekend. If you've never been to Vail, it's absolutely stunning. But this was not a fun weekend at the snow.

When I got back to Venice on the Monday, I finally made it into my psychologist's office. Brad had an office high above Beverly Boulevard, on the top floor of a stunning medical building. His office looked from the ocean in the west all the way to the snow-capped mountains in the east. Sitting on the edge of a chair with my feet on the floor and my elbows on my knees, I told him that the world was ending and I was the only one who knew about it. If he were smart he'd pack up his family and drive up to the mountains surrounding the city and hide, because the civil unrest that would tear LA apart would probably kick off around sunset that day. He calmly listened and nodded, then quietly and gently tried to explain to me that I was experiencing paranoid delusions.[2]

My first thought was, 'Oh, shit ... he doesn't know! Either that or he must be in on the climate change denial conspiracy ...' But by the grace of god or Buddha or Prince or whoever watches over me, I had a brief moment of realisation that if I was too sick to trust my shrink, I was going to be in real trouble. My mentor David had told me on the phone the day before, 'The problem with crazy people is that they don't know they're crazy', and in my case he was absolutely right. Now in question was everything I had ever trusted about my ability to rationalise and appreciate the visual, auditory and sensory input related to the reality I shared with other people. I knew right there in Brad's office, sitting on his glorious

---

2 Paranoid delusions are false, irrational beliefs that can't be changed by evidence and aren't shared by other people from the same cultural background.

original Eames reclining chairs, that if at that moment I chose to believe the delusions in my head over the highly trained, sane, calm and well-meaning doctor sitting across from me, I would slip right off the edge of reality.

Within a breath, I stepped back in my mind's eye to look at where I had been. I could see back down into the abyss of the psychosis that was enveloping me, a place where everything that you see and hear is distorted through a lens of panic and fear, and I knew at that moment that if I believed what I wanted to believe, I might never come back. I had to go against every fibre of my being and trust that what Brad was telling me was true. It was like someone was sitting in front of me saying, 'I know you think that right now you're in a swimming pool – but you're actually on dry land.' Couldn't they see the water all around me? Weren't they wet too? It took absolutely everything that I had to believe what Brad was telling me just 1 per cent more than what my terrified brain was convincing me was utterly real. So I took another breath and listened.

Brad told me that neurosis is the pain caused when the brain is having trouble accepting what is happening in reality: a breakup, a major illness, the loss of someone close to you. Psychosis happens when that pain gets so great that in order to protect itself from the pain caused by reality, the brain simply reinterprets it. This was a lot to take in. To be told you're experiencing psychosis is heavy for anyone to hear. To be told that what you believe to be absolutely real is actually a fabrication of your mind? That is even more challenging to accept – especially with a mind that's clearly malfunctioning. With all my heart I didn't want it to be true. When I thought about it a bit more, it made sense. I was suffering massive anxiety because of my on-again, off-again romance, plus my father's serious illness, plus uncertainty about my work future and finances, it was everything all at once.

My psychologist told me that treatment would probably involve medication, and that he could refer me to a psychiatrist who could help. But I was so reluctant to go back on meds *even in this incredible crisis* that I said I'd think about it. I was making a decision about taking medication with a brain that needed medication to make a clear decision about taking medication. It was not a good idea to wait.

That night I went to my regular fellowship meeting in Venice. It was the most hip meeting I went to.[3] The room was packed, and I must have been the only one in there without a successful fashion brand, start-up or neck tattoo, but the message of recovery was very strong. As different people put their hands up to share about the difficulties they'd encountered that week and how they had overcome them, all I wanted to do was run out of the room. As far as I was concerned, no one knew how much grave and immediate danger all of us were all in right now.

We were in there talking about taking steps and not drinking and none of it mattered because you wouldn't be able to drink anything when there was no fucking fresh water left, would you? The thoughts were inescapable.

I rode my bike home and got ready for the flight to Israel the next day.[4] As I was packing up my toiletries I threw in my last packet of SSRIs. I'd stopped taking them so I still had

---

3   When you can no longer go to bars and clubs, and often have to cut ties with the friends that you used to drink and use with, meetings tend to become a new and healthier social life.

4   Of course I rode a fixed-gear bike. I was a vegan who changed his name for spiritual reasons living in Venice Beach.

a whole box left and I figured I'd have them on hand just in case.

The flight to Israel was fine but the moment I landed in Tel Aviv I was drowning in fear. It was an unusually warm winter's day and everyone I met said, 'I can't believe how *warm* it is!' My head was screaming. This was evidence that the world was ending, and they didn't know about it here either! I headed out on my usual running route, south to the ancient city of Jaffa, turning around at the lighthouse and back to the hotel.[5] As I ran, the hallucinations started again. Every step brought another vision of the entire shorefront submerged and the population fleeing up into the hills around Jerusalem, where it's safe to say there's a bit of an issue as to who's allowed to live where. I was in agony.

I had arrived a day or two early so that I could get aligned with the time zone before I started shooting, so no one seemed to mind if I hid in my hotel room. The thoughts got worse and worse. Trapped in a repetitive behavioural loop, walking from the bedroom to the bathroom, in mental anguish and great physical pain, I was continuously flinching, and sometimes grunting or even shouting, 'No!' as doom washed over me. The thoughts were coming about every five to eight seconds. They just wouldn't stop, no matter how often I wrote out rational responses to each one of them, as I'd been taught to do. Nothing could convince me that things were different from my imaginings. I was trapped in an unstoppable loop of inescapable physical pain and mental anguish and I was very, very frightened about how to live the rest of my life if it was going to be like this.

---

5   Yes, in this part of the world you take your run to ancient cities which are name-checked in the Bible and past ancient mosques that date back to the dawn of Islam.

When I bodysurfed at Bronte Beach in Sydney I'd often stay out until I got too cold to move. When I was out there, unable to feel my feet or fingers, getting an ice-cream headache from the cold, I'd fantasise about the shower back in my apartment. I thought about how good it would feel to stand under that shower in my wetsuit, peeling it off as the warm water washed over me, slowly bringing my core temperature back up. The thoughts of that warm shower were just delicious and ever so seductive.

That's exactly what suicide felt like now.

It was the simplest, and easiest way to make my incredible pain and suffering go away. I was staying on the thirteenth floor after all, and my room had a balcony with a door that opened all the way. The interesting thing is, the idea of killing myself didn't feel scary. It was a perfectly simple solution to the horror I was going through. It would be the most gentle, kindest thing that I could do for myself. I looked forward to it. I *wanted* it. Death would wrap me up in a warm towel plucked fresh off the oil heater, holding me tight while the noise and pain and fear gently went away. It seduced me with promises of tranquillity and serenity. Finally I would be able to rest.

Once again, I was incredibly lucky to know that something was wrong. In tiny glimpses of light amidst the turbulent chaos, I was able to see that my brain was sick, distorting reality and giving me false ideas about what was actually happening. That same brain was telling me that killing myself was probably a great idea. Suicide seemed to me like the best and smartest idea I'd ever had, and because of that I knew I couldn't do it – because this was probably a distorted thought too.

I got on the phone to Dr Chung back in Sydney. It was late in the evening in Israel so Australia was just waking up.

I finally managed to get a message through for him to call me back. While I waited for that call, I FaceTimed two of my brothers, one in Brisbane and one in Melbourne, talking to them each for ages, grateful they were able to talk to me. Then I called all the people that I knew would be awake and able to talk to me.

After an hour or two, Dr Chung called me back. He told me I should really go to the emergency ward, but that would be dangerous because I was in a foreign country and I'd probably get committed and held without my own consent. Well I clearly couldn't do that, I had a TV pilot to shoot the next day. I told him that I had some Lexapro with me and he said that while it wasn't the best drug, that I would need something far more powerful than that to control what was happening, I should probably start on the highest allowable dose and see a psychiatrist as soon as I got back to LA. I promised him that if opening the balcony door became a good idea, I'd head straight to the hospital.[6]

I necked those Lexys quicker than you can say Sarah Tonin. On the phone afterwards I promised my mentor that I would head to ER if things got bad. The problem is, drugs like Lexapro take weeks to start to work. I was in for a rough ride. I couldn't sleep, so I must have Skyped or FaceTimed people all over the world for hours that night, just trying to connect with reality as much as I could, trying to get a healthier perspective on what I was so terrified about.

---

6   I should point out here the difference between active and passive suicidal ideation. Active suicidal ideation involves an existing wish to die accompanied by a plan for how to carry out the death – such as me planning to open that balcony door and simply step over the railing. For me, the will to carry out the plan hung around from sometimes as short as one minute to up to five and even twenty minutes at a time. Passive suicidal ideation involves a desire to die, but without a specific plan for carrying out the death. For me, this one hangs around your neck like a chain sometimes for hours. I have struggled with both forms of suicidal ideation.

The next day was the first day of shooting the pilot. And, just like at every other time in my life, being on camera was the one thing that made all the noise stop. The focused attention on a task allowed me to block out all the other noise. Of course it came roaring back the moment they yelled 'Cut', but those minutes of respite were glorious.

With a few days to spare in between wrapping the pilot project and starting at THNK in Amsterdam, I headed to London to visit friends. A passenger on the plane was reading a newspaper, and the front page screamed in capital letters: 'EUROPA UNTER WASSER IN 50 JAHREN!' My German's not great, but I could roughly translate. The newspapers were now writing about it. It was real. It was going to happen. And still no one gave a shit. As we flew from Tel Aviv to London, I looked out the window down at all the low-lying countries that lay below us. All I saw was reshaped coastlines and displaced populations, food insecurity and endless war over who gets to live where. By the time I landed in Heathrow I was a fucking mess. I got to my friend's house, then ran around Kensington Gardens for an hour with visions of the trees stripped of all their leaves, lying dead at the bottom of a new ocean.

This chaos went on for weeks. Every day something new would trigger me and I would plunge into a vortex of fear. I'd have a panic attack and then seriously consider suicide as a simple solution to the inescapable pain in my head five, ten, sometimes twenty times a day. It is nothing short of a miracle that I didn't pick up a drink. That would have been the quickest exit from the pain, and there's no question that if I had, I'd have just said, 'Fuck it' and jumped to my death. However, fellowship meetings in London and in Amsterdam gave me somewhere to be, someone to talk to and someone to be accountable to when I said, 'I'll see you tomorrow.' Without those meetings, I wouldn't be writing this right now.

When I started my course at THNK in Amsterdam, I was deep in the darkness. I was barely able to put on a brave face during the day, and as I hid in my Air B'n'B at night. The thoughts trapped me in the room; the unstoppable rumination freezing me to the spot in terror. But then I found something that did help, however briefly.

I had learned Vedic meditation a few years before. It involves repeating a nonsense sound in your head, and after a while your brain (if healthy) lets go of everything and you reach a peaceful altered state. I also used another technique called noting, where you just note what pops into your head during meditations. You can learn a lot from observing where your mind goes when there's no stimulus. Now, no matter what I thought about, every single thing I sensed was going through a filter of cataclysmic doom. Every single thing would relate back to my paranoia. I noted this and while the thoughts did not stop, I could separate myself from them just a little.

Through meditation, I could clearly see that something was wrong with my ability to perceive reality. I'd test my theory by looking around the room, and seemingly benign objects like a candle or a book about soup would send my brain flying into wild tangents about the environmental destruction wrought by the sourcing of beef tallow to make that candle, or the astonishing waste of energy and plumes of environmentally destructive CO_2 that would be released should I light the gas-powered stove in the apartment to cook the delicious looking soup on the cover of the book.

Every single piece of input was being run through this neural pathway of horror, and thankfully in meditation I was able to see that it was happening. It still hurt physically, and it still terrified me – but having that tiniest space between my thoughts and the ability to see that my thoughts were being distorted saved my life that night.

As each thought came around every five to eight seconds, I ran through a cycle of reminding myself that I was sick, and that my ability to see what was real was being severely compromised.

It was like getting a tiny gasp of air in between waves crashing over your head, just enough to get you through the next tumble in the surf until another break in the waves allowed a breath that could keep you going for a few more seconds.

It didn't work every time, in fact it barely worked at all – but it was something that with practice I was able to make more effective as time went on. However, this was a very long, very slow process, and when the Lexapro kicked in about two weeks later, all it did was bring the suicidal thoughts down from twenty times a day to three or four. Every single day for months, suicide was there, sitting next to me, holding out his hand for me to just follow him up the gentle and welcoming path to where all the pain would stop.

Back in LA I carried on as best I could, working on developing new TV formats and trying to keep positive despite the triggers. I kept seeing my psychologist but that didn't help much. The smallest thing would set off the hallucinations again, and after a few hours of it, the idea of suicide would seductively seep into my brain offering itself as an antidote to the pain.

Not long after I got back, the second season of *The Bachelor Australia* finally got the green light and soon I was on a plane back to Australia for another go around with the roses. By now Dad was doing OK, back at work, although he had absolutely refused to change his lifestyle. Doctors are the worst for that.

For the second season, we had a new shooting location: a spectacular Victorian-era mansion on Sydney Harbour. Instead of driving to and from work, I could now ride my bicycle. I absolutely loved riding to work and back, and I highly recommend it if you can do it too. It's a great way to get your brain fired up for the work you're about to do, and an equally great way for your brain to calm down when you're done for the day. From the apartment in Bondi where I was staying it was eighteen kilometres, 250 metres of climbing and 650 calories of riding to get to work. At the time I had a great dislike for going to the gym, so it was a pretty excellent way to get the exercise in. Riding to and from work helped my head enormously, even though my route took me over three bridges across parts of Sydney Harbour, and every time I crossed the water my head was filled with very realistic apocalyptic visions of the bridge being swept away by rising sea levels. But riding home from late shoots through Sydney at three in the morning is very special. The whole city is yours and you're travelling from one side of it to the other, all under your own power. It's a great feeling.

Alas, every day my brain would find something to trigger me. I'd become averse to putting on the air conditioner in the car I'd rented because it was June and if I put the AC on in winter it meant that climate change was real and the world was ending. Anything weather-related set off this awful pattern. Just as when I'd returned from NYC after 9/11, I could no longer even look at a newspaper just in case there was anything on the front page that would trigger me. I couldn't listen to radio because they were always giving the time and temperature. I preferred to ride my bike because on the bike I didn't have a temperature gauge staring back at me telling me that it was 27°C in Sydney in July. The worst trigger was work colleagues exclaiming with glee, 'Wow, I can't believe how warm it is today! How good is it?' They don't give acting awards for reality shows, but I'll take my *TV Week* Logie for 'Best reality presenter pretending he's actually interested in what he's talking about while all he can think about is suicide' as a given. Thankfully when the cameras were rolling, all of those thoughts once again went away. Those small moments were a welcome respite.

It's important to say that during this time I had a meeting with Stephen Tate, my executive producer at Network Ten who'd not only hired me for *Australian Idol* but also this incredible second chance at a career with *The Bachelor*, and disclosed to him that I was struggling with my health but that I was getting help. He was incredibly supportive and assured me that whatever I needed he'd be there. I can't thank him enough for not only trusting that I could still do the job even though I was having a rough time – but also for being a great friend.

Season two of the show meant being able to ask for one or two extra things to make the job a little easier to do. One was that Carla Mico, the makeup artist I'd worked with at Channel [v] and *Australian Idol*, would now be working with me. The camera sees colour and shadow differently from the human eye, so unless you want to look like a ghoul crawling out of a van on *The Walking Dead* you're going to need makeup. A big-shot film producer/director in LA once told me that when he's putting a film together the first head of department he hires after his cinematographer is the head of makeup. This is before he's even cast the talent. He told me, 'The makeup artist gets the talent three hours before I do. Their job isn't just to make the talent look great, it's also to make them feel great. A good makeup artist can turn a crying and anxious actor into a confident stud in the time they're in the chair. The job is not all about powder puffs and hairdryers.'

He's absolutely right. Doing hair and makeup is a very intimate job, involving a stranger touching your face all day while you're at work. For me, that person has to have a positive energy. When your makeup artist has negative energy, it rubs off on you. It's not like you can move to another desk in the office. And this is where Carla comes in. A true shining light of pure positivity, Carla is the kind of person who brings warmth to any room she's in. She's also very, very good at her job and has been the official curator of my hair since 2014. Any time you see a joke or a meme about my hair, that's Carla's work. When I go about my day when I'm not working, I don't put in nearly that much effort.

Having Carla on set helped enormously because I had known her for so long that I could speak to her about what was going on in my life. I wouldn't talk to her about the suicidal thoughts, but I did confide in her about other things that were bothering me. Particularly how much difficulty I had dating.

Because of the job I do, Tinder was not a place for me, nor was any kind of internet dating site. The last thing I needed was a photo of a Tinder profile in the paper when I was working on a show all about finding love. The press were doing that to many of the participants in our show and I didn't want them doing it to me.

After a few weeks of my whining about how hard it was to meet women, particularly as pubs were out of the question, Carla finally had enough.

'Listen,' she said with a stamp of her foot. 'I'm going away next week for a job I booked before this one came along. I'll be gone for a week. I've got someone to come in and look after you, and you're welcome.' She told me her replacement's name was Audrey Griffen.

When we would arrive at the Hunter's Hill mansion for work, we'd gather in the carport (oh, the glamour of TV) while waiting for a break in the shooting of the cocktail party so that we could travel down to the room where we got ready without being seen on camera. Audrey was waiting with the other crew members as I arrived, meeting me for the first time in my natural state – sweaty and nervous on the back of a bicycle. I said hello, my face streaming with sweat, and stripped off my day-glo jacket. I took one look at her and saw her glorious Disney-princess eyes looking back at me, and the kindest smile I'd had thrown my way in a long time. Given that I was still dealing with a thought storm from crossing the Gladesville bridge, with visions of every one of the beautiful homes that I saw underwater, I probably looked terrified. Not the best first impression.

I was attracted to Audrey immediately, but that first week I played it very cool. Everyone has the right to turn up to work and not be hit on. We're all professionals and we're here to do a job. I found out later that in that first week I was so subtle about my interest in her that Audrey was convinced that I was not into women at all, given the complete lack of sexual signals I was pointing her way.[7]

As we got to work and she started to apply makeup, I tried to get the conversation started – so I deftly asked, 'So ... did you watch *Game of Thrones* last night?'

_____

7 I'm sticking with that double entendre and I don't care what anyone says.

She replied, 'Well, I've read all the books – so none of it comes as a surprise.' By the beard of Zeus! Smart, funny, beautiful *and* she read books? I had to figure out how to move this forward.

To work out whether she had a boyfriend or not I casually told her that my standup-comic friend Luke Heggie was taping his new TV special that Saturday at the Comedy Store. A few of us were going, and if she was interested she could text me her name, plus that of a guest, and I'd see they got in.[8] She did, and the other name wasn't a man's. That Saturday night, while we waited outside the Comedy Store for her friend to show up Audrey said, 'Well, I hope you like blondes, because my friend is blonde.'

'Thank you, but I'm not interested in your friend,' I replied.

She didn't miss a beat. 'Oh, I wish you'd told me – I would have showered, I've just come straight from work!'

After that we went out together a few times. I was very shy and she didn't really know whether I was interested at all. This was partly because the 'falling in love' parts of my brain were running at around 10 per cent capacity from the effects of the meds I was taking. The hormones released when you find someone new, the warm fuzzy feelings, the chemicals in your body that cause arousal, were barely a trickle instead of *flooding* my brain. This wasn't because I wasn't into her – I most definitely was – but with the meds I was on all of my body's responses were dulled, not just those dealing with anxiety.

But I *knew* this woman was very special and I wanted very much for her to be in my life. She was stunningly beautiful and

---

8   Pretty slick way of getting her number, eh?

the kindest person I'd ever met, with a warmth and empathy unlike anyone I'd ever known. She was smart and quick, too, with a rapier wit. Life had not always been easy for her. She had migrated from Fiji with her parents after the coup in the mid-1980s and told me she had broken up with her boyfriend while she was unexpectedly pregnant with their baby – yet had chosen to have her daughter regardless, even though she was only twenty-three and had to drop out of a promising academic career. She spoke about her daughter with such love. In the past, initial physical attraction had been a dominant factor early on in my relationships. However, because of my medication situation and even though intense physical attraction was playing out, I got to focus on *who she was* as well as what she looked like.

Audrey finally came over to my house for a dinner date and cooked me the most wonderful eggplant and chickpea curry. She even made the dough and rolled the roti that went with the meal, and I'd never eaten such a delicious curry. I'm sure she sprinkled magic Fijian herbs and spices into the food because, that night as I chatted with her in my kitchen, I remember feeling that I could really fall in love with this woman. At the same time, I was far too afraid to admit this to myself or to her. After dinner we sat on the couch together, each awkwardly waiting for the other to make the first move. The parts of my body that were supposed to be reacting to her might not have been firing on all cylinders, but with a *lot* of concentration I was able to respond. Anyone who's dated while on medication will understand how difficult it was. This stuff is of course icky to talk about, but it's important that we do talk about it.

Having a new relationship in my life made me feel a bit better. A few weeks after we got together Audrey covered for

Carla again. It felt very naughty to have shared a bed the night before and be professional on set the next morning.

My brain was oscillating between excitement about seeing Audrey again and despair at the prospect of starting a new relationship while the world was burning all around us. In the same day I'd feel my heart beat faster when I got a cheeky text from the woman who was now my lover, and later I'd then feel my heart nearly stop when I accidentally saw an article about drought or famine. It's not easy to enjoy those first few weeks of getting to know someone when you're also grappling with thoughts about killing yourself five times a day.

It all started to become just too much, so I went back to see Dr Chung and asked him for help. He gave me a drug called Zyprexa and told me to take a quarter of a tablet only when I needed it, and then only on the really bad days. I didn't have to wait long for a *really* bad day. As I battled with my brain trying to tell me that the best way out of this pain was to remove myself from the situation permanently, I decided to take a tiny piece of one pill.

When I cut it up as Dr Chung had shown me, it was just a little bigger than a grain of sand. I didn't see how such a tiny amount could do anything of significance, but I swallowed it anyway. Within twenty minutes all the noise, all the chaos and fear and thoughts of suicide just vanished. It was as if someone had just pulled the power cord out of that part of my brain. That night, I slept better than I had done in years.

Seeing how such a tiny dose of a chemical could change my state of mind so intensely made me think of the times I'd snorted gigantic lines of mystery powder off closed toilet seats in nightclubs with strangers, and how those huge amounts of drugs had changed my brain too, apparently in some ways permanently. I researched Zyprexa and saw that it was an anti-psychotic, which made me very reluctant to take it. This was a prime example of a sick brain not making a good decision, because I now performed the trick of the mentally ill that is as old as psychiatry itself: 'If I take the drug, that means I've got psychosis, right? Therefore, if I *don't* take the drug that means I *don't have* psychosis! Brilliant!'

Allow me to state the bleeding obvious to you. This is *not* a smart strategy. Rather than seeking the relief this medication so clearly gave me, I gritted my teeth and refused to take it. Taking it would be an admission that I *needed* it to live, and with all my heart I didn't want to *need* it.

Like most things left untreated, the trigger responses and the suicidal ideations got worse and worse. I could barely do my job, so I went back to Dr Chung. When I told him I wasn't taking the Zyprexa, for the second time in our relationship he became very angry with me, and with good reason.

I couldn't tackle this alone, he said. It was bigger than me, and I needed better ideas than I had to deal with it. It was like the first two steps of a twelve-step program: I had to admit I was powerless over this disease, that my life had become unmanageable and only a power greater than myself could restore me to sanity. I alone couldn't fix things: I needed something outside of myself and, more importantly, something other than my ideas if I wanted to get better. And if I wanted to get better, I had to accept that this was the brain I was born with, which meant accepting what my brain was doing and how it was reacting.

From that moment I started taking my meds as instructed. Not long afterwards I began to feel a little less horrible. At first, the addict in me roared back to life and I'd crave the sedative effects of Zyprexa. My mentor assured me that as long as I was using the drug in the prescribed manner and I wasn't abusing it, that craving would soon go away. It did.

Antipsychotics are great because they work, but they're not great because they have side effects. Soon I started to gain weight as the drug began to alter the way my body metabolised food. These meds also affect your sex drive, but because Audrey and I were still in the 'pants-ahoy!' phase of our relationship, the spiking hormones were thankfully strong enough to override that.

As the second season of *The Bachelor Australia* came to a close, the weight gain was becoming a problem at work. Even though I was riding my bike to and from work three to five times a week, the kilos were still piling on. To counteract this, I'd eat less and I'd ride more but it was without success. Travelling to South Africa for the final episodes, we took a few suitcases of wardrobe options because we weren't sure what I'd need to wear on the big finale day. These were suits that had been tailored for me at the start of the season and I was now ballooning out of them, looking like sausage meat squeezed out of a rubber glove.

Thankfully, though, my relationship with Audrey was growing stronger by the day – but we were now faced with a common problem of couples in our situation. The tricky thing when you're dating a woman who has a child is figuring out when to introduce the child to the fact that you exist. At first Audrey would only visit me on nights when her mum could look after Georgia, and even then only after Georgia had gone to sleep. I enjoyed the late-night adventure part of this, but it did limit Audrey's ability to stay over.

After a few weeks Audrey invited me over for dinner to meet her parents and her daughter Georgia. Her mum and dad were the epitome of welcoming love that defines Fijian hospitality, and I became instantly fond of the tall, funny and whip-smart Georgia the moment I met her. But I played it super-cool and at first Georgia believed I was just Mum's friend. However, once I started staying over, it was obvious I was more than a friend and that became a problem. Georgia was used to being able to crawl into her mother's bed when she was afraid in her own, and more than once I woke up with a long-haired child standing over me like the creepy kid in *Paranormal Activity*.

It was clear to me that Audrey would always put Georgia first, and nothing could have made me happier. I wasn't just dating one woman – I was getting into a relationship with two people, each of whom had very different needs. The first glimmers of what a life could be with just the three of us started to emerge, and it looked like something I really wanted. If only I could convince my brain that it was safe to move forward. However, that was too much for me to bear. For that to happen, it took Audrey being brave in the face of pure paranoia.

Being open with Audrey about my thoughts of self-harm was important and I can't thank her enough for listening to me on the phone for hours while I just spurted fountains of delusion about the world ending. It was in one of these rants that with great kindness she stopped me mid-sentence and said words that pierced the veil of spiralling fear.

'If it does come to that. I'll be with you, and it will be OK.'

In all of my very real cataclysm visualisations, I had been alone. I was usually on a hill, watching the sea below me swallow entire South Pacific countries, engulfing cultures, washing away homes and infrastructure and entire communities, while streams of people ran past me in panic, escaping to higher ground.

For the first time, in that deluded fantasy, Audrey was now with me. Her arm lovingly around me. And thanks to the meds that by now had started to work their way into my mind's constant doom-loops, that thought felt like it could also be true. Audrey's fearless love for me in that moment, when she was clearly talking to a deluded person, absolutely saved my life.

Despite this fearless show of affection, I still needed to get over my stupid ego and man up when it came to our relationship.

When the filming for season two of *The Bachelor* was over and I was preparing to head back to LA, Audrey and I had to have The Talk. I was moving away for an indefinite amount of time and we needed to see where we were. For a relationship that had lasted only a matter of weeks we had covered a lot of ground, but at a much healthier pace than some of my previous attempts. However, given how great my brain was at catastrophising, I was thinking, 'If I invite her to LA we will suddenly be serious and then we will get married and then I will have to move her over and find her a visa and ... Aaargh!' With plenty of playful teasing (including convincing me that she was already planning the wedding), she talked me down from the ledge. We decided we would keep talking to each other and just see what happened.

After I got back to LA, I headed straight out to Utah to meet the Summit Series people. They own a mountain out there and hold regular weekends where entrepreneurs from all over the world gather to talk to each other, find out how they might work together and do things that they'd otherwise never do.[9] Through my work at THNK in Amsterdam I was much

---

9   It was on that trip that I learned how to escape from a set of handcuffs behind my
    back.

more aligned with the triple-bottom-line business models that people were running, and it was great to get a healthy dose of inspiration. The Summit parties were legendary and stacked with some of the smartest young women and men in the world, running businesses that were not only making money but often helping their communities. As I watched from the back of the room while a big-name DJ playing under an alias rocked the basement dance party, I cradled my soda water and I was still overwhelmed with fear. These were some of the best, brightest young people around, and they were joyfully dancing while the world was on fire around them – and they didn't seem to care.

I couldn't live like this any longer. Something had to change.

twenty-three

the brain i was born with

Back in Los Angeles, my off-season life continued as normal. Because I knew I might soon need to pursue something outside television I landed a job at THNK, the school in Amsterdam I'd been attending for the previous eighteen months. I'd be running their Forum program, rather like TED talks but in an interview format.

I adore Amsterdam and would move there in a second if I could. My first trip there had been traumatic, and I spent my days climbing the walls and feeling suicidal, but on my second trip I was just a little better and could begin to appreciate how wonderful it was there. Thanks to Air B'n'B I was staying for the week in a house owned by the editor of one of Holland's leading design magazines. It was a classic walk-up terrace house, all compacted onto one floor with a big glass window facing the beautiful Haarlemmerstraat. I was blown away at how little stuff he had. He was the editor of a high-selling magazine and he had maybe ten separate outfits. His fridge was a little bigger than a hotel minibar fridge and he only seemed to have objects in his home that conveyed significant meaning. Two or three trips to Amsterdam later I realised that his place wasn't the only one like this. Life there wasn't focused on the acquisition of stuff, it was about what you did with your life.

Landing back in LA, I would look down over the junction of several freeways to see 100,000 cars in a slow-moving car park that stretched out to the horizon, each car probably containing only one person. In Amsterdam, every one of those people would be on a bicycle. Every message beamed into my ears and eyeballs in the USA was based on the premise that buying more stuff would make everything better. A bigger TV, a bigger truck, more clothes, more food. But I'd seen a society where that wasn't the case, and everything was pretty fucking excellent. The first thing I did on my return to LA was sell the massive fridge that had come with the apartment. It was big enough to feed my whole building and probably burned more energy in a day than my tiny replacement fridge did in a week.

For me LA and the USA had represented the pinnacle of what an educated and developed society could achieve. Now I'd been to Amsterdam and was beginning to know the Netherlands (most of it by bicycle, as I'd come to add weeks on either side of my trips there to go for 100-kilometre rides around the dykes hunting for windmills), my view of what America meant to me was beginning to shift. I had seen a society where nobody cared about your sexuality or what you looked like: all they cared about was whether you were a good person or not. Maybe living in the USA wasn't the be all and end all of my life.

Back in LA the wind was starting to leave my sails. I was pushing less and less for an on-camera job. The reality was that I was now hitting forty and clearly starting to age out of the market. With *The Bachelor Australia* helping pay the bills I wasn't on the hunt for a job here or there, I was just one of the guys waiting to pounce if any network started sniffing around for a big, shiny-floor TV show.[1] Unfortunately for us, shiny-floor TV was not as hot as it once was. It's a tough reality of a job like mine. You either hit hard in your twenties and thirties and vanish forever or you are one of the very, very few people who get to live out their golden years of broadcasting throwing to infomercials on the mid-morning talk show.[2]

My manager John Ferriter and I strategised about how best to approach this situation. John totally believed in me, knowing my skills and where I was in my career. We decided I would keep working on format developments and keep an ear to the ground for anything going over at the networks. It was during one of these meetings that I spoke with Andy Cohen, one of John's colleagues. Andy rightly sensed that I wasn't 100 per cent and recommended I go and check out Dr Stephen Johnson, a psychologist out in the Valley who had a great reputation.

Dr Johnson's office was in Woodland Hills, deep in the heart of the San Fernando Valley. The office had the usual subdued lighting and comfy chairs, and there were also various artefacts from the indigenous people of the area, including wolf totems, a bear carved of wood and an animal skin drum. Dr Johnson was not only a PhD psychologist, he was one of the original 'men in the woods beating a drum as a way of spiritual awakening' leaders. He was absolutely my kinda guy. He had a PhD in psychology and had been practising for more than forty years when we met. He was working on

---

1   Shiny-floor is a kind of television show, almost always light entertainment, and always shot in front of a live studio audience, always with a shiny floor. *Australian Idol*, *Dancing with the Stars* and *The Voice* are all examples of shiny-floor TV. I fucking love a shiny-floor show.

2   FYI this is totally my plan. Jono Coleman and I will sail into the sunset together riding on a ship built entirely of ab exercise machines, lubricated with anti-ageing serums, while Daryl Braithwaite serenades us over the horizon.

the very fringes of where traditional psychology ends and the exploration into the true meanings of consciousness begins.

I was still plagued by fears about a climate apocalypse, which sucked because he practised out in Woodland Hills which would often get over 38°C even in the winter. And here I was utterly unable to turn on the A/C in my car because doing so would prove that the world was indeed ending. I would often turn up to his office sweating and smelly.

Stephen guided me through some breathing exercises, which at first were quite strange, but by now I was willing to do anything to stop my constant fear and thoughts of suicide. One particular exercise had me on my back hyperventilating for what seemed like forever.[3] He calmly talked me through what I was feeling in my body. Then when I was ready he told me to breathe out and hold it for as long as I was comfortable. I won't say how long but it was a *really* surprisingly long amount of time. When I finally breathed in, he asked me to say what was on my mind. When I did speak, it was in the third person. It was the first time that the 'observer' in my head had used my mouth. I spoke as if I was observing the thoughts, filtering through my fear. It was a truly profound exercise and I'd never try to replicate it without him, because I don't know how safe it is to expose that observer to a point where he is suddenly able to control my body.

When I finally sat back up, Stephen read back to me what I'd told him while in that state. I wrote it down in my phone, and I've copied and pasted it from the day it happened, which was 19 December 2014. 'I'm so sorry that might happen, but if it does happen, I will help you deal with it.'

---

3   Unless you're lying down next to Stephen, do not try this. Please.

This might sound a little too much like beating drums in the woods, and if you want to skip forward a bit I won't be upset. For those of you still with me, I was realising that despite my constant swirling thoughts of doom and horror there was a deep part of my consciousness that knew that I would be able to deal with whatever happened. But while I *knew* on that level that I would ultimately be OK, the rest of me refused to believe it. I still couldn't break out of the thought patterns and triggers that punished me ten or twenty times a day, nor work out how to make them stop permanently.

We repeated the exercise twice more, days apart. The second time I said, 'I'm sorry that you might feel this pain – but you may see that self preservation is communal preservation – and you just might find that by letting go of selfishness there is joy.' Who knew that inside me I had a part of my consciousness that was capable of spouting such wisdom?

The third and final time I said, 'It's OK to feel the fear, know that I will know what to do. I am in the unknown, and I know what to do.'

I remember saying those words, I remember feeling my mouth making the sounds, but it wasn't me who directed the muscles in my face and throat to do it. I honestly don't care whether I was just out of my gourd with hypoxia or that my brain was firing in every direction at once because I had no CO_2 in my blood. At the time I didn't care that it might have even been a parlour trick, like John Edward's cold reading.[4]

---

4   Which I must point out it certainly is not. Numerous research studies show that breathwork can indeed be a form of effective psychotherapy treatment. Personally I'd prefer to do it under the guidance of someone as expert as Dr Johnson. I'm not really into lying around on the floor with strangers listening to someone tell me to breathe while they're surrounded by an altar of crystals, even if he's an expert at guiding this kind of exercise. For me it opens up something a little too fragile to do in a group setting.

It just made me feel so reassured that deep inside me existed thoughts that weren't all cataclysm and constant doom, that somewhere in my brain there was actually a thought that was positive. When you've been unable to see anything but darkness for as long as I had, it was nice to know that just one of the switches in my head could still turn on a light.

The problem was getting those thoughts to stick. No matter how many times I read and reread the things I'd said to myself, no matter how hard I tried to will myself into believing them to be true, they were no match for the doom and catastrophe that made so much noise in my head that I sometimes couldn't even work, let alone sleep. So Dr Johnson recommended that I go and see a psychiatrist colleague of his, a man with whom he often shared treatment of patients. Each of them would work an angle in consort with each other.

This is how I came to meet Dr Jehangeer Sunderji. Jehangeer was a total rock star. He was the first doctor I ever saw who was younger than me; he had left a successful career in the corporate world and spent years retraining to become a psychiatrist because he just *loved* the challenge. The first day I went to see him, I told him how horrible my life was and that I was willing to do just about anything not to feel like topping myself every day. He then uttered a line I'll never forget. 'I'll get you better. Don't worry, I never lose.' He started me on another antipsychotic called Seroquel, which I was to take in the mornings. At this point I honestly didn't care how many drugs I had to take; I just wanted the thoughts to stop.

Now I was taking more antipsychotics that were not only making me fatter but affecting my sex drive, I worried whether I'd be up for a visit from Audrey who was talking about coming to see me, and I was umming and aahing about it. I was so scared of being in another relationship, so afraid of getting into a relationship and then driving it until the wheels fell off that I was very reluctant to keep going with her. Thankfully for me, she ignored my logic and flew over to LA regardless. I was so worried about her arriving that *the day before* she came for what we hoped would be a very romantic week together, I got a cold sore on my lip.[5] I was so ashamed. When Audrey arrived at LAX, she was a stunning vision in white. She came in for a kiss and I quickly diverted to her cheek.

'What the fuck?' she asked, aptly. I pulled back and showed her the pet cornflake on my face and I could see her heart sink. I wanted to kiss her *so* badly – but when you have face herpes, that's off the menu. Despite this major setback, we got by. There was enough excitement at seeing her again that even though I was on three separate medications that threw a cold wet towel over my sexuality, I was actually able to break through and rise to the occasion.[6]

It was great exploring the neighbourhood of Venice together and spending time on the beach, but the week wasn't without its challenges. During a late-night conversation about our relationship status, I went on a long riff about wanting to acknowledge her feelings, ending with the line, 'I just want to make you feel heard.' With that, my body had endured enough

---

5 I've struggled with my body manifesting my mental problems into physical problems in the past, notably when I was in my twenties and super-hung up about sex, I'd break out in psoriasis on my genitals. Is that too much to know about your friendly neighbourhood rose-counter? I honestly don't care. It's important for you to know that sometimes your brain can take something you're worried about and turn it into a related or unrelated physical problem. In the months leading up to my divorce my left testicle *ached* so badly that I went to go and see a specialist because I thought that something was drastically wrong. After one of the more interesting ultrasound sessions I've experienced it turned out that there wasn't that much wrong at all. And what do you know, from the moment we broke up, the pain disappeared.

6 I promise that's not a stiffy joke. OK, it is.

talking and decided that sleep was needed. Despite my desire to ensure Audrey of my commitment to listening to her, I took a long blink and fell asleep. Her solid punch in the arm woke me up. You can be sure I'm still hearing about that one.

That week in Venice Beach I basked in the glow of Audrey's love and kindness. But because I was still pretty sick, part of me was pushing her away at the same time as wanting so much for her to be near to me. Inside me was a two-headed monster of come here/go away, and thankfully Audrey saw this and rose above it. She is an absolute expert in reading people; her ability to analyse micro-expressions and intentions in others is a serious ASIO interrogation skill. When I'd say something that would diminish how I *really* felt about her, my face and body would say another, and Audrey would call me out on it and verbalise *exactly* the thought or feeling I actually had.

Initially it was quite confronting dealing with someone I couldn't hide from, but without Audrey calling bullshit on what I was doing I wouldn't have been able to work past the fears that were hiding my actual emotions from her. I was very frightened of ruining what we were starting by running my usual pattern of 'complete, totally intense emotional focus and engagement that's initially flattering, but soon so utterly unrelenting that the woman I'm focused on just gets the hell out of there and I'm then justified in my belief that I'm not worthy of love and I'll die alone'. But thanks to Audrey's far more developed emotional intelligence, she called bullshit on me every single time, and if she hadn't I'd still be alone in that apartment in Venice Beach, staring at the walls.

She managed to show me that I was worth her love and kindness, and that what we had was something that could really work. Outwardly I was still too scared to call her my girlfriend, but in my heart I knew I absolutely didn't want to be with anyone else. It would still take me a few weeks to tell her this, but thankfully Audrey had the resilience not to let go. That week Audrey showed me what we had was love that was not only worth pursuing, it was worth fighting for.

Once Audrey had headed back to Sydney, my psychiatrist Jehangeer started exploring a different hypothesis. He figured out that I not only suffered from generalised anxiety but also obsessive compulsive disorder, aka OCD. With OCD there's a trigger and then a compulsion, and once you've been triggered you can't rest until you've done what your brain is compelling you to do.[7] In my experience most compulsions were physical acts such as washing my hands or checking door locks or ovens. However, Jehangeer's hypothesis was that my trigger was anything related to climate change and my compulsion was the mental torture loop that resulted in the physical pain and flinching I'd have to endure.[8] I could whirl around in this for hours until the pain felt so inescapable that my super-smart solution of ending it permanently would arise. Now we had a new hypothesis we could start treating for it, which involved *another* drug called Wellbutrin, known as Zyban in Australia.

The first day that I started taking all four medications (Lexapro, Zyprexa, Seroquel and Zyban) I recorded a podcast with Meshel Laurie for her show *The Nitty Gritty Committee*, sitting by the pool at the fabulous Roosevelt Hotel in the

---

7 OCD is a very misunderstood disease, and if they want a clean house people often say something like, 'I am so OCD about my cushions.' Well, you're not. I wouldn't wish OCD on anyone, even a person who likes things being overly neat.

8 As I was in a hyper-alert state, that trigger could have been pretty much anything at all – I'd get agonisingly triggered from an overly large SUV next to me in traffic to seeing a plane fly overhead, or even as I've described previously, a disposable coffee cup.

heart of Hollywood. It was the first day everything had been loaded up in my system, and I felt as if I was surrounded by a thick gel which was slowing down my every thought and movement. Sitting with someone I trusted (we'd met a few times and connected strongly when she was on my podcast about a year before), when Meshel asked me how I was doing I answered honestly. If you listen to the podcast you will hear the very first time I 'came out' about what I was living with.[9] We discussed the reframing tool – using 'of course' – during this show, and I spoke about the very early stages of my relationship with Audrey. I'm eternally grateful to Meshel for giving me the chance to be open. When I think about what made me suddenly choose to start speaking about it, something my mentor once told me just stuck in my head. I had been talking to him about my reluctance to come clean in a fellowship meeting back in Sydney because I was so famous and worried about my words being used against me (I see it was all ego now, of course). He told me to pull my finger out of my arse, stick my hand up and speak because I might just save someone's life. So that's what I did.

That was a very important moment in my life and career. I would never pressure anyone to come out or disclose their mental illness; stigma is still attached to that, and it might not be safe in your workplace or community, or even for your own health. But I just knew I had to speak up because I had been lucky enough to know something was wrong with my brain, that I had a brain in distress. Others may not be so lucky.

Now I was taking multiple kinds of medications at once, life was changing. Jehangeer was a master at subtle adjustments of

9   Check it out – the episode 'Osher Gunsberg gets realer than real' was posted on Meshel's website on 14 March 2016.

dosage to get the right effect – up a few milligrams here, down a few there – whatever it took to hit the sweet spot. It took a few weeks, but soon enough I had a day when I didn't have to think about killing myself. That was a really, really nice day.

I was still freaked out by my triggers, and despite doing my best to avoid them I'd still get hit once or twice a day. But this wasn't the non-stop mental punishment I'd endured for so long. And because I was finally starting to experience respite from those thoughts, I didn't really mind the side effects of taking the antipsychotics. I was riding every morning, I'd do two to three hundred kilometres a week up and down proper mountains, and yet I was still gaining weight. I could drink nothing but kale smoothies all day and I'd still gain weight. Luckily cycling clothes are made of lycra and a flannel shirt can hide love handles, so for the moment I was OK with it.

The other big side effect, of course, was the change in my sexual response. What used to be something I chased down like a hungry wolf in the woods didn't even cross my mind now. I'd gone from having subtle sexual urges injecting themselves into every part of my day to absolute zero. Sexual thoughts tend to cross the mind of a healthy male a number of times per day. However, now it was as if being a man meant sitting in a comfy chair with a nice cup of tea listening to podcasts while looking out the window. I could sit at a traffic light and a beautiful, voluptuous woman could walk right in front of my car and I wouldn't even notice. Even if she had walked past in slow motion and winked at me as if in a deodorant ad I couldn't have cared less. This wasn't so bad because I was away from Audrey and didn't really notice it was a problem.

With Audrey back in Australia I just kept on with my routine. Ride, meet, pitch, repeat. Every day I was out there hustling.

I got one or two projects some distance along the way to a show, but it's a long *long* way from 'we love it' to 'premiering tonight, 7:30'. Jehangeer upped my meds some more as I was slipping backwards a bit, but with him and Dr Johnson working together I was finally making some progress. I like to think of it as analogous to rally driving. The psychiatrist is the mechanic making sure everything is firing properly, and the psychologist is the navigator calling out the corners as you hurtle through the forest. It was a great combination for treatment and one I have kept to this day.

Knowing I was alone in LA on New Year's Eve my dear friend Mel Nahas, who had relocated to LA from Sydney, invited me out to a house party in Calabasas.[10] It was at a super-secret recording studio built into the granny flat of a house way out in a gated community. Everywhere I looked there were platinum records hung on the walls, all of them from artists I'd been talking about on *The Hot Hits Live From LA* for the past three years. The team of producers who worked out of that room were absolute hit machines, and this was their party. The room was packed solid with incredibly successful men and women, all with enormous momentum behind their careers, and all at least fifteen years younger than me. This was the next generation, the next group of people to run whatever the music industry was morphing into. Mel had spent her career back in Australia working in music and had cultivated and nourished relationships with heavy hitters in LA the entire time.

As I stood in the corner of the room and looked at the young and successful people dancing the night away, it hit me like a

---

10 If you're famous, you buy a big house in the Canyons above Sunset Boulevard. If you're *really* famous, you buy a compound out in Calabasas. It's miles from anywhere and anyone and you can pretty much get away with anything.

tonne of bricks. I was done. Mel had spent a decade creating the perfect combination of people to help her take the next step in her career, and I'd been narcissistically waiting for the knock on my door with the prime-time gig. Mel was hitting the ground firing on all cylinders, and this room of smart and successful people were all there ready to help her.

Mel was doing exactly what I hadn't done ten years before. She understood that everything in LA is business, and that you need to work to create your own work. I'd only just grasped that concept and while I'd arrived in LA in August of 2005 with huge momentum pushing me up the mountain, I'd put no effort into keeping that going and had just coasted off that energy ever since.

But now I'd seen what I could have back in Sydney with Audrey and Georgia, I was no longer interested in playing the LA game. What was I doing in this city so far from home when I could be laughing with Audrey and Georgia, building a life together that would bring me more happiness and fulfilment than any TV show ever could? What I had wanted out of life had changed, and the words of Craig Bruce echoed in my ears yet again. I wasn't excited about the game any more. It was time for me to get out of the way and let these people with more smarts and energy have a shot at the title.

Audrey and I had made plans for her to visit again, this time bringing Georgia with her. They were coming to spend a week with me in early January and we would participate in the pilgrimage that almost every family coming to California completes at some point – a visit to Disneyland. If you've been there you'll know what I mean, and if you haven't you'll know what to expect, but nothing compares to going to Disneyland with a ten-year-old. On the last two days in Disneyland,

Georgia wore a Snow White costume, and we walked around the park with each highly trained employee bowing as she walked past, saying things like, 'Oh good morning, Snow White, we hope you have a wonderful day.' It was fucking awesome.

On one of the mornings that we were getting ready to go into the park I watched the tenderness with which Audrey mothered Georgia, and the penny finally dropped. I was falling wonderfully in love with Audrey, and it was unlike any kind of affection I'd had before. Instead of just putting the pedal to the metal in all-guns-blazing unhealthy obsession, I was able to walk slowly and safely towards the glowing warmth of this woman and the love embodied in her every action. I just wanted to be around her, to talk with her, to laugh with her, and to love her in return. But I still couldn't tell her, for fear of ruining it all.

It must have been tricky for Georgia because her whole life had only really been her and her mum, and suddenly I had shown up. While I guess I might have been a threat to her and her mum's relationship, I've got to hand it to Georgia – she handled the situation really well. Sure she was understandably suspicious, but as I was the only one brave enough to go with her on the scary rides I saw how much joy you can have in your heart when a child you care for is enjoying herself. Her happiness was my happiness, and it was unlike anything I'd ever felt before. Those three days with Audrey and Georgia in Disneyland told me that yes, it could work, and yes, I was definitely up for the challenge of being a stepfather. Sure, every day I was haunted with visions of the tops of the roller coasters peeking out above the new sea level, but I was still able to see what the three of us could be, even if the world was ending. I wanted us to be a family. I just had to figure out how to make that happen.

After Audrey and Georgia went home, and with about six weeks left before I headed back to Sydney to go around again on *The Bachelor Australia*, I had to talk to Dr Sunderji about a big problem. I was running out of clothes. On all of these drugs, I was gaining about a kilogram a week. The last few times I saw him, I went in track pants. With a rapidly approaching on-camera date coming up, I needed to be looking my best, and right now I couldn't get away with counting roses looking like the Stay-Puft marshmallow man.[11] While I was still pretty sick, I was worried that coming back off the antipsychotics would make the delusions, panic attacks and suicidal ideations return. He told me, 'Osher, I could make all the thoughts stop at the click of a finger if you wanted, but you'd gain 50 pounds.'[12] That simply wasn't an option. I couldn't go back on TV with three chins. Slowly he and I began to safely reduce the dosages and agreed that he'd hand me over to the care of a psychiatrist in Sydney, who would take things from there.

Back in Sydney I initially moved into a hotel provided by the network, but before long I was spending almost every night of the week at Audrey's house, so I simply packed up the hotel and moved in. I don't have to tell you that when you fall in love with someone it's pretty special. A magic dust gets released and settles down over you and your partner and everything you do. With Audrey I was on such a slow burn

---

11 OK, now I'm getting really old with my references. You'll need to watch *Ghostbusters* to get that one.

12 That's 22.68 kilograms for those of you using the metric system. Which is everyone. Come on, America, get your shit together. Jesus, how did you ever put people on the moon using fractions of inches?

towards that special feeling, taking the long way around to releasing that magic dust, that I'm lucky that every day she had the stamina to pull us towards it. I'd been testing the bubbling waters of the hot tub of love, reluctant to commit to shifting my weight. But as I finally sat down and relaxed into the warm and welcoming feeling of what it was to be in love in a healthy way for the first time as a sober person, all my fear of ruining the relationship by going too hard too fast began to dissipate.

What happened next really knocked me for six. They don't tell you that when you fall in love with a woman who already has a child, you fall in love with the child too. All the things I loved about Audrey were present in Georgia, along with a whole other part of her personality that I was just besotted by. It only took a few weeks of us living together as a family for something profound to happen within me. From one day to the next Georgia had gone from being my girlfriend's kid to someone I would lay down my life for. I simply woke up one day to find that the paternal instinct had kicked in. While Georgia and I were not biologically related, I could now feel deep in my heart that if I needed to push her out of the way of an oncoming train to save her life, even though that train would then squish me like a grape, I would do it without question.

This was surprising for someone as self-centred as I was. As much as I had to find food and water and shelter for myself, it was more important to feed, clothe, house, protect and provide for this little girl. Something just shifted within me, and it was now a part of who I was.

Between falling in love with Audrey and my feelings for Georgia, I had found incredible happiness. Whatever LA promised, I no longer wanted a part of it. Nothing could feel better than this. What did I possibly hope to find in LA that could be better than waking up every day to bask in the love and kindness of Audrey and working with the singular purpose to provide for her and Georgia?

After ten years away, I was done.

twenty-four
catching the wind

When the third season of *The Bachelor* and the first season of *The Bachelorette* wrapped in August of 2015, I headed back to LA for three days to pack up what I wanted to take back and give away everything I didn't need. A quick trip to Amsterdam for one final stint of work, and I was finished with living away from Australia.

I was in LA packing for Amsterdam when my phone rang, and I saw it was my mum. It was odd that she'd call, as she wasn't the kind of person to initiate contact; I called her every week, she didn't call me. There could be only one reason I'd see her number pop up in my phone and I could tell by the sound of her voice that I was right. If you haven't had this phone call yet, I'll promise you now that it will happen at least once in your life.

'I've just had a scan and it doesn't look good,' she said.

Mum's physio had found an odd lump on her collarbone and suggested that she get an X-ray to see what it was. Being a good doctor she went straight to the radiology place, ordered herself up some images and waited for the results. But also being a doctor, she didn't need the on-call radiologist to tell her what was wrong. 'Osher, I held the scan up to the light and my body is peppered with tumours. It looks like I've been hit with a shotgun. I'd give myself six to nine months.'

Of course I was devastated by her news. We talked for a while, and I could see that her clinical way of looking at the world was helping her deal with the situation. 'I woke up this morning a fit seventy-five-year-old doctor who was still working, and I'm going to bed tonight as an old lady dying of cancer,' she told me. Her medical experience was also able to inform the way she talked about the treatment she would probably be offered. Mum had seen first-hand what it means to start chemotherapy. She was reluctant to give it a go because she had seen so many times what it really means to go through it.

I just let her talk. Even though I was reeling from what she was telling me, I knew the best thing I could do was to show her I would support her as she talked out what she was going through. She told me that as a doctor for more than fifty years she had seen death hundreds of times and wasn't afraid of it. We talked about a near-death experience she'd had when she was seven, trapped between a reversing truck and a wall at a refugee camp in Germany. She said that in that moment she had seen herself from above, and that behind her something warm and welcoming was waiting, so she was curious. Then she said the bravest and most dignified thing I'd ever heard anyone say. 'I'm not frightened, or surprised. I'm just disappointed that I won't get to see more of life.'

While I was still reeling from this bomb of wisdom dropped on me, Mum hit me with a classic Ruth Günsberg zinger. 'I'm a bit pissed off that it was the cancer causing my weight loss,' she said. 'I'd been working so hard at following that diet for my diabetes.'

In terms of career, some people get dealt a shitty hand, but I am nothing if not lucky. I didn't ask for luck, I don't know what

I have done to deserve it, but the number of times that things have gone my way when they so easily could have gone badly is too significant to ignore: the intention of working at Channel [v], the intention to work in LA, the universe giving me a year after my divorce before putting me into unemployment when everything could have so easily all blown up at the same time. This time was no different.

When I decided to move back to Australia I was committed to making up for lost time. Last time I had been on TV I had squandered so many opportunities by either being an unreliable drunkard or simply hiding in my house and not answering the phone. Not this time. I wanted to haul as many sails up the mast as I could and catch every breath of wind that was blowing at my back.

A few months earlier I'd begun to approach radio networks in Australia about a possible role on a breakfast show. I was pushing for Sydney, but I was woefully unqualified for the gig. A job joining the Brisbane team at Hit 105 was on the table and I went all in. I headed up at the end of November for some trial runs and by the start of December I was locked in to join Stav and Abby on the breakfast team. Not only was this a dream job, it allowed me to spend precious time with my family in Brisbane too. Once again, the universe provided.

I was living back in Australia with two prime-time TV shows on air every year and a major metropolitan breakfast radio gig. I was finally making the most of the momentum I had, and it had only taken me fifteen years to make it happen. Now all I needed was to show Audrey that I was just as committed to her.

I can never thank her enough for the fact that she fought for us. Because she did, I saw how much love and kindness I could be a part of, if only I stuck with it. I'd been digging deep in therapy in doing work in sobriety to find all of the reasons I had torpedoed relationships before, because there was absolutely no way I ever wanted to put anyone through that pain again.

What absolutely made me sure I wanted to marry Audrey were some words that Adam Sher, my old LA agent, had once said to me. 'There's no such thing as *the one*. There's only the one *who's willing to work on it with you*.' Those word described Audrey perfectly.

During a glorious sunset on Heron Island in Queensland I asked Audrey if she would marry me – and thankfully she said yes. Eleven months later, on 27 December 2016, surrounded by 200 friends and family members in the glorious bush of Woollombi in New South Wales's Hunter Valley, we were married. There had been times when I honestly had not believed I'd be able to find happiness again, and yet here I was, barefoot under some ancient melaleuca trees looking into the same Disney-princess eyes I'd first seen years before, saying, 'I will.' In the past I had had trouble staying in an emotional moment and I would often reach for something – a drink, porn, gambling, even my phone – to avoid engaging with or dealing with that emotion. But I was absolutely *not* going to miss the moment that I committed to Audrey and she committed to me. I felt the earth beneath my bare feet and we lit a glorious scented candle that Wil Anderson's partner, Amy, had lent us, so that even my sense of smell was anchored into this moment. That day when Audrey read me her vows they went straight into my heart. And I spoke from that same place when I read vows not only to Audrey but also to Georgia, because when you commit to a woman with a child, you're committing to them both. I was just lucky to be allowed to join their team.

Any good team needs a coach. Sensing that neither of us had the skills to guide Georgia through her rapidly shifting family structure, Audrey sought help. Every week down at the Randwick Children's Hospital a brilliant child psychologist named Deborah talked us through what might be going on in Georgia's mind as she saw the dynamic shift from one parent to two. She helped us with coming together as a family unit and gave us a whole new set of skills for when things were tough. I was coming to live with a child on the cusp of her teens without the ten-year experience of parenting that Audrey had. Deborah helped us both enormously, and I wouldn't be where I am in terms of Georgia without her.

Now I was back in Sydney Jehangeer handed over the reins to a clever psychiatrist named Adam Bayes, who was again significantly younger than I. While I had been busy forward-selling the latest ballad from Bryan Adams in the middle of the night, he had probably still been in high school. It was strange at first but soon I realised that he was incredibly smart and committed to trying to get me better. Despite all the happiness in my life I was still feeling pangs of agony most days and suicidal ideation cast its shadow over me every other day. I never got used to it, and it felt bloody grim. It stopped me from enjoying anything because the spectre of death was constantly hanging over my head. Adam decided that a change of meds to focus solely on the OCD was the next strategy for us, and so we gradually reduced my medication over a number of weeks, then had a full week with nothing, before slowly coming onto a new medication.

We chose a period where I was between on-camera gigs to minimise impact on those around me, but I was still doing radio every morning. I talked to my team about it, telling them I might come across a little differently for a few days as my brain untethered from the regular medication while I was trying to flush my system.

On breakfast radio you've got to be fast. And I mean *fast*. Stav and Abby were experts: by the time I'd thought of something funny to say Stav had already come up with a line and Abby had hit the tag while Dave our anchor was already calling out the time and temperature and playing the next song. Sure I was a little out of practice, but I felt that the meds were holding me back and I found it really frustrating – just another side effect I had to deal with.

During the time between meds Adam had given me some Valium to take the edge off when I needed it. Because I'm an addict with a history of treating Valiums like TicTacs, I gave the bottle to Audrey and asked her to hide it, only giving me one if I asked for it. I stopped taking meds one Friday after we finished the radio show, and the first two days off were across a weekend.

By Monday's show I was completely free from the slowing effects of the meds as I hit the 6am news. After the second or third talk break each person on the team separately told me, 'Geez, you're *funny* today.' I was on fire, I was fast, I got laughs. But it was unsustainable. I was getting wound up into the space I used to get when on stage with the band, the engine in my head just whirring faster and faster. This was great in the quick-fire world of breakfast radio, but terrible when I was talking to Audrey or getting on with the day. As I no longer had booze to help me come down from the high of the show, I'd grit my teeth and climb the walls until the evening I asked Audrey for a Valium to help me sleep.

It broke my heart that I was faster and funnier off meds. I was everything I wanted to be on air but everything I could not handle when the microphone was off. I was a complete pain in the neck during meetings about the show, grumpy and antagonistic, and even I wouldn't have wanted to work with me. With some reluctance I started on a new regime of Anafranil, an old-school drug specifically used to treat OCD. Once I'd worked up to my therapeutic dose I finally, finally started feeling better.

This drug came with side effects too, but what it did for me was incredible.

For the first time in years the rational part of my brain began to successfully challenge the irrational thoughts I was having. I'd see a picture of a lone iceberg in a bay that used to be frozen solid, and instead of reacting as if the world was going to end that very day I could say to myself, 'Well, that's concerning. I can't be the only person who is worried about this. I can't do anything about it today except try to minimise my personal impact.' After a little while I would start to feel better. Finally, the plasticity was beginning to return to my brain and with hard work I could redirect those neural pathways one at a time. It took a long while, but eventually I was no longer reacting in ghastly horror to my triggers.

Adam began to use a technique called exposure therapy. He got me to write a list of ten experiences, from least terrifying to most terrifying. The idea was to challenge myself with something just a little more confronting every time so that slowly the reaction to the stimulus would become less and less extreme. To give you an idea of how sick I was when I first met Adam, I looked at the list I'd written to him. Number ten on the list, the most extreme thing I could do, was to look at maps that showed the expected new coastlines when sea levels rose. My handwriting on the list is so shaky and angular that I'm clearly freaking out just writing it.

Number one on the list was to go outside on a warm day and feel the sun on my skin. Even with all of the drugs I was on, that was still something that made me horribly uncomfortable. However, I'd learned that trusting my doctors was a better idea than trying to figure out how to get better on my own, and on a perfect, blue-sky Sydney day I went outside. I felt the warmth of the sun on my skin and I just wanted to run. But I just kept breathing and remembering that the point of this was to build up my tolerance to the triggers. After about ten minutes it was a little better, and half an hour later it was OK. Yes, it was warm. Yes, it was warmer than usual. But I was OK. Over a few months we worked our way through the list, and slowly things got better.

Suicidal ideation became a rare occurrence, and if it did happen I was gradually able to rationalise my way around it. The obsessiveness had calmed right down, and I was feeling pretty good. Pretty fat, but pretty good. Back when I'd done *Live To Dance* I had managed to work myself down to seventy kilograms and stay around there for a few years. I stood on the scales in November 2016 and I was now ninety kilos. My interest in sex was up there with my interest in studying air-conditioning systems for container ships. Minimal. It was nice not to be crazy. It was not nice to be fat and frigid.

But when you're on meds, you have to weigh up the benefits against the side effects. Adam and I took our time, but slowly over nearly a year we decreased my dosage down to the minimum therapeutic dose. I'd gone from swallowing five pills a night to just one, which was a relief. However, every time I reduced the dosage I had to deal with my system flaring up again. I'd settle down for a few weeks and then drop another pill off the regimen and boom! I'd be all over the place again.

This was pretty tough on Audrey and Georgia, who were constantly having to recalibrate how to deal with me, and starting to see a side of me they hadn't signed up for. It was as if the tethers on the hot-air balloon of my brain were being released one by one, and the upward pressure was increasing on those tethers still attached to the ground. I had to slowly learn how to handle the world again every few weeks, and then after about a month of having it together we'd drop another half tablet off the regime and it would happen all over again.

As I was readjusting to experiencing the world at a much higher intensity every few weeks, Mum's condition started to deteriorate. Once while walking with her around the U-shaped cancer ward at the Wesley Hospital in Brisbane, I prepared for us to head back to her room when Mum said, 'Let's just keep going straight ahead. I'll probably end up here anyway.' With that we wandered through the serene palliative care area of the floor. Different from the harsh light and loudly beeping machines of the cancer ward, the palliative ward was painted in warm earthy colours, had calm soft lighting and the only machine there was a blanket warmer.

Despite intense treatment, after a few short months her very good partial remission had decided to escalate to stage IV multiple myeloma. Having already been through one round of chemotherapy and even though she was offered a second, Mum refused. Refusing chemotherapy is apparently not uncommon in doctors who find themselves as patients. Mum faced the last stage of her life with incredible calmness, bravery and dignity, and I hope I have even a fraction of that when my time comes. She passed away surrounded by her family in June 2017.

At her funeral there were a few people I didn't recognise. As a doctor in the community for close to thirty years, my mother had helped a lot of people. One woman told me a story that absolutely summed Mum up. This woman had been to see Mum for a recurring problem, one that she'd already needed many, many operations to treat. She was very scared about going under general anaesthetic again and she didn't want to have the surgery that she needed. Mum told her not to worry; she'd be there. Sure enough, on the day of the operation Mum showed up to the hospital. She just walked in, put on scrubs and started washing her hands in the special way that doctors do in their sinks just outside the operating theatre. When her patient arrived on the rolling bed Mum just marched in with her and despite the surgeon's protestations of trespass and privacy she simply refused to leave. I guess the surgeon knew he'd have a fight on his hands if he resisted, so Mum stayed with her patient when the anaesthetic kicked in and was there when she came out in recovery.

That's the kind of woman my mum was. Like all of us she had her faults. My experience of her as a parent is different from that of my brothers, and now she's no longer here I've learned through therapy that she could have done some things better along the way. However, at her core, she was guided by her sense of doing things because they were the right thing to do. She was utterly devoted to her kids and she sacrificed everything for us. I miss her every day.

When Mum died, I didn't cry. I was on low meds, but not no meds. Emotions were still difficult to access, especially pain or sadness. We were knocking my meds down half a tablet at a time in an effort to start to re-engage with those feelings. Every time we did, the edges of the world felt a little more spiky, and I'd occasionally get so anxious I would flip up into a hypomanic state. Adam my psychiatrist occasionally brought his rescue greyhound into the office. When I was first seeing him, the enormous dog could sense my hyper state and would go from sitting placidly on the floor watching his owner to going into full zoomies mode in the small office.[1] Once or twice Adam had to take the enormous dog out of the room to prevent utter calamity. However, as I learned to deal with my brain at full volume, the dog started to become more and more calm. Now when I go to see Adam the dog just sleeps on the floor, and every time that he does I consider it a massive win.

In December 2017 Adam and I decided to stop the meds altogether.

Within two weeks, even though it was rocky, I started to notice a change. The most significant one occurred at the Sydney red-carpet premiere of the Hugh Jackman film *The Greatest Showman*. It's a big, bombastic musical with uplifting songs of triumph and love, all of them with huge key change after huge key change.

It was during one of these songs ('This is me' to be exact) when for the first time in over a decade I felt goosebumps to the sound of music. I used to feel them all the time when I was younger; I would play a particular part of a song over and over so I could feel that chill up my spine as the cadence changed and the singer hit the big, big note. As I sat there holding Audrey's hand, something else happened for the first time in years. I started to cry. I was crying because I could feel music

---

1 If you've never had a dog, zoomies are when the dog gets excited about being excited and just runs around in circles.

again. I turned to Audrey and wept into her shoulder, tears of happiness streaming down my cheeks. She'd never seen me cry, and it was only the second time I'd cried in fifteen years.

Initially, coming off the meds altogether was easy for me but a challenge for Audrey. I was now different to be around, and it was difficult for me to understand that, especially when I didn't feel too much of a difference.

I guess the meds had been masking pattern behaviour I'd been hiding in the back of the brain, but now those old patterns and ways of reacting came back. Everything felt pretty much the same to me, but I had to trust that Audrey's reading of a situation was the healthy one, no matter what I thought I was doing. I am grateful to have had her perspective.

Despite this positive, it was a difficult few weeks as I adjusted to experiencing the world at full intensity. I'd again chosen to go off meds between jobs, on holiday with Audrey and Georgia to Quebec in Canada, a cold and beautiful place full of nothing but icebergs in the bay and polar bears in the zoo. Triggers everywhere.

It was grim. My brain was back in full-blown doom mode, and I was *not* fun to be around. My head was spinning so fast in fear that I just couldn't engage emotionally with Audrey and Georgia, and they were feeling it. My head was just too full to experience things like joy, empathy or intuition.

On our third day there, I woke up in agonising anxiety, ready for another day of mental punishment. I was washing my hands and my head was full of doom-laden thoughts looping around and around. I could deal with it, but it just took up so much bandwidth that I couldn't feel or think about anything else, let alone show my family that I care about them and love them, or heaven forbid enjoy my holiday. I looked at myself in the mirror and let out a big sigh, thinking: 'Oh, here we go, another fucking day of this.' And then I just laughed.

I laughed at how ridiculous it was that I still had this issue in my head. I suddenly found it hilarious to be in this living museum of Quebec City (we were staying in a fortress built in the seventeenth century) with me being pummelled by these fucking thoughts again. I laughed at how ridiculous the whole thing was – that after four years, when I was trying to live without meds I was still being punished by my own brain. I tried to laugh again but couldn't, so I just started a fake laugh until I actually laughed for real. I don't know if the physical act of laughing shook my diaphragm out of the loop of anxiety breathing, or it was the effect of my facial muscles finding a smile amidst all the turmoil, but the horror thoughts were suddenly further away from me than ever before. The challenge through the day when I repeated this to find respite was coming up with reasons when Audrey or Georgia asked, 'What's so funny?'

I am not a doctor and I would need this claim to be backed up by a double-blind placebo controlled study, but I think my brain had changed while I was on the meds. I felt like the neural pathways that were shortcuts to terror were no longer the guaranteed thought path, that my brain had healed enough to allow me to put new thought patterns in there with a bit of deliberate work. What is nice is that after a bit of practice, the new thought patterns were actually beginning to stick.

I've since learned to keep the smile on the inside, but from time to time I still giggle as the Grim Reaper tries to bowl another thought of death and doom through my brain.

This is just one of the many ways that I'm learning to live with life off of medication. As of writing this, six months has just ticked over since I last took a drug to help my brain approach normality. But I must point out, there's a big difference between not taking meds, and not *needing* to take meds. To keep myself from *needing* to take meds, I work every day to make sure that I'm giving myself the best chance of managing life without them.

I have a structured morning routine, that involves getting up early if need be so that I can write for at least twenty minutes, journaling all the fears out of my head so I can challenge them on paper and get them out of the way before the day begins. I then write at least ten things I'm grateful for, to show myself that while those fears exist and might even be based in something that is quite tangible, they don't represent the totality of my life and indeed I have a lot more to be grateful for than fearful of.

I keep regular appointments with my psychologist, where she and I work through what we need to work through, in order to help me handle life at full volume, and I see my psychiatrist regularly to check in every month or two so that we can be sure that I'm not sliding backwards.

I have taken what I learned when I was eighteen, when I figured out that walking around the block lifted my mood – and I've now brought that to a whole new level, doing near-daily resistance training and high intensity cardio in between sets, either in the gym under the guidance of husband and wife training team, Emilie Brabon-Hames and Chief Brabon, or in the backyard with some kettlebells.[2]

---

2   It's fair to say that my trainers have taught me so much about my own body. Sure I'd been physically active before – yet resistance training always eluded me. Em and Chief have given me the gift not only of teaching me how to move my body correctly, but in doing so they've given me a whole new set of tools to change my mood at will.

On top of this, I try as hard as I can to also get at least an hour in on my bike trainer every day.[3] Almost all of the editing process of this book has been done on that bike trainer – and while my digital avatar rides up and down the mountains on the online bike experience Zwift for hours on end, I've got a laptop propped up on an old photography light stand so I can work while I'm pedalling the pent-up energy out of my body.

To fuel all of this exercise, I've gone from being what's known as a 'junk food vegan' – existing on mainly a toast-based diet – to someone who diligently and meticulously prepares meals with just the right ingredients to be sure that I'm fuelling my body with everything that I need to be the strongest, healthiest person that I can be.

I am relishing in finally beginning to learn about plant-based nutrition, appropriate portion sizes, and how to cook properly. While I enjoy experimenting in the kitchen, I've still got way less experience and knowledge than my teenage step-daughter who's been cooking complex meals since she was just a kid. It's never too late to learn something new, right?

Taking the time to prepare the food, taking the time to enjoy the food when I eat it, and then looking in the mirror and seeing the results of what proper nourishment and a diligent exercise regime does to my body is changing what I see in the mirror in nothing short of miraculous ways. The

---

3 I use what's called a 'smart trainer' where you take the back wheel off your road bike, and bolt it onto a variable-resistance flywheel that's controlled by a program on my laptop called Zwift. When the little man on the bike on the monitor goes up a mountain, it gets harder to pedal. When he goes downhill, it gets easier. I ride for hours through imaginary mountain passes with other people all around the world also sweating away in their garages and spare rooms.

wonderful thing is that it's not only changing my body, it's changing my mind as well.

What's undeniable is that as my body gets stronger, my mind follows suit.

I do my best to prioritise sleep, and defend the time in my calendar when I'm not working so that I can spend time with my family.

When I am with them, I'm working hard to learn new ways to connect emotionally with Audrey and Georgia, their presence in my life giving me incredible joy and fulfilment, and being of service to them is a true privilege.

All of these things aren't optional. They are things that I need to do so I stay healthy and not need to take meds again. You can't expect to just stop taking meds and think everything is going to be OK – I learned that the very hard way.

It's like sitting ten people down to dinner, sawing one leg off the table and expecting everything to not topple onto the floor. You have to prop the table up with something.

All of these action steps are not only what's propping me up, they're providing a solid foundation to a level of emotional resilience that I don't ever remember experiencing in my life before. It sounds like a lot but, as I'm learning in the gym, you don't just do one set of sit-ups to get the six-pack of an underwear model. Abs like that take months if not years of hard work, repeated action of increasing intensity, and a diligent adherence to diet, rest and recovery.

The same goes for my head. I can't just go to my psychologist once a fortnight and expect things to be OK. It's in the daily practice that things get to stay OK. While it might sound like a lot, I must promise you that the freedom this discipline gives me is worth every second of the work I put into it.

Of course there's always ways that I can improve, and I enjoy the challenge of trying to be a better person, husband, stepfather and employee every day.

what i have learned

So here we are. The end of the book, a memoir written by someone only halfway through his life. You're not far away from the feeling when you finish a book and go, 'Well, what am I supposed to do now?' I'll try to make it worth your while.

First, here's what I've learned about work. Some things you hear about work sound trite, but they're true. 'The harder you work, the luckier you get' is one of them. Without the shadow of a doubt, I have found that to be a truth. I might never have been the best, the fastest, the funniest or the smartest, but goddammit I would work the hardest. The benefits of having a brain that absolutely will not stop until something is done is that you can achieve incredible focus when you need to, and hard work seems like simply another step towards where you want to go.

My LA manager John Ferriter once told me, 'You're the only one who knows how hard you've worked to make your dreams come true.' He's absolutely right. If something doesn't come your way and it's because you didn't work that hard, you know that in your heart, and you know to go harder next time. But if something doesn't come your way and you did absolutely everything in your power to make it happen, you can sleep well that night knowing that you did your part and the time just wasn't right.

My dad once gave me a piece of advice that when translated from Czech into English goes like this: 'Make friends with the steps on the ladder, because you'll need them to come back down.' Not that I'm on the way back down, but nearly every person I've met on the way up in my career still works in my industry. The way you leave a person feeling when you leave the room is like a calling card that's there to cheer for you when you're not around. Remember how I got the job on CBS? The meeting I'd had with the person who made the final decision was *four years* before I got the job – but I'd left her with a good memory of me, and that's what got me the gig.

The biggest breaks in my career all happened because of someone who knew what I could do. They say it's not who you are, it's who you know, but in my experience it's who knows what you know. From my first gig in radio to my job at Channel [v], to the massive break at CBS with *Live To Dance* and even to *The Bachelor Australia* – every one of those jobs came about because someone I knew or had met was aware of what I could do, and was willing to give me a heads up or vouch for me based on how I had treated them last. Everyone you ever meet in your career might be the person you ask for a job in twenty years, so make sure you leave them feeling like you're worth hiring every time and you'll never be out of work.

Obviously I can't say I've been kind and great to work with for my whole career, there were times there when even I wouldn't have wanted to work with me, but like the man said – progress, not perfection.

The best thing I ever decided to do in my career was to try to make everyone else's job on set easy. If I made everyone else have an easy day it was because I was doing the best job I could possibly do. Rather than an interior focus, I shifted that around to trying to be there for others – and that's what has fuelled my TV work since *Live To Dance*.

When it comes to getting work, I've learned that if you want work, you have to make it happen. Through creating something you're passionate about, like my podcast, while it might not be making oodles of cash, it's something that has changed the way people see me and what I'm capable of and it's worth every single hour I work on making it happen every week. I've learned you can create your way out of unemployment, which is something I've now proudly done twice, and if I ever have to do it again I know it will be scary but I'll be fine. Yes, I work in a seasonal industry and it's an industry not without its uncertainty, but as Hyman Roth said to Michael Corleone, 'This is the business we have chosen.'[1]

One final thing I've learned about work is that for a long time you have to be prepared to be quite ordinary at what you have set out to do. Sure you might have a natural talent that guides your career and gives you a head start, but it's the days, months and years of continuous work that make the difference. So often we are flashed images on social media of a get-rich-quick scheme or a person who sold their company to Google for $20 million after only a year in development. Those things aren't the norm. You can't expect anything like that, nor can you be upset when it doesn't happen. You just have to spend hour after hour, day after day, year after year sharpening the blade and perfecting your thrust so that on the day that Bill finally darkens your doorway, you're ready for him.[2] I did

---

1   The context of that speech doesn't *really* work here, but now you'll have to watch *The Godfather Part 2* to get the full context. It's bloody good.

2   OK that's the last of the movie references. But seriously, *Kill Bill* is pretty great.

five years of midnight–dawn radio, mostly being *terrible* at it, and then four years of Channel [v] being slightly better than terrible but still not great. That's seven years of work before I stepped onto the stage at *Australian Idol.* In my experience, it's the people who've done the work and hit the big stage with a wealth of knowledge that have the momentum to keep things going.

As far as problem drinking is concerned, if you're able to stop once you start, good for you. But it's important to realise that not everyone is like you. Some people, like me, can't stop once they start. I have an allergy to alcohol. If I drink it, I break out in fuckwit. At first when I drank it was fun, then it was fun with problems, then it was just problems. During my drinking I know I hurt people and lived a life that was self-centred and self-seeking. I can't make all of it better, but I do try as hard as I can to live every day in amends to the hurtful things I did. I've learned that if you can't control when you stop drinking, everywhere I've travelled on this earth there are fellowship meetings of people who are willing to be of service to help you stop. I've been thousands of kilometres from home and walked into a room full of people I've never met, yet I have felt the warmth of acceptance and support. I wish more people knew that for free, a group of strangers is prepared to help you stop drinking and be grateful they've had the chance to help you. I wish I'd known about that earlier, but I had to wait until I was as low as I could go before I looked up for help.

I was always ashamed to score drugs from strangers, and felt worse about buying them from friends. But doing the job I did, drugs were always around. I've learned that while yes, ecstasy is an incredibly powerful drug that can bring about states of euphoria unsurpassed in regular human experience, it is *not* worth a life filled with the wreckage of intense anxiety and psychosis that follows. Some people I know necked five pills a night every weekend for five years and walked away scot-free. I dropped a daisy-cutter into my brain and it exploded, apparently taking my ability to produce oxytocin and serotonin with it. Justice Vs Simian's 'We Are Your Friends' is a fucking good song and I'll never forget how it felt to sing it with everyone else at the top of my lungs on a sweaty dance floor, but it isn't so good that it's worth a life plagued with powerful anxiety, psychosis and suicidal ideation. Not that everything that happened to my brain is due to that one pill, but I just know that after that summer nothing was ever the same again.

I've learned it's important to share. When I hit my lowest point after my divorce, hearing other people talk during fellowship meetings helped me feel less alone. Hearing men I lunched with tell me that it was going to be OK gave me hope. When we hear someone with a story similar to ours, the magnitude of our story diminishes and it's no longer something we have to tackle alone, it's now something we can get help dealing with – because someone else has dealt with it before and they can show us a path out of the pain.

I started my podcast back in September of 2013 and one day not long afterwards, I just opened the mic and talked about how I was doing that week. I didn't plan it, it just happened. Sharing how I'm going at the start of each podcast episode is something that so many people have written to me about. The power of hearing that someone else is going through the same thing you are makes the problem appear smaller.

When given the chance to talk about my mental health in public, I used the forum that the brilliant team at Story Club gave me to talk about the day I lost my mind. It was that story that ultimately led to me writing this book. When I first knew what feeling suicidal can feel like, I knew I had to talk about it. It's not necessary to go on stage and share about the day your brain turned on you; something as small as a phone call or even a text message will do, but sharing your experience and being open to someone sharing their experience with you is incredibly powerful. As you've read here, in the past that has saved my life.

Since coming out about my brain and living with a mental illness, I've learned that people are calm about it if they see you're serious about managing it. If I had Type 2 diabetes and shovelled donuts down my cakehole all the time, you'd probably be uncomfortable. Being self-destructive in such a way, I'd look as if I didn't care about myself at all, or you either. The same goes for mental health. If someone's got a mental illness issue and they're self-medicating with drugs, alcohol, sex or gambling, everyone is uncomfortable. However, if they're seen to be taking responsibility for their situation and visibly take steps to manage what's going on, people are far more cool about it. I've learned that it's important to say that while I'm off meds now, by the time this book is published I may very well be back on them. But at this point my brain seems to be healthy enough to do without medication.

I've learned that except for when I was *really* ill and going through psychosis, exercise can be an incredibly powerful tool. My brain already has a lot of the chemicals that can make me feel better, I just need to do the right things to release them. Now my brain is healthier those effects are more powerful. But even when I was really sick, just a short walk could make me feel way better than I did. Don't underestimate the power of moving your body if you can.

I'm learning how to fall in love in a healthy way. In my earlier relationships I was often emotionally unavailable or trapped in obsession and unable to slow it down to experience true bonding.[3] Audrey was patient and kind enough for me to take it slowly and learn from her what it is to be in love. As my brain heals and starts to operate more normally, I work every day at reacting in a more human way. I work every day at matching the incredible love Audrey sends towards me. I can be a self-centred arsehole sometimes, but I'm learning how not to be. Most of that comes from Audrey. She never flinched at the fact that I was sick. I told her from the moment we started seeing each other about what was happening in my head, and that suicidal ideation was a part of my day. When she met me I was on two different kinds of antipsychotics, but she had the ability to see my illness and me as two separate things. I'm very, very lucky that I fell in love with Audrey. Through the course of our relationship I've had the chance to heal in so many ways, and each moment of healing is accompanied by 'levelling up' in my love for her. It's a pretty good feeling.

Feeling the paternal instinct kick in with regard to Georgia was one of the most surprising things about our relationship. I've never been so focused to provide and protect and be there for these two women. The work I did before was from a place of wanting to achieve something that would make it all better (if I can just get on a *big enough* TV show, *then* I'll feel OK) and of course it never did, even when I was on US network prime-time TV. The work I do now is great and I love it, but I do it with the purpose of providing for my family. To have

---

3   For the scientists among you, I've had it explained that in obsession I was stuck in a loop and high on dopamine. In that state I was unable to release any oxytocin, which is the hormone that helps humans bond emotionally with each other.

a purpose like this driving me when I get out of bed every morning and push through all the way to 4am on a big shoot day just makes it all so great.

I was lucky to arrive as the last rays of sunlight set upon Georgia's childhood. I got there *just* in time for a blissful period where she warmed to me enough to allow me to be in bed with her and Audrey at night and read bedtime stories to her. It was only about six weeks, but I'll treasure every night we did that together. My Hit 105 colleague Stav once told me that one day he would put his young daughter down after carrying her and while he wouldn't know it, that would be the last time he would ever do so, and it was a thought that made him sad. Similarly, one day Georgia didn't want a bedtime story and that was it. We never lay in bed reading to her again. Her journey to becoming an independent and driven teenager had begun.

Being a stepfather is not without its challenges. I have to remember when I get things wrong that while I'm trying to parent a teenager, I'm doing so with less than four years' experience in parenting. I consider being a stepfather a privilege and I work every day to be the best that I can be at doing it. I love these two women with all of my heart and I'd do anything to protect and provide for them.

I am a long way from where I was, but I am still a work in progress. Writing this all down does bind me to a commitment to stay sober, to stay sane, to stay married, and to stay employed. While I work every day with all my might to achieve each of those things, there's a possibility I might yet fail. However, with Audrey in my life, with the great doctors I have in my life, with my mentor and with the excellent team I am surrounded by at work, my chances of sticking to that commitment are as good as they come.

acknowledgements

Any project of merit is a sum of the people who worked on it. All I did was the writing bit; however, there are quite a number of other people who were a massive part of helping make this book a reality.

First and foremost, I must thank Audrey for her incredible support during the writing of this book. When digging in the dirt in an effort to find the authentic emotions of difficult events long gone, the energy of those moments would not only go onto the page, but also linger with me afterwards, sometimes for hours. Audrey has been so understanding in supporting me through reliving those difficult emotions, and unwaveringly provided a safe place for me to come back to at the end of a day of writing and reconnect with her in the present moment. She has also been incredibly generous and gracious in allowing me to share the intimate details of our relationship that were affected by my illness and the medication, always with the idea that in sharing our experience we may hopefully help others. For that, I am eternally grateful.

I have to thank Georgia for coming into my life, and for giving me even more reasons to make a daily effort to be the best and healthiest man I can be. I'd seen a similar thing happen to those close to me when they became parents, and when I was suddenly overcome with the need to protect and provide for Georgia, she gave my life an entirely new meaning and purpose, and helped me immeasurably.

To my mentor David I offer enormous gratitude. As you've read, he has guided me through the darkest and scariest of times in my life, helping to guide me back to sanity and all the while helping me to stay sober through the chaos. I hope that if you need a mentor of your own, you can go out and find someone like David. I wouldn't be here without him.

Thanks also to my doctors and therapists, without whom I would have fallen off the edge of the world, never to return. When our brains turn on themselves, we are lucky that there are people who've dedicated years of their lives to helping us get back to health, safety and sanity.

Thanks must also go to Will Cate, who formally introduced me to Dom Knight during my early days of searching for podcast guests. It was Dom who I asked for any way that I could be involved in the world of *The Chaser*, and who then introduced me to the incomparable Zoe Norton Lodge, co-founder of *Story Club*. It was during my fourth appearance at *Story Club*, in the safe space that Zoe and her co-founder, Ben Jenkins, had created between the storyteller and the audience that I told the tale 'The Day I Lost My Mind', which was the first time I'd spoken publicly about my experience with psychosis and the medication required to bring it under control. Without those people, this book would never have happened.

Thanks must go to Jack Heath, CEO of SANE Australia who has listened to me tell the more detailed and intense version of my story to select audiences behind closed doors as part of my role as a director at SANE Australia. It was Jack who gave me the confidence to write this book, and impressed upon me how important it could be to others facing similar struggles, if I shared publicly what I'd been through. It was Jack who introduced me to my extraordinary publisher and collaborator at HarperCollins, Catherine Milne.

Catherine has shepherded many people in my position through the process of writing their memoirs, and she expertly guided me through this journey with love, compassion and patience in the face of many panicked phone calls about being vulnerable in print. I couldn't have asked for a more fearless and capable captain for this voyage into the unknown.

My editor Shannon Kelly has been nothing but patient and understanding with effortlessly rearranging deadlines and milestones to embrace the hectic production schedule that I keep – one that can lurch a day to the left or right at any given moment. Through his work, he's helped me become a better writer and at all times made me feel that what I was writing was indeed worth writing about. Catherine asked for eighty thousand words, and I gave her an initial draft pushing one hundred and fifty thousand. The real skill and craft of what Shannon and my other editor, Jacquie Kent, did was in culling all the chaff that came along with the kernels of story you just read. My gratitude must also go to Annabel Adair, my proofreader, who tirelessly undid twelve years of me not paying attention in grammar and punctuation lessons. Also, my thanks to Graeme Jones, who worked on typesetting this book. Line breaks are like a deep breath after hearing good or bad news, and Graeme made sure each one was in the most effective place that it could be.

Sourcing photos for this book was tricky, but thanks to too many people to name we managed to get some pictures that helped me timestamp what was going on. Steve Murphy at

FremantleMedia Australia found a box inside a box behind a cupboard full of *Idol* Archives (not really, they were on a hard drive) and helped with those pictures, and Scott Forbes assisted with culling my hundred-and-forty-plus personal photos down for the picture selection while Megan Bond did the illustration section design.

Speaking of photos, the story of the cover of this book could be an entire podcast episode in itself, which I hope to do one day with the extraordinarily talented photographer who captured the moment, Steve Baccon. Steve was my first choice to shoot the cover, and the stars and planets aligned in such a way that he happened to be free on the day that we were to shoot it. Gratefully too, I was able to have my exceptional styling team with me – as without them, I'm a very daggy dresser. My long-time hair and makeup artist, Carla Mico, and Melissa Byrne, my stylist, who I get to work with every day in my TV life were able to be a part of making this very special photograph. We share a very intimate workplace and, indeed, an intimate job – one where personal energies are important as you're sometimes shoulder to shoulder with each other for hours and days on end. These two women are so wonderful to have in my life, and I'm grateful for every day that we get to work together. Once we shot the photo, we handed it over to Mark Campbell, who put together a cover design that shouted at you from the bookstore shelf and got you to first hold this book in your hands. The fact that you even know this book exists is thanks to Kimberley Allsopp and Kajal Narayan who ran the marketing for this project at HarperCollins.

This wouldn't have been a book without Lauren Miller, Hayley Van Spanje and Rachel Barrett, my management team, who helped me work so well with HarperCollins.

Hayley diligently defended my calendar so that I could find the time to write, but also to not write and instead reconnect with my family. Hayley and Lauren protected me at all times from feeling overwhelmed, and somehow managed to help me keep my robust podcast interview and output schedule uninterrupted, get me to set on time, and make sure I'd be where I said I'd be – all while ensuring there was time to give this book the energy and focus it deserved, and afterwards enough time to practice the self-care and family connection that fuelled more work. Lauren has launched a lot of books in her career, and her guidance and experience in telling stories of a more delicate nature has been invaluable.

I must thank my brothers. This is my story, but parts of my story are shared with these fine men. Through their incredible generosity, I have been able to go into detail about our shared history, and all through the writing of this book they have been there for me. As I've written, I wouldn't still be around if I hadn't had them to speak to on those dark nights during the first few weeks of my sickness, and that support has continued to today. I'm very grateful that I get to share my life with them.

During the early drafts of this book, I had the privilege of interviewing Benjamin Law for my podcast and in five minutes he gave me the three best writing lessons I'd ever get:

Break it down into manageable chunks, then into smaller and smaller chunks of those chunks and then just link those chunks together.

Approach writing like you would any other job. Turn up, log in, get to work, then clock off.

Write with the door closed but edit with the door open. You can't write about the pot of gold you found at the end of the rainbow if you don't first write the rainbow. If the story is about gold, you can lose the rainbow and still have what you came for.

After he and I spoke, I was buoyed with confidence to start to write in earnest, breaking the shackles of stilted notes I'd begun to make and opening the floodgates for the torrent of words that followed.

Thanks and acknowledgement must go to the fine body of men who are defined by the group chat name 'Bondi Poker Boys'. Even though only one of us still lives in Bondi (well, Bondi Junction), we have kept the same Wednesday-evening gathering around the card table in one way or another for over fifteen years. The stories, support and laughter shared around that table has given me so much strength over the years – and in writing this book, that support has been invaluable.

To my Warner Brothers family, especially Shaun Murphy and Janine Cooper, the two greatest executive producers I've ever had the chance to work with. Their love, support and guidance while I was going through the darkness allowed me to still come to work and be of value, and feel like things indeed could be OK.

To my Network Ten family, especially Hilary Innes and Stephen Tate, I owe enormous thanks – for allowing me to come to them and let them know I wasn't well, but that I was working to get better; and for trusting that my ability to manage what was happening with me wouldn't affect my ability to do the job they wanted me to do. For giving me space when I needed it, and work to do when I needed something to keep me busy. I am eternally grateful for their friendship and leadership.

And lastly, to the incredible listeners of my podcast. Each week I open the mic and simply check in. By trying to share an authentic version of what's going on in my head that week, I've been able to connect with people from all walks of life, from all over the world. And those people have let me know time and again that, after hearing me talk openly about what I'm going through, they had similar conversations with people close to them – conversations that led to people getting help and getting better. Without you listening, I'd never have kept making the podcast; without the podcast, I'd never have connected with Dom Knight; and without him, this book wouldn't exist. Thank you for helping me make conversations about mental health normal to hear. Together we can hopefully help more people have similar conversations that will lead to them also feeling better.

support services

Support Services (Australia)

Alcohol and Other Drugs

Australian Alcohol and Drug Foundation
1300 85 85 84

Alcohol and Drug Information Service (ADIS)
ACT: 02 6205 4545
NSW (Sydney): 02 9361 8000
NSW (Regional): 1800 422 599
NT: 1800 131 350
QLD: 07 3837 5989 or 1800 177 833
SA: 1300 131 340
TAS: 1800 811 994
VIC: 1800 888 236
WA (Perth): 08 9442 5000
WA (Regional): 1800 198 024
A 24-hour confidential information, advice and referral
    telephone service.

Cannabis Information and Helpline
1800 30 40 50
11am–7pm, Monday to Friday (including public holidays)

Family Drug Support
1300 368 186
24 hours a day, 7 days a week
Support for families faced with problematic drug use.

QUIT line
13 7848
8am–8pm, Monday to Friday
Support for those quitting smoking or going smokefree.

Ted Noffs Foundation Helpline
NSW/ACT: 1800 151 045
QLD: 1800 753 300
24 hours a day, 7 days a week
Counselling and support for young people and their families.

Mental Health

beyondblue Support Service
1300 22 4636
24 hours a day, 7 days a week
Support for depression, anxiety and related disorders.

headspace
1800 650 890
eheadspace.org.au
Online and telephone support and counselling to young people
aged between 12 and 25, and their families and friends.

Kids Helpline
1800 55 1800
24 hours a day, 7 days a week
Free and confidential telephone and online counselling
service for young people aged between 5 and 25, as well
as parents, carers, schools and teachers.

Lifeline Australia
13 11 14
24 hours a day, 7 days a week
Confidential telephone counselling and crisis support.

Reachout
reachout.com
Information for young people experiencing mental health
issues.

SANE Australia Helpline
1800 187 263
9am–5pm, Monday to Friday
Information and referral about mental health issues.

Suicide Call Back Service
1300 659 467
24 hours a day, 7 days a week
suicidecallbackservice.org.au
Provides immediate telephone counselling and support in a
crisis.

Support Services (New Zealand)

Alcohol and Other Drugs

Alcohol Drug Helpline
0800 787 797 or text 8681
alcoholdrughelp.org.nz
Confidential, non-judgmental advice and support.
If you are concerned about your own or someone else's
    drinking or other drug use, the Helpline can support you
    to make the changes that you want to make.

Mental Health

Mental Health Foundation of NZ
mentalhealth.org.nz
Lifeline – 0800 543 354 or (09) 5222 999 within Auckland
Suicide Crisis Helpline – 0508 828 865 (0508 TAUTOKO)
Healthline – 0800 611 116 (Mental health crisis team)
Samaritans – 0800 726 666